THE ARM

OF THE
KINGDOM

2014–2015

Editor – Charles Heyman

ISBN 978 1 78346 351 0

Price £9.99

Pen & Sword Books Ltd
47 Church Street
Barnsley S70 2AS

Telephone: 01226-734222   Fax: 01226-734438
www.pen-and-sword.co.uk

The Information in this publication has been gathered from
unclassified sources.

Front Cover: Type 45 Destroyer HMS Diamond on sea trials before joining
the Fleet. (MoD Crown Copyright 2013)

Rear Cover: RAF Regiment Forward Air Controllers guide a Typhoon from
6 Squadron RAF onto a land target during training in Scotland. (MoD Crown Copyright 2013)

Printed and bound in India by Replika Press Pvt. Ltd.

CONTENTS

CHAPTER 1 – THE MANAGEMENT OF DEFENCE

GENERAL INFORMATION

Populations – European Union – Top Five Nations

Germany	80.5 million
United Kingdom	64.2 million
France	63.8 million
Italy	59.6 million
Spain	46.9 million

Note: The above are the latest European Union (EU – 2013) estimates. The total estimated EU population is 498 million (27 countries). This compares with the population of the United States (315 million) the population of China (1,300 million), India 1,200 million and Russia 143 million.

UK Population – 63.2 million
(2011 census figures)

England	53.0 million	Wales	3.1 million
Scotland	5.3 million	Northern Ireland	1.8 million

Figures rounded to the nearest whole number.

UK Population Breakdown – Military Service Groups
(2011 census figures)

Age Group	Total		
0 14	11 million	5.4 million	5.4 million
15–19	4 million	1.8 million	1.8 million
20–24	4.3 million	1.8 million	1.8 million
25–29	4.3 million	1.8 million	1.8 million
30–64	24.3 million	14.5 million	13.9 million

Age Group	Total
0–14	11 million
15–19	4 million
20–24	4.3 million
25–29	4.3 million
30–64	24.3 million

There are 5.6 million males and 5.4 million females in the 0–14 age group and 20.7 million males plus 20.9 million females in the 15–64 age group.

Figures rounded to the nearest whole number.

UK Area (in square kilometres)

England	130,423
Wales	20,766
Scotland	78,133
Northern Ireland	14,160
Total	243,482

Note: Comparisons include Germany 356,854 sq kms and France 550,000 sq kms. The total area of the European Union is 4,324,782 sq kms. The United States is 9,826,630 sq kms; Canada 9,984,670 sq kms; China 9,640,821 sq kms India 3,166,414 sq kms and Russia 17,098,242 sq kms.

GOVERNMENT

The executive government of the United Kingdom is vested nominally in the Crown, but for practical purposes in a committee of Ministers that is known as the Cabinet. The head of the ministry and leader of the Cabinet is the Prime Minister and for the implementation of policy, the Cabinet is dependent upon the support of a majority of the Members of Parliament in the House of Commons. Within the Cabinet, defence matters are the responsibility of the Secretary of State for Defence.

National Security Council This council is where the UK Government decides on the national defence and security objectives and the best way in which these objectives can be met using national resources. The National Security Council is chaired by the Prime Minister, and generally meets weekly with representation from across the major Departments of State. The Secretary of State for Defence attends as does the Chief of the Defence Staff when the need arises.

MILITARY TASKS AND DEFENCE PLANNING ASSUMPTIONS OF THE UK'S ARMED FORCES

The latest Strategic Defence and Security Review (SDSR) stated that the contribution of the UK Armed Forces to the national security effort is defined by a number of Military Tasks (MT) and Defence Planning Assumptions (DPA).

Military Tasks
The seven military tasks are:

♦ Defending the UK and its Overseas Territories
♦ Providing strategic intelligence
♦ Providing nuclear deterrence
♦ Supporting civil emergency organisations in times of crisis
♦ Defending the UK's interest by projecting power strategically and through expeditionary intervention
♦ Providing a defence contribution to UK influence
♦ Providing security for stabilisation

Defence Planning Assumptions
These assume that in the future the UK Armed Forces will have the size and shape that will enable them to conduct operations of the following type:

An enduring stabilisation operation at around brigade level (possibly up to 6,500 personnel) with maritime and air support as required, while also conducting:

One non-enduring complex intervention (up to 2,000 personnel), and
One non-enduring simple intervention (up to 1,000 personnel):

or alternatively:

Three non-enduring operations if the UK Armed Forces are not already engaged in an enduring operation:

or

For a limited time period, and with sufficient warning, committing all the UK's effort to a one-off intervention of up to three brigades with air and maritime support at a level of about 30,000 personnel.

FUTURE FORCE 2020

In general terms the planning framework provided by the Military Tasks and Defence Planning Assumptions provides an outline for structure which the UK Government aims to establish by 2020.

The proposal is for the Future Force 2020 to have three main combined service elements:

- ◆ The Deployed Force
- ◆ The High Readiness Force
- ◆ The Lower Readiness Force

The Deployed Force
This will consist of those forces that are actually engaged in operations. Therefore aircraft engaged in operations (including the defence of the UK's airspace), forces involved in operations in the South Atlantic, forces operating in Afghanistan (until late 2014) and other expeditionary operations plus the nuclear deterrent will all form elements of The Deployed Force.

The High Readiness Force
This force will consist of a range of maritime, air and land based units capable of deploying at short notice to meet the requirements of the Defence Planning Assumptions. Such forces would enable the UK to react quickly to a range of scenarios that might threaten our national security interests. These force elements would be capable of operating with allies or where necessary on 'stand-alone' UK operations.

The High Readiness Force will include an enhanced Special Forces capability.

We would expect the new Joint Forces Command to have operational control of the majority of future High Readiness Force (Deployed Force) operations.

The Lower Readiness Force
The Lower Readiness Force would consist of elements that have either recently returned from operations, or those that are preparing and training for inclusion in The High Readiness Force. Many Lower Readiness Force units (especially logistic) would be involved in supporting The Deployed Force on operations.

Royal Navy
Under the terms of the Future Force 2020 proposals the Royal Navy will provide a continuous nuclear deterrent system at sea, maritime defence of the United Kingdom and defence of territories in the South Atlantic. Forces assigned to these roles will include:

The Vanguard submarine force equipped with Trident submarine launched inter-continental ballistic missiles. Current plans are for the Vanguard class submarines to be replaced in the late 2020s (with the first submarine possibly being delivered in 2028).

Seven Astute class nuclear powered hunter killer submarines equipped with Tomahawk land attack cruise missiles. Astute class submarines are capable of operating at sea indefinitely.

Two new aircraft carriers, one of which will be kept at extended readiness. The aircraft carrier at sea will be equipped with Joint Strike Fighters and a range of helicopters that (depending on the operational requirement) could include Apache attack helicopters and possibly Chinook and Merlin support helicopters.

A balanced surface fleet of 19 frigates and destroyers.

Up to 14 mine counter- measures vessels to be based on the existing Hunt and Sandown class vessels. In addition there will be an ice patrol ship and an oceanographic survey capability.

The Royal Marine's 3 Commando Brigade will provide an important maritime response capability to the High Readiness Force. 3 Commando Brigade will be able to land significant forces anywhere in the world.

Strategic transport will be provided by a force of up to 6 x roll-on, roll-off ferries.

The Royal Fleet Auxiliary will continue to supply and refuel Royal Naval vessels at sea worldwide.

Land Forces
Land force capabilities will be based around eleven brigades as follows:

A Reaction Force of three multi-role brigades in 3 (UK) Division each consisting of around 6,500 personnel that are comprised of main battle tanks, armoured reconnaissance units, armoured, mechanised and light infantry elements, plus artillery, engineers, army aviation units in support and a complete range of logistic support units. One brigade would always be part of the High Readiness Force and where necessary these brigades could be self supporting.

16 Air Assault Brigade would be the fourth brigade and would provide parachute and air assault units for rapid intervention operations at very short notice. This brigade would be self supporting for short duration operations.

All of the above could form part of a much larger organisation (possibly divisional size) under the command of a deployable UK divisional headquarters. For multinational operations the headquarters of the Allied Rapid Reaction Corps (HQ ARRC) would be available.

Another seven brigades in 1 (UK) Division. These brigades would be equipped at lighter scales and be composed of a mix of regular and reserve personnel. They would be at a lower state of readiness, and if required individual units could be attached to formations in the Reaction Force. Many of the units in these brigades would be able to provide 'depth' in any enduring operation.

The Royal Marines 3 Commando Brigade (a Royal Naval formation) would be available for Land Force operations as required.

There are plans for all UK Army units to have been withdrawn from their bases in Germany by 2020. A majority of land force units will be returned to the UK well before that date.

Royal Air Force
The Royal Air Force will continue to provide the air defence of the United Kingdom and territories in the South Atlantic. To meet this requirement, in the longer term, a fast jet force of both Eurofighter Typhoon and Joint Strike Fighter aircraft will provide air defence, precision ground attack and combat ISTAR capabilities.

In the short term elements of the Tornado fleet will be retained to support operations in Afghanistan and elsewhere should the operational requirement arise.

The Royal Air Force will also provide a fleet of strategic and tactical airlift aircraft based around approximately 7 x C-17, 22 x A400M and 14 x Airbus A330 tanker and transport aircraft. The Chinook helicopter fleet will be increased by 12 new aircraft and Merlin helicopters will be retained.

ISTAR capabilities will be enhanced to include a range of unmanned air systems that will complement existing manned aircraft. The UK may purchase 3 x KC-135 Joint Rivet signals intelligence aircraft to improve the existing ISTAR capability.

TOTAL BRITISH ARMED FORCES (MID 2013)

Regular: 170,710; Regular Army 99,730; Royal Navy 33,960 (including about 7,800 Royal Marines); Royal Air Force 37,030. (Figures are for trained and untrained)

By 2020 Regular Forces levels are planned to be about: Army 82,000; Royal Navy 30,000; Royal Air Force 33,000.

Note: Army figure includes about 3,800 Gurkhas and small numbers of Full Time Reserve Service (FTRS) personnel deployed overseas.

Volunteer Reserves: Army 24,690; Maritime 2,620; Royal Air Force 1,360. There are probably over 50,000 Regular Reserves who could be recalled in a major emergency.

Cadets: Army 75,360; Royal Navy 18,920 ; Royal Air Force 44,970 (includes Combined Cadet Force).

MOD Civilians: 65,400 (mid 2013)

CURRENT FORCE LEVELS

Strategic Forces: 4 x Vanguard Class submarines capable of carrying up to 16 x Trident (D5) Submarine Launched Ballistic Missiles (SLBM) deploying with 40 x warheads per submarine. If necessary a D5 missile could deploy with 12 MIRV (multiple independently targetable re-entry vehicles). Future plans appear to be for a stockpile of 120 operationally ready warheads and 58 missile bodies. Strategic Forces are provided by the Royal Navy.

Current plans appear to be for the Vanguard Class submarines to be replaced in the '2030s'.

Army: 93,940 (trained strength I) : moving to – 1 x Corps Headquarters (HQ ARRC – NATO Deployable HQ);1 x Reaction Force Divisional HQ (1 x Headquarters plus 5 x Brigades);1 x Adaptable Force Divisional HQ (1 x Headquarters plus 8 x Brigades); Force Troops Grouping (1 x Headquarters plus 8 Brigades); 8 x Regional Headquarters;1 x District HQ (London District).

These figures include: 3 x Armoured Infantry Brigades, 1 x Air Assault Brigade; 7 x Regional Infantry Brigades; 3 x Logistics Brigades; 1 x Artillery Brigade; 1 x Engineer Brigade; 2 x Signal Brigades;1 x Medical Brigade; 1 x Intelligence & Surveillance Brigade; 1 x Military Police Brigade. Major Units: 9 x Armoured Regiments; 32 x Infantry Battalions; 13 x Artillery Regiments, 16 x Engineer Regiments/ Major Units; 12 x Signal Regiments; 4 x Army Air Corps Regiments; 7 x Equipment Support Battalions; 12 x Logistic Regiments; 10 x Medical Regiments/ Field Hospitals.

Royal Navy: 31,420 (trained strength – including some 6,850 Royal Marines): 4 x Nuclear Powered Ballistic Missile firing (UK Strategic Deterrent); 7 x Nuclear Powered Submarines (attack type); 4 x Amphibious Assault Ships; 6 x Destroyers; 13 x Frigates (future combined total of 19); 15 x Minehunters and Minesweepers (future total of 14); 4 x Ocean survey vessels; 1 x Antarctic patrol ship; 2 x Patrol vessels and 16 x Patrol craft (fishery protection and patrol duties).15 x Fleet Air Arm Squadrons; New construction: 5 x Nuclear Attack Submarines; 2 x Aircraft Carriers. 6 x Destroyers (Planned to enter service from 2018).

Fleet Support Ships (Manned by Royal Fleet Auxiliary personnel. Supply fuel, stores and ammunition at sea to fleet units) 2 x Fast fleet tankers; 2 x Small fleet tankers; 1 x Support tanker; 3 x Replenishment ships;1 x Casualty receiving facility/Aviation training ship; 1 x Forward repair ship; 3 x Landing Ships.

Royal Marines: 6,850: 1 x Commando Brigade Headquarters; 3 x Royal Marine Commando (Battalion Size); 2 x Commando Assault Helicopter Squadrons; 3 x Commando Assault Helicopter Squadrons; 1 x Commando Regiment Royal Artillery; 1 x Commando Squadron Royal Engineers; 1 x Commando Logistic Regiment; 4 x Commando Assault Squadrons (Landing craft); 1 x Fleet Protection Group; 4 x Nuclear Security Guarding Squadrons; 4 x Special Boat Service Squadrons.

Royal Air Force: 35,350 (trained strength) : 11 x Strike/Attack/ Fast Jet Squadrons; 2 x Unmanned Air Vehicle (UAV) Squadrons; 2 x Airborne Early Warning Squadrons; 2 x ISTAR Squadrons; 5 x Transport Squadrons; 3 x Air to Air Refuelling Squadrons; 7 x Support Helicopter Squadrons; 2 x Search and Rescue Squadrons; 8 x Ground (Field) Defence Squadrons (RAF Regiment). With the following aircraft (numbers approximate): 108 x Typhoon (total of 160 on order); 88 xTornado GR4/4A; 84 x Hawk (all types); 5 x Tristar (being withdrawn during 2014); 8 xVoyager (total of 14 on order replacing VC10

& Tristar); 4 x Sentry AEW; 3 x Sentinel; 5 x Shadow R1; 24 x Hercules C1/3/4/5 (8 x C1/C3 being withdrawn); 8 x C-17; 2 x BAe 146; 5 x Bae 125; 16 x Sea King HAR 3/3A; 5 x Reaper; 30 x Tucano (Training); 119 x Tutor (Training); 38 x Chinook (JFH) – 14 x Mk 6 on order; 25 x Merlin (JFH); 24 x Puma (JFH); (Mk 2 entering service); 22 x A400M Atlas will replace Hercules C1/C3 later in the decade; RAF Chinook, Merlin and Puma helicopters are assigned to the Joint Force Helicopter (JFH); RAF Merlin helicopters will transfer to the Royal Navy's Commando Helicopter Force beginning in 2014.

Joint Forces: 1 x Joint Forces Command HQ; **Joint Helicopter Command:** 4 x Royal Naval Helicopter Squadrons; 5 x Army Aviation Regiments (already listed in the above Army entry plus 1 x TA Regiment); 7 x Royal Air Force Helicopter Squadrons (including 1 x RAuxAF Helicopter Support Squadron). **Joint Special Forces Group:** 1 x Regular Special Air Service (SAS) Regiment; 2 x Volunteer Reserve Special Air Service Regiments; 4 x Special Boat Service (SBS) Squadrons; 1 x Special Reconnaissance Regiment; 1 x Special Forces Support Group; 1 x Joint Special Forces Air Wing; **NBC:** Defence CBRN Wing: **Defence Medical Services:** Ministry of Defence Hospital Units; The Royal Centre for Defence Medicine: The Defence Medical Rehabilitation Centre (Headley Court); Defence Medical Services Training Centre (Aldershot); Defence Dental Services; Defence Medical Postgraduate Deanery.

National Police Forces: England and Wales 125,000 Scotland 14,000, Northern Ireland 11,000.

MINISTRY OF DEFENCE (MOD)

In 1963, the three independent service ministries (Admiralty, War Office and Air Ministry) were merged to form the present MoD.

The UK MoD is the government department that is responsible for all defence related aspects of UK National Policy. This large organisation, which directly affects the lives of about half a million servicemen, reservists and MoD employed civilians, is controlled by The Secretary of State for Defence.

The Secretary of State for Defence has the following principal deputies;

◆ Minister of State for the Armed Forces
◆ Minister of State for Defence Personnel, Welfare and Veterans
◆ Parliamentary Under Secretary of State for Defence Equipment, Support and Technology
◆ Parliamentary Under Secretary of State for International Security Strategy
◆ Parliamentary Under Secretary of State and the Lords Spokesman on Defence

The Secretary of State for defence is assisted by two advisers, one a civilian and the other a senior military officer:

Permanent Under Secretary of State (PUS): The PUS is responsible for policy, finance and administration in the MoD. As the MoD's Principal Accounting Officer he is personally responsible to Parliament for the expenditure of all public money voted to the MoD for Defence purposes. The PUS is the most senior civilian in the MoD.

Chief of the Defence Staff (CDS): The CDS acts as the professional head of the Armed Forces and he is the principal military adviser to both the Secretary of State and to the Government.

Both the PUS and the CDS have deputies; the Second Permanent Under Secretary of State (2nd PUS), and the Vice Chief of the Defence Staff (VCDS). The VCDS acts as the Chief Operating Officer in the Armed Forces Chain-of-Command.

DEFENCE COMMITTEES

In general terms defence is managed through a number of major committees that provide corporate leadership and strategic direction:

Defence Ministerial Committee – chaired by the Secretary of State for Defence
Defence Council – chaired by the Secretary of State for Defence
Defence Board – chaired by the Permanent Secretary
Chiefs of Staff Committee – chaired by the CDS
Service Boards (Admiralty Board, Army Board and Air Force Board)

Defence Ministerial Committee
This committee is chaired by the Secretary of State for Defence and enables ministers and high ranking officials to discuss the overall business of defence. The committee meets about eight times a year.

Defence Council
The Defence Council is the senior committee which provides the legal basis for the conduct and administration of defence and this council is chaired by the Secretary of State for Defence, The composition of the Defence Council is as follows:

Secretary of State for Defence
Minister of State for the Armed Forces
Minister of State for Defence Personnel, Welfare and Veterans
Parliamentary Under Secretary of State for Defence Equipment, Support and Technology
Parliamentary Under Secretary of State for International Security Strategy
Parliamentary Under Secretary of State and the Lords Spokesman on Defence
Permanent Secretary
Chief of the Defence Staff
Vice-Chief of the Defence Staff
Chief of the Naval Staff and First Sea Lord
Chief of the Air Staff
Chief of the General Staff
Chief of Defence Materiel
Chief Scientific Adviser
Director General Finance
Second Permanent Under-Secretary of State for Defence

Defence Board
Chaired by the Secretary of State for Defence this board is the MoD's main corporate board providing senior leadership and direction to the implementation of defence policy. It is responsible for the full range of Defence business other than the conduct of military operations.

The current membership of the Defence Board is:

Secretary of State for Defence
Minister of State for the Armed Forces
Permanent Under Secretary
Chief of the Defence Staff
Vice Chief of the Defence Staff
Chief of Defence Materiel
Director General Finance
Audit Committee Chair (Non Executive Director)
Investment Approvals Committee Chair (Non Executive Director)
Appointments Committee Chair (Non Executive Director)

The Mod describes the objectives of the Defence Board's core tasks as follows:

◆ Role of Defence: To help define and articulate the Department's strategic direction, and provide a clear vision and set of values for defence.

- Targets and Objectives: To establish the key priorities and Defence capabilities needed to deliver the strategy.
- Resource Allocation: To ensure that Defence priorities and tasks are appropriately resourced.
- Performance Management: To manage corporate performance and resources in-year to deliver the required results.

Chiefs of Staff Committee
This committee is chaired by the CDS and is the MoD's senior committee that provides advice on operational military matters and the preparation and conduct of military operations.

Single Service Boards
There are three single service boards: Admiralty Board, Army Board and the Air Force Board all of which are chaired by the Secretary of State for Defence. In general the purpose of the boards is the administration and monitoring of single service performance. Each of these three boards has an executive committee chaired by the single service chief of staff; Navy Board, Executive Committee of the Army Board and the Air Force Board Standing Committee.

MOD HEAD OFFICE

The MoD Head Office allocates resources to Top Level Budget Holders (TLB) who are then accountable to the Chief of the Defence Staff and the Permanent Under Secretary. TLB holders are now far more responsible for the way in which their resources are allocated than they were previously.

There are seven TLB holders:

- Navy Command
- Land Command
- Air Command
- Joint Forces Command
- Head Office & Corporate Services
- Defence Equipment & Support

- Defence Infrastructure Organisation

In general terms the Head Office structure resembles the following:

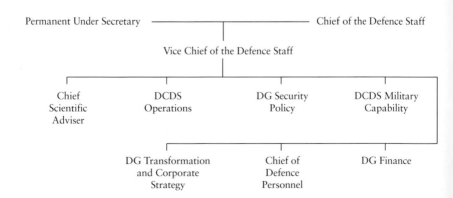

Permanent Under Secretary ——————————————— Chief of the Defence Staff

Vice Chief of the Defence Staff

| Chief Scientific Adviser | DCDS Operations | DG Security Policy | DCDS Military Capability |

| DG Transformation and Corporate Strategy | Chief of Defence Personnel | DG Finance |

CHIEF OF THE DEFENCE STAFF

The Chief of the Defence Staff (CDS) is the officer responsible to the Secretary of State for Defence for the coordinated effort of all three fighting services. He has his own Central Staff Organisation and a Vice Chief of the Defence Staff who ranks as number four in the services hierarchy, following the three single service commanders. The current Chief of the Defence Staff is:

GENERAL SIR NICHOLAS HOUGHTON GCB CBE ADC GEN

General Nick Houghton was born in 1954 in Otley, West Yorkshire. He was educated at Woodhouse Grove School in Bradford, RMA Sandhurst and St Peter's College, Oxford, where he completed an in-service degree in Modern History.

Commissioned into the Green Howards in 1974, he had a variety of Regimental and Staff appointments before attending the Army Command and Staff Courses at both Shrivenham and Camberley. Thereafter he was Military Assistant to the Chief of Staff British Army of the Rhine and a member of the Directing Staff at the Royal Military College of Science, Shrivenham. At Regimental Duty he was both a Company Commander in, and Commanding Officer of, 1st Battalion The Green Howards in the Mechanised and Airmobile roles, and in Northern Ireland.

General Houghton was Deputy Assistant Chief of Staff, G3 (Operations & Deployment) in HQ Land Command 1994–1997 and attended the Higher Command and Staff Course in 1997. He commanded 39 Infantry Brigade in Northern Ireland from 1997 to 1999 and was the Director of Military Operations in the Ministry of Defence from December 1999 to July 2002.

General J N R Houghton GCB, CBE, ADC Gen. (MoD Crown Copyright 2013)

He was Chief of Staff of the Allied Rapid Reaction Corps from July 2002 to April 2004 before becoming the Assistant Chief of the Defence Staff (Operations) from May 2004 to October 2005. He was the Senior British Military Representative Iraq and Deputy Commanding General of the Multi-National Force-Iraq from October 2005 until assuming the appointment as Chief of Joint Operations at PJHQ (UK) in March 2006.

From 2009 General Houghton was the Vice Chief of the Defence Staff and in July 2013 he became the Chief of the Defence Staff.

Vice Chief of the Defence Staff

Where appropriate the Vice Chief of the Defence Staff deputizes for the Chief of the Defence Staff. On a day to day basis he is responsible through the Central Staff for running defence business (with the Second Permanent Under-Secretary).

As of May 2013 the Vice Chief of the Defence Staff is Air Chief Marshal Sir Stuart Peach who had been Chief of Joint Operations/Commander Joint Forces Command since March 2009.

CHAIN OF COMMAND

The Chief of the Defence Staff (CDS) commands and coordinates the activities of the three services through the following chain of command:

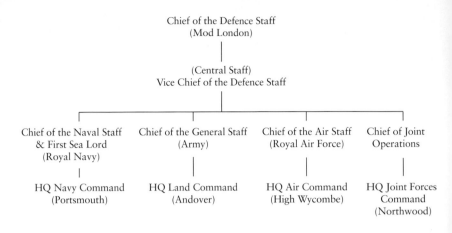

The three single service commanders exercise command of their services through their respective headquarters. However, the complex inter-service nature of the majority of modern military operations, where military, air and naval support must be coordinated, resulted in the establishment in April 2012 of Joint Forces Command (JFC). More detail regarding the JFC can be found in Chapter 5.

DEFENCE EQUIPMENT AND SUPPORT (DE&S)

Following the establishment of PJHQ (now Joint Forces Command) at Northwood it became important to combine the separate logistics functions of the three Armed Forces. As a result, in 2000 the three distinct separate service logistic functions were fused into one and the Defence Logistic Organisation was formed.

From 1 April 2007 the Defence Procurement Agency (DPA) and the Defence Logistic Organisation (DLO) were merged to form Defence Equipment and Support (DE&S). More detail regarding the DE&S can be found in Chapter 5.

STAFF BRANCHES

The Staff Branches that you would expect to find at every military headquarters from the Ministry of Defence (MoD) down to Brigade level are as follows:

Commander	Usually a starred officer (see note) who commands the formation.
Chief of Staff	The officer who runs the headquarters on a day-to-day basis and who often acts as a second-in-command. Generally known as the COS.
Gl Branch	Responsible for administration, personnel matters including manning, discipline and personal services.
G2 Branch	Responsible for intelligence and security
G3 Branch	Responsible for operations including staff duties, exercise planning, training, operational requirements, combat development and tactical doctrine.
G4 Branch	Logistics and quartering.
G5 Branch	Plans
G6 Branch	Communications and IT
G7 Branch	Training
G8 Branch	Resource Management (finance and contracts)
G9 Branch	CIMIC (Civil affairs and cooperation with other agencies)

Note: Commander – The senior officer of the formation who in a large headquarters could be an Admiral, General or Air Marshal. The Army often refers to the commander as the GOC (General Officer Commanding), the Royal Air Force to the AOC (Air Officer Commanding) while the Royal Navy uses the term Flag Officer.

NATO OVERVIEW

The United Kingdom is a member of NATO (North Atlantic Treaty Organisation) and the majority of military operations are conducted in association with the forces of NATO allies.

The following nations are members of the NATO Alliance.

Albania, Belgium, Bulgaria, Canada, Croatia, Czech Republic, Denmark, Estonia, France, Germany, Greece, Hungary, Iceland, Italy, Latvia, Lithuania, Luxembourg, Netherlands, Norway, Poland, Portugal, Romania, Spain, Slovakia, Slovenia, Turkey, United Kingdom, United States.

In 1993, NATO was reorganised from three into two major Commands with a further reorganisation of these two commands in 2003. The first is ACT (Allied Command Transformation) with headquarters at Norfolk, Virginia (USA) and the second is ACO (Allied Command Operations), with its headquarters at Mons in Belgium. NATO operations in which the United Kingdom was a participant would almost certainly be as part of a coalition force under the command and control of Allied Command Operations (ACO).

The current Supreme Allied Commander Europe (SACEUR) is General Philip M. Breedlove. SACEUR, (a US officer) is responsible for the overall command of NATO military operations and conducts the necessary military operational planning, including the identification of forces required for the mission and requesting these forces from NATO countries, as authorised by the North Atlantic Council and as directed by NATO's Military Committee.

The Deputy Supreme Allied Commander Europe (DSACEUR) is General Sir Richard Shirreff, a British Officer. General Shirreff assumed the post in March 2011

SACEUR – GENERAL PHILIP M. BREEDLOVE

General Philip M. Breedlove assumed duties as Supreme Allied Commander, Europe and Commander of US European Command in May 2013'.

General Breedlove was commissioned in 1977 as a distinguished graduate of Georgia Tech's ROTC (see note) program and was raised in Forest Park, Georgia. A Fighter Pilot by trade, General Breedlove is a Command Pilot with over 3,500 flying hours primarily in the F-16. He has flown combat missions in Operation Joint Forge supporting the peacekeeping operation in Bosnia and Operation Joint Guardian to implement the peace settlement in Kosovo.

From 1993–1994, General Breedlove commanded the 80th Fighter Squadron in Kunsan AB, South Korea.

From 1997–1999, he commanded the 27th Operations Group at Cannon AFB, New Mexico. From 2000–2001, he was the commander of the 8th Fighter Wing, Kunsan AB, South Korea. From 2002–2004, he was the commander of the 56th Fighter Wing at Luke AFB, Arizona followed by another wing command from 2004 -2005 of the 31st Fighter Wing at Aviano AB, Italy.

General Breedlove. (US Air Force Image)

From 2008–2009, General Breedlove commanded 3rd Air Force, Ramstein AB, Germany.

From 2012–2013, he was Commander, U.S. Air Forces in Europe; Commander, U.S. Air Forces Africa; Commander Headquarters Allied Air Command, Ramstein; and Director, Joint Air Power Competence Centre, Kalkar Germany.

In addition to General Breedlove's command assignments he has served in a variety of senior leadership positions for the U.S. Air Force including: the senior military assistant to the Secretary of the Air Force; the Vice Director for Strategic Plans and Policy on the Joint Staff; the Deputy Chief of Staff for Operations, Plans and Requirements for Headquarters U.S. Air Force; and Vice Chief of Staff of the U.S. Air Force.

General Breedlove earned a Master of Science degree in Aeronautical Technology from Arizona State University and a Master's degree in National Security Studies from the National War College in 1995.

General Breedlove also attended the Massachusetts Institute of Technology in 2002 as a Seminar XXI Fellow.

He is a distinguished graduate of both Squadron Officer School and Air Command and Staff College.

General Breedlove holds various decorations and awards, including the Distinguished Service Medal, the Defense Superior Service Medal and four awards of the Legion of Merit.

Note: The Reserve Officers' Training Corps (ROTC) is a college-based program for training commissioned officers of the United States armed forces.

NATO COMMANDS

There are two major NATO Commands:

◆ Allied Command Operations (ACO)
◆ Allied Command Transformation (ACT)

Allied Command Operations (ACO)

Allied Command Operations, with its headquarters, SHAPE, near Mons, Belgium, is responsible for all Alliance operations. The levels beneath SHAPE have been significantly streamlined, with a reduction in the number of headquarters. The operational level consists of two standing Joint Force Commands (JFCs) one in Brunssum, the Netherlands, and one in Naples, Italy – which can conduct operations from their static locations or provide a land-based Combined Joint Task Force (CJTF) headquarters, and a robust but more limited standing Joint Headquarters (JHQ), in Lisbon, Portugal, from which a deployable sea-based CJTF HQ capability can be drawn. The current organisation of Allied Command Operations is as follows:

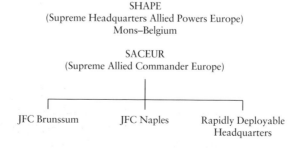

SHAPE
(Supreme Headquarters Allied Powers Europe)
Mons–Belgium

SACEUR
(Supreme Allied Commander Europe)

JFC Brunssum   JFC Naples   Rapidly Deployable
                                          Headquarters

Component Headquarters at the tactical level

The component or tactical level consists of six Joint Force Component Commands (JFCCs), which will provide service-specific land, maritime, or air expertise to the operational level. Although these component commands will be available for use in any operation, they will be subordinated to one of the Joint Force Commanders.

Joint Forces Command – Brunssum

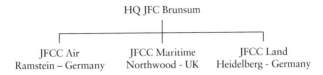

Joint Forces Command – Naples

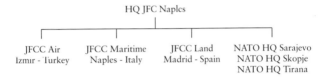

Static Air Operations Centres (CAOC)

In addition to the above component commands there are four static Combined Air Operations Centres with two more deployable as follows:

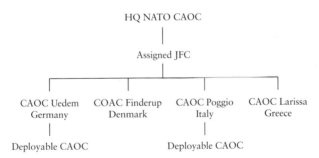

As the deployable CAOCs will need to exercise their capability to mobilise and deploy, the current facilities at Torrejon Air Base in Spain will probably be the primary site for training and exercising in that region. A small NATO air facility support staff would be stationed at Torrejon to support this capability.

Deployable Immediate Reaction Forces (IRF) available:

Immediate Reaction Forces (Maritime) – There are four Maritime Immediate Reaction Forces that provide NATO with a continuous naval presence and can be deployed NATO-wide, when required.

ACE (Allied Command Europe) Rapid Reaction Corps (ARRC) – The ARRC is prepared for deployment throughout Allied Command Europe in order to augment or reinforce local forces whenever necessary. The Headquarters of the ARRC are located in Rheindahlen, Germany (2009) and will move to the UK during the next two years.

Reaction Forces (Air) Staff – With headquarters at Kalkar in Germany.

ACE Mobile Force (AMF) – With headquarters at Heidelberg in Germany.

Deployable National Corps – These deployable corps are available with headquarters provided by Italy, Turkey, Germany / Netherlands, Spain and Greece.

NATO Airborne Early Warning Force (NAEWF) – The NATO Airborne Early Warning Force provides air surveillance and command and control for all NATO commands. It is based in Geilenkirchen, Germany, and Waddington, United Kingdom.

NATO Programming Centre (NPC) – The NATO Programming Centre maintains NATO Air Command and Control Software and provides system expertise to nations and NATO agencies and headquarters. It is located in Glons, Belgium.

Allied Command Transformation (ACT)

Allied Command Transformation, with its headquarters in Norfolk, US, has the responsibility for the transformation of NATO's military capabilities. In doing so, ACT enhances training, improve capabilities, tests and develops doctrines and conduct experiments to assess new concepts. It also facilitates the dissemination and introduction of new concepts and promotes interoperability. There is an ACT Staff Element in Belgium primarily for resource and defence planning issues.

ACT commands the Joint Warfare Centre in Norway, a Joint Force Training Centre in Poland and the Joint Analysis and Lessons Learned Centre in Portugal. ACT Headquarters will also supervise the Undersea Research Centre in La Spezia, Italy and the NATO School at Oberammergau in Germany. There will be direct linkages between ACT, Alliance schools and NATO agencies, as well as the US Joint Forces Command. In addition, a number of nationally or multinationally-sponsored Centres of Excellence focused on transformation in specific military fields support ACT.

THE 2003 NATO CONCEPT

Under the 2003 concept, NATO forces are able to rapidly deploy to crisis areas and remain sustainable, be it within or outside NATO's territory, in support of both Article 5 and Non-Article 5 operations. The successful deployments of the Allied Command Europe Rapid Reaction Corps (ARRC) to two NATO-led Balkan operations (the Implementation Force (IFOR) to Bosnia Herzegovina in 1995 and Kosovo Force (KFOR) to Kosovo in 1999) are early examples of non-Article 5 crisis response operations outside NATO territory. The 2011 deployment of coalition assets to the Libyan no-fly zone (in support of a UN Resolution) is a recent example of rapid deployment in a crisis situation.

The 2003 concept has its largest impact on land forces. Maritime and air forces are by nature already highly mobile and deployable and often have a high state of readiness. Most of NATO's land based assets, however, have been rather static and have had limited (strategic) mobility. In the new structure, land forces should also become highly deployable and should have tactical and strategic mobility. The mobility requirements will have great impact on the Alliance's transport and logistic resources (sea, land and air based). The need for quick reaction requires a certain amount of highly trained forces that are readily available. Further, interoperability (the possibility of forces to co-operate together with other units) and sustainability (the possibility to continue an operation for an extended period of time) are essential in the new force structure.

Note: Article 5 operations commit each NATO member state to consider an armed attack against one state to be an armed attack against all states. Non-Article 5 operations are operations that are not concerned with collective defence.

HIGH READINESS FORCES AND FORCES OF LOWER READINESS

There are forces at two different kinds of readiness posture. First, forces with a higher state of readiness and availability, the so-called High Readiness Forces (HRF) who react on short notice. Second, forces with a lower state of readiness (FLR) to reinforce and sustain the main effort. Graduated Readiness Headquarters have been developed to provide these forces with command and control facilities.

Nato Response Force – Land Component Command (NRF LCC)

An NRF is a coherent, high-readiness, joint, multinational force package of up to 25,000 troops that is technologically advanced, flexible, deployable, interoperable and sustainable. Its role is to act as a stand-alone military force available for rapid deployment. NATO designates NRFs on a rotating basis, and they traditionally comprise land, air and sea components, volunteered and provided by NATO members.

High Readiness Forces (Land) Headquarters candidates available:

The Allied Command Europe Rapid Reaction Corps (ARRC) HQ in Gloucestershire with the United Kingdom as framework nation;

The Rapid Deployable German-Netherlands Corps HQ, based on the 1st German-Netherlands Corps HQ in Munster (Germany);

The Rapid Deployable Italian Corps HQ based on the Italian Rapid Reaction Corps HQ in Solbiate Olona close to Milan (Italy);

The Rapid Deployable Spanish Corps HQ based on the Spanish Corps HQ in Valencia (Spain);

The Rapid Deployable Turkish Corps HQ based on the 3rd Turkish Corps HQ near Istanbul (Turkey);

The Greek 'C' Corps HQ near Thessaloniki (Greece).

The Multinational Corps HQ North-East in Szczecin (Poland) sponsored by Denmark, Germany and Poland;

The Eurocorps HQ in Strasbourg (France) sponsored by Belgium, France, Germany, Luxembourg and Spain.

Note: The Eurocorps Headquarters which has a different international military status based on the Strasbourg Treaty has signed a technical arrangement with SACEUR and can also be committed to NATO missions.

High Readiness Forces (Maritime) Headquarters:

Headquarters Commander Italian Maritime Forces on board of the Italian Naval Vessel GARIBALDI.

Headquarters Commander Spanish Maritime Forces (HQ COMSPMARFOR) on board of LPD CASTILLA.

Headquarters Commander United Kingdom Maritime Forces (HQ COMUKMARFOR) onboard a UK vessel.

THE ALLIED RAPID REACTION CORPS (ARRC)

The concept of the Allied Rapid Reaction Corps was initiated by the NATO Defence Planning Committee in May 1991. The concept called for the creation of Rapid Reaction Forces to meet the requirements of future challenges within the alliance. The ARRC provides the Supreme Allied Commander Europe with a multinational corps sized grouping in which forward elements can be ready to deploy within 14 days (lead elements and reconnaissance parties at very short notice).

As stated by SHAPE the mission of the ARRC is: "HQ ARRC, as a High Readiness Force (Land) HQ, is prepared to deploy under NATO, EU or coalition auspices to a designated area, to undertake combined and joint operations across the operational spectrum as:

♦ a Corps HQ
♦ a Land Component HQ
♦ a Land Component HQ in command of the NATO Response Force
♦ a Joint Task Force HQ for Land-centric operations

These formations will enable support for crisis support management options or the sustainment of ongoing operations."

As NATO's most experienced High Readiness Force (Land) Headquarters the ARRC is actively engaged in the NATO Response Force (NRF) transformation initiative.

Currently the ARRC trains for missions across the spectrum of operations from deterrence and crisis management to regional conflict.

Currently (early 2014) Headquarters ARRC is located in Innsworth (UK) with a peace-time establishment of about 400 personnel. It comprises staff from all the contributing nations. As the Framework Nation, the UK provides the infrastructure, administrative support, communications and 60 per cent of the staff.

HQ ARRC moved from Rheindahlen (Germany) to Innsworth in the UK during the summer of 2010.

The Commander (COMARRC) and Chief of Staff are UK 3 Star and 2 Star Generals and the Deputy Commander is an Italian 2 Star General. The other appointments, as with the training and exercise costs, are shared among the contributing nations.

Outline Composition of the ARRC Headquarters (Allied Command Europe Rapid Reaction Corps)

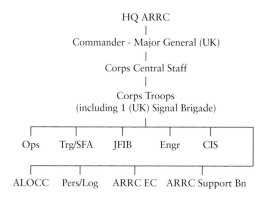

Abbreviations: Ops – Operations; Trg – Training; SFA – Security Force Assistance; JFIB – Joint Fires & Influence; Engr – Engineer; CIS – Command Information Systems; ALOCC – Airland Operations Coordination Cell; ARRC EC – Allied Rapid Reaction Corps Enabling Command.

Although having no permanently assigned formations. HQ ARRC has five Divisions affiliated for operations and training.

1st UK Division	HQ York
3rd UK Division	HQ Bulford
1st Danish Division	HQ Haderslev (Denmark)
Acqui Division	HQ San Giorgio a Cremano (Italy)
1st Panzer Division	HQ Hanover (Germany)

The operational organisation, composition and size of the ARRC would depend on the type of crisis, area of crisis, its political significance, and the capabilities and availability of lift assets, the distances to be covered and the infrastructure capabilities of the nation receiving assistance. It is considered that a four-division ARRC would be the maximum employment structure.

The main British contribution to the ARRC is 3 (UK) Armoured Division. In addition, and in times of tension the assets of 1 (UK) Division could be allocated together with the assets of 16 Air Assault Brigade and 3 Commando Brigade. In total, we believe that should the need arise some 30,000 British soldiers could be assigned to the ARRC together with substantial numbers of Regular Army Reservists and some formed TA Units.

Command Posts and Deployment
Due to the need to be able to respond flexibly to the whole range of potential operations, HQ ARRC has developed the capability for rapidly deployable and modular HQs. Deployment begins with the despatch of a Forward Liaison and Reconnaissance Group (FLRG) within 48 hours of the order to move being given which can then be quickly followed up.

Within four days the key enablers from 1 (UK) Signal Bde would be within theatre and three days later HQ ARRC Forward and HQ Rear Support Command (RSC) Forward – as required – could be established. The forward-deployed HQs are light, mobile and C-130 transportable. While there is a standard 'default' setting for personnel numbers, the actual staff composition is 'tailored' to the task and can vary from approximately 50 to 150 staff, depending on the requirement. The 'in-theatre' task would then be supported by the remainder of the staff, using sophisticated 'Reachback' techniques and equipment.

The Early Entry HQs are capable of sustained independent operations if required but can also be used as enablers if it is decided to deploy the full HQ ARRC. This deployment concept has been tested and evaluated on several exercises and has proven its worth. In parallel, HQ ARRC is continuously looking to make all of its HQs lighter and more survivable

EUROPEAN UNION (EU)

The following countries are members of the European Union:

Austria; Belgium; Bulgaria; Cyprus; Czech Republic; Denmark; Estonia; Finland; France; Germany; Greece; Hungary; Ireland; Italy; Latvia; Lithuania; Luxembourg; Malta; Netherlands; Poland; Portugal; Romania; Slovakia; Slovenia; Spain; Sweden; United Kingdom.

During 2013 the countries of the EU spent approximately 190 billion euros on defence. The largest defence budgets were the UK, France, Germany, Italy and Spain (in that order). Between them these five nations spent about 76 per cent of the total.

Note: 190 billion euros equates to about £158 billion or US$237 billion.

Council of the European Union
The Council of the European Union represents the governments of the Union's 27 nations in the legislature of the European Union. Each nation provides one minister whose portfolio includes the subject being discussed. In the case of defence – the ministers responsible would attend (in company

with their own National European Commissioner). The other legislative body is the European Parliament.

European Common Security and Defence Policy (CSDP)
The EU CSDP is the successor to what used to be known as the European Security and Defence Policy (ESDP). As such the CSDP is an important component of the EU's Foreign and Security Policy (CFSP) and provides the framework for policy and plans relating to all aspects of European defence and security.

CSDP Objectives – EU Helsinki Headline Goal 2010
The EU has adopted the following illustrative scenarios which form the basis for force planning to meet the EU Helsinki Headline Goal 2010 proposals:

◆ Stabilisation, reconstruction and military advice to third world countries
◆ Separation of parties by force
◆ Assistance to humanitarian operations
◆ Conflict Prevention
◆ Evacuation Operations in a non-permissive environment

To ensure that the requirements of the CSDP and the objectives of the Headline Goal 2010 are met, the following command and planning elements have been established:

European Political and Security Committee (PSC)
The PSC keeps track of the requirements of the EU's Common Foreign and Security Policy and defines how those requirements can be incorporated into the Common Security and Defence Policy. Reporting to the Council of the EU the PSC is composed of EU Ambassadors who have the responsibility for providing a coherent And response to a crisis or emergency.

European Union Military Committee (EUMC)
Under the leadership of its current Chairman General Patrick de Rousiers (France) the EUMC is composed of the Chiefs of Defence of the EU member nations. Under normal circumstances these Chiefs of Defence are represented by officers seconded to the EUMC from each of the EU member nations. The EUMC provides advice and recommendations on all aspects of EU security and defence matters to the PSC. General de Rousiers was appointed in November 2012 for a three year term.

Committee for Civilian Aspects of Crisis Management (CIVCOM)
This committee works closely with the EUMC and provides the PSC with information and recommendations relating to all civilian aspects of crisis and emergency management.

In this section we outline the organisation and functions of the following:

◆ The European Union Military Staff (EUMS)
◆ The European Defence Agency (EDA)

EUROPEAN UNION MILITARY STAFF (EUMS)

Working directly to the Chairman of the EUMC the staff is composed of military and civilian personnel who are responsible for planning and coordination of EU security and defence objectives within the framework of the CSDP.

The EUMS have a major focus on operations and the creation of future military capabilities, co-ordinating where possible the military aspirations of the Member State Defence Staffs, the European Defence Agency, the European Commission, NATO, UN, AU and strategic partner countries. This is done in concert with partners in the EU Diplomatic Staff and specifically with the EU Crisis Management Planning Directorate and other crisis response agencies.

EU military forces can be used across the full spectrum of crisis prevention, response and management activities; ranging from support to Humanitarian Assistance, Civil Protection, Security Sector Reform, stabilization and evacuation of citizens, to more complex military operations such as Peace Keeping and Peace Enforcement.

Director General of the EU Military Staff Lieutenant General Wolfgang Wosolsobe (Austria)
Lieutenant General Wolfgang Wosolsobe assumed the responsibilities of Director General of the EU Military Staff, Brussels, on 28 May 2013.

Born in 1955, Lieutenant General Wolfgang Wosolsobe started his military career in 1974 at the "Theresianische Militärakademie" in Wiener Neustadt, Austria and was commissioned as an Infantry Officer in 1977. Assignments as Company Commander (infantry) and instructor at the Military Academy followed by the General Staff Officers Course of the Austrian Armed Forces (1982 -1985) and during two following years, occupied a post in Defence Planning.

In 1987 and 1988, he joined the French "École Supérieure de Guerre Interarmées" and the "Cours Supérieur Interarmées" which offered him the full range of joint staff training and a good command of the French language. Two additional years as a Defence Planner (1989 -1990) were accompanied by functions as lecturer for strategic management methods at the Austrian Defence Academy and as Chief of Staff of the Territorial Command of Salzburg.

In 1991, he joined the Austrian Diplomatic Mission in Geneva as a Military Advisor for Disarmament. This 15 month period in Geneva offered, beyond a first experience in multilateral military diplomacy, a broad range of contacts with other Geneva

General Wolfgang Wosolsobe. (Photo EEAS)

based institutions, including the Graduate Institute for International Studies. His international career continued with the assignment as Defence Attaché (colonel) to France, from 1992 to 1997. Back in Austria, he took over command of the Austrian Special Forces for the period 1997–1998, where continued the efforts of his predecessors to pave the way for the international employment of this force.

After his return to the Austrian MoD, he was appointed Director for Military Policy in 1999, a post which he occupied until 2005. He was promoted to Brigadier General in 2001. During these 6 years, he contributed to shaping the international posture of the Austrian Armed forces. During the defence reform process, conducted during this period, Brigadier General Wosolsobe largely contributed to the adaptation of Austria's defence policy to new realities, particularly to the European Security and Defence Policy (ESDP).

This laid the groundwork for his appointment as Defence Policy Director during the Austrian presidency of the EU Council in 2006. From there, he joined Brussels as Military Representative in 2007 and was promoted to Major General in June of the same year. During his period as Military Representative, he served as Dean of the EU Military Committee in 2009 and 2010. In 2012, he was elected to the post of Director General of the EU Military Staff. He takes over this appointment on 8 May 2013. In March 2013, he was promoted to Lieutenant General.

The Deputy Director General is Rear Admiral B N B Williams CBE BSc CCMl (Royal Navy) appointed in September 2011.

EUMS OUTLINE STRUCTURE (BRUSSELS)

Note: ACOS External Relations has links with the UN, NATO and the SHAPE EU Liaison cell.

EU Operations Centre
During January 2007, the EU Operations Centre was established in Brussels. This Headquarters can command a small force of about 5,000 troops (possibly a Brigade).

In March 2012 the EU Operations Centre was activiated for the first time to command and control three different EU Operations in the Horn of Africa.

In addition to the EU Operations Centre, there are 5 x national operational headquarters which have been made available for use by the EU. These are:

◆ Mont Valerien (Paris)
◆ Northwood (London)
◆ Potsdam (Berlin)
◆ Centocelle (Rome)
◆ Larissa (Greece)

CURRENT EU MILITARY OPERATIONS (LATE 2013)

EUFOR (Operation Althea)
The EU launched Operation Althea in Bosnia and Herzegovina (BiH) – in December 2004. This follows the decision by NATO to conclude its SFOR mission.

The EU deployed a large force of 6,300 personnel to ensure continued compliance with the Dayton/ Paris Agreement and to contribute to a safe and secure environment in BiH.

The key objectives of Operation Althea are to provide deterrence and continued compliance with the responsibility to fulfil the role specified in Annexes 1A and 2 of the Dayton/Paris Agreement (General Framework Agreement for Peace in BiH) and to contribute to a safe and secure environment in BiH, in line with its mandate, and to achieve core tasks in the Stabilisation and Association Process (SAP).

The headquarters of EUFOR is in Sarajevo and in mid 2013 the personnel strength for Operation Althea was in the region of 830.

Operation Althea has been authorised by the United Nations Security Council Resolution 1575.

EURONAVFOR (Operation Atalanta)
In December 2008, the EU established operation ATALANTA to protect World Food Programme and other vulnerable shipping transiting through the Gulf of Aden. The UK has provided the Operation

Commander and Operation Headquarters at Northwood since its inception and will continue to do so until the end of the mandate.

EURONAVFOR currently includes warships, support vessels, and the delivery of shipping advice and reassurance from Belgium, Denmark, France, Germany, Greece, the Netherlands and Spain. Maritime Patrol aircraft are provided by Portugal, Spain, Germany, France

Personnel strength is in the region of 1,050.

EUTM (Somalia)
During January 2010, the EU established a training mission for Somali security forces which commenced during early May. Training actually takes place in Uganda and EUTM has a personnel strength of around 80.

The mission also includes a liaison office in Nairobi and a support cell in Brussels.

EUTM (Mali)
Established in April 2013 EUTM Mali supports the formation and training of four battalions (approximately 3,000 soldiers) of the Malian Army.

The mission consists of about 390 personnel (includes 200 instructors) from a variety of European Armed Forces.

Civilian Planning and Conduct Capability (CPCC)
Working directly to the Political and Security Committee (PSC) this group is responsible for the command and control of civilian (non-military) elements of CSDP crisis and emergency related operations.

Current EU Civilian Missions (late 2013)

Mission	Area	Role	Established	Personnel
EUPM	Bosnia	Police Support	2003	281
EULEX	Kosovo	Rule of Law	2008	2,140
EU SSR	Guinea Bissau	Security Reform	2008	16
EUSEC	Congo	Security Reform	2005	79
EUROPOL RD	Congo	Police Reform	2007	60
EUROPOL COPPS	Palestinian Territories	Police Support	2006	96
EUBAM Rafah	Palestinian Territories	Border Assistance	2005	8
EUBAM	Moldova and Ukraine	Border Assistance	2006	105
EUBAM	Georgia	Border Assistance	2008	395
EUPOL	Afghanistan	Police Support	2007	540
EUJUST LEX	Iraq/Baghdad	Legal Training	2005	59
EUCAP	Niger/Sahel	Security Assistance	2012	44
EUAVSEC	South Sudan	Aviation Security	2012	33
EUCAP Nestor	Horn of Africa	Maritime Training Mission	2012	53

EUROPEAN DEFENCE AGENCY

The European Defence Agency (EDA) was established in July 2004 following a unanimous decision by European Heads of State and Government. It was established under the Council Joint Action 2004/5 51/CFSP on the basis of Article 14 of the treaty on the European Union (Maastricht).

The purpose of the European Defence Agency is to support the Member States and the Council of Europe in order to improve European defence capabilities in the field of crisis management, and to sustain and develop the European Security and Defence Policy (ESDP).

UK Government position on membership

The UK is currently a participant in the activities of the European Defence Agency. The following is an extract from a statement made by the Secretary of State for Defence Philip Hammond on 12 February 2013:

> *"I am announcing today that following a review of our membership of the European Defence Agency the UK will at the present time remain a member of the agency.*
>
> *In 2010 the UK reviewed its membership of the EDA following the strategic defence and security review. Subsequently, my predecessor, my right hon. Friend Dr Fox, recommended that the UK should remain a member of the EDA with a stocktake after two years.*
>
> *In consultation across Government, my Department has reassessed the benefits of remaining in the EDA and reviewed progress made by the agency since 2010 against identified shortfalls.*
>
> *The EDA has made progress in some areas requiring reform, but there is more to be done to improve its operational effectiveness and so the case for continued membership remains finely balanced. Overall, I have concluded that for now the UK should remain a member of the EDA with our continuing membership to be reviewed again in late 2013 in light of progress made during the year."*

On 6 March 2013 a question was asked in the UK Parliament regarding the decision of the UK Government to to remain a member of the European Defence Agency and to the annual cost of membership. The reply by Lord Astor of Hever ((Parliamentary Under Secretary of State, for Defence) was as follows:

> *"As set out in the Statement of 12 February, the Government have concluded that the agency has achieved some progress against identified shortfalls. There is, however, further work to be done to improve its performance. We will work with the agency and its member states to achieve this, and review our continuing membership in late 2013. Our European Defence Agency membership costs some £3 million to £4 million per annum and is calculated on gross national income."*

The EDA has the following tasks:

◆ To improve the EU's defence capabilities in the field of crisis management.
◆ To promote European armaments cooperation.
◆ To strengthen the European defence industrial and technological base and create a competitive European defence equipment market, in consultation with the Commission.
◆ To promote research, in liaison with Community research activities, with a view to strengthening Europe's industrial and technological potential in the defence field.

EDA Organisation

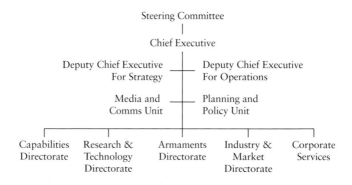

In the longer term the EDA will achieve its goals by:

♦ Encouraging EU Governments to spend defence budgets on meeting tomorrow's challenges and not, in their words, yesterday's threats.

♦ Helping EU Governments to identify common needs and promoting collaboration to provide common solutions.

♦ The EDA is an agency of the European Union and therefore under the direction and authority of the European Council, which issues guidelines to, and receives reports from the High Representative as Head of the Agency. Detailed control and guidance, however, is the responsibility of the Steering Committee.

The Steering Committee, the principal decision-making body of the Agency is made up of Defence Ministers from participating Member States (all EU members except Denmark) and a member of the European Commission. In addition to ministerial meetings at least twice a year, the Steering Committee also meets at the level of national armaments directors, national research directors, national capability planners and policy directors.

The EDA's Chief Executive is Claude-France Arnould who was appointed in January 2011. She has more than 20 years' experience in External Relations, Common Foreign and Security Policy and the European Common Security and Defence Policy.

The EDA Headquarters is in Brussels (Belgium) and there is approximately 120 staff.

The Agency had a budget of €30.5 million (US$40.4 million/£25.9 million) in 2013.

European Union Institute for Strategic Studies (EU-ISS)

The EU-ISS is based in Paris and was established in 2002 and is an independent think tank that researches issues relevant to EU defence and security. Much of the work is published and the EU-ISS organises conferences and seminars on all aspects of EU related defence and security.

EUROCORPS

The Eurocorps was inaugurated in January 1989 and declared operational in October 1991 and comprises military contributions from its five framework nations: Belgium, France, Germany, Luxembourg and Spain. The Headquarters is located in Strasbourg (France). Greece, Italy, Poland and Turkey have military liaison staff co-located at Eurocorps HQ.

The Commander Eurocorps (COMEC) is a Lieutenant General (3 stars). The Deputy Commander (DCOM) is a Major General (2 stars). The staff is directed by the Chief of Staff (COS), also a Major General and he is supported by two Deputy Chiefs of Staff (DCOS) for Operations and Support, both of whom are Brigadier Generals (1 star).

The posts of Commanding General and the other general officers as well as some key functions are filled by EU framework nations on a rotational basis. COMEC, DCOM and COS are always of different nationalities. Their tour of duty generally lasts for two years.

In general terms the Eurocorps is at the disposal of the European Union and available for service in support of NATO. The command language is English.

The Eurocorps consists of formations under direct operational control and formations earmarked for assignment during a crisis or emergency:

Under direct operational control:

♦ Franco German Brigade (GE-FR Bde)
♦ Multinational Command Support Brigade (MNCS Bde)

Formations earmarked for assignment during an emergency:

French Contribution

Etat-Major de Force numéro 3 (EMF3) in Marseille (equivalent to a divisional HQ) composed of:

1 x Armoured Brigade
1 x Mechanised Infantry Brigade
Specialised support units

German Contribution

The 10th Armoured Division, with its HQ in Sigmaringen, composed of:

2 x Brigades as required
Specialised support units

Belgian Contribution

Belgian Operational Command Land, with its HQ in Evere, composed of:

1st Medium Brigade in Leopoldsburg Support units

Spanish Contribution

1st Land Forces Command its HQ in Burgos, composed mainly of 1st Mechanised Division.

Luxembourg Contribution

Luxembourg assigns a reconnaissance company composed of about 180 personnel. During operations this unit would be integrated into the Belgian contingent.

Operational Experience

During the past decade the Eurocorps HQ has been involved in operations as follows:

SFOR (Bosnia) 1999–2000
KFOR III (Kosovo) 2000
ISAF IV (Afghanistan) 2004–2005
HQ Eurocorps Standby Element of Nato Response Force (2006–2007)
HQ Eurocorps Standby Element of Nato Response Force (2010–2011)
Afghanistan Training Deployment – 300 personnel (2012–2013)

Note: If all earmarked national contributions were committed to operations, the Eurocorps would number approximately 60,000 personnel.

FRANCO – GERMAN BRIGADE (FGB)

The FGB is essentially a wheeled mechanised Brigade. It is the core entry group for Eurocorps operations and in concert with the EU Battlegroups the immediate EU reserve formation.

The Brigade is a joint formation consisting of both French and German units and under the direct command of the Eurocorps.

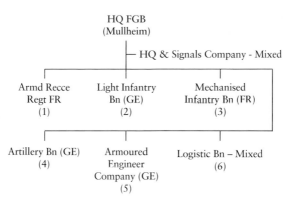

HQ FGB
(Mullheim)

— HQ & Signals Company - Mixed

Armd Recce Regt FR (1)

Light Infantry Bn (GE) (2)

Mechanised Infantry Bn (FR) (3)

Artillery Bn (GE) (4)

Armoured Engineer Company (GE) (5)

Logistic Bn – Mixed (6)

Approximately 5,200 personnel

Notes:

(1) 3e Regiment de Hussars

(2) Jagerbataillon 291

(3) 110e Regiment d'Infanterie

(4) Panzerartilleriebataillon 295

(5) Panzerpionierkompanie 500

(6) Logistic Battalion with: Supply Company; Maintenance Company; Transport Company; Administration & Support Company; HQ & Suport Company.

Jagerbataillon 292 is available to reinforce the FGB should that be necessary.

EU BATTLEGROUPS

There are EU plans to be able to provide at least one coherent Battlegroup package at any one time to undertake Battlegroup-sized operations in support of the EU Helsinki Headline Goals.

Full Operational Capability (FOC) was reached at the end of 2007 when all Battlegroups became available. The EU now has the capacity to undertake up to two Battlegroup-size rapid response operations, including the ability to launch both such operations nearly simultaneously.

There are usually two EU Battlegroups on standby for operations and trained to respond to emerging contingencies at any one time. They would be deployed following a unanimous decision of the European Council of Ministers, with the nations providing the Battlegroup having a veto on any deployment decision.

EU Member States have indicated that they will commit to Battle Groups, formed as follows:

1	United Kingdom
2	France
3	France and Belgium
4	Italy
5	Spain
6	France, Germany, Belgium, Luxembourg and Spain
7	Germany, the Netherlands and Finland (BG 107)
8	Germany, Austria and Czech Republic
9	Italy, Hungary and Slovenia
10	Spain and Italy (Amphibious)

11	Italy, Romania and Turkey
12	Poland, Germany, Slovakia, Latvia and Lithuania
13	Sweden, Finland, Estonia, Ireland and Norway
14	United Kingdom and the Netherlands
15	Greece, Bulgaria, Cyprus, Romania and Slovenia
16	Czech Republic and Slovakia
17	Spain, Germany, France and Portugal

Expect a battle group to have between 1,500 and 2,000 personnel.

Each Battlegroup will have a 'lead nation' that will take operational command, based on the model set up during the EU's peacekeeping mission in the Democratic Republic of the Congo (Operation Artemis). Two non-EU NATO countries, Norway and Turkey participate in the EU Battlegroup program.

Battlegroups would have to be able to deploy within 5–10 days and be sustained initially for 30, but possibly up to 120 days while operating up to 6,000 km from Brussels.

As yet (late 2013) EU Battlegroups have not been deployed.

EU RELATIONSHIP WITH NATO

In a joint declaration by both the EU and NATO during 2002, a previously slightly confused relationship was clarified under a number of major headings that included partnership, mutual cooperation and consultation, equality and due regard for the autonomy of both the EU and NATO, plus reinforcing and developing the military capability of both organisations.

The 'Berlin Plus Agreement' of March 2003 allows the EU to use NATO structures to support military operations that do not fall within the remit of NATO responsibilities. In addition, there is considerable exchange of information between both organisations and they are EU/NATO liaison cells situated in the headquarters of both organisations.

Because in many cases nations that are members of the EU are also members of NATO, the same forces are often assigned to both EU and NATO missions. It is therefore likely that the EU will only act if NATO first decides that it will not do so.

ANGLO – FRENCH DEFENCE COLLABORATION (DOWNING STREET DECLARATION)

In November 2010 the UK and French Governments announced treaties and agreements relating to mutual defence and security:

◆ Defence and Security Cooperation Treaty
◆ Nuclear Stockpile Stewardship Agreement

Defence and Security Cooperation Treaty
This treaty allows for the British and French Armed Forces to cooperate across a wide spectrum of defence activities including training, equipment, access to joint facilities, access to defence markets and industrial and technical cooperation.

Nuclear Stockpile Stewardship Agreement
This agreement related to collaboration on nuclear stockpile stewardship with access to the Joint UK Technology Centre at Aldermaston and the Joint French Centre at Valduc.

In addition:

A 'Letter of Intent' establishing a new framework for collaboration between French and UK Armed Forces on **operational matters** was also signed.

This declaration also outlined a decision to create a **Combined Joint Expeditionary Force** (CJEF) capable of reacting to the complete spectrum of military operations. These would range from high intensity to peace support operations and would be available for NATO, EU and if necessary UN tasking. The CJEF would have land, sea and air components. Full capability could be expected by 2015.

There would be cooperation between France and the UK regarding their **aircraft carriers** with the possibility of being able to deploy an integrated, French – UK carrier group during the 2020s.

Agreements were also made regarding equipment and capabilities with cooperation a wide range of in-service **defence equipment and systems**. This would include strategic plans for the French/UK weapons sector and focus on priority R&D programmes important to both nations. France and the UK would also cooperate on cyber security.

Both countries would concentrate on cooperation in the whole spectrum of **counter-terrorist** activities to ensure the protection of their populations and critical infrastructure. Joint efforts would be made to assist in the creation of counter-terrorist structures in other (especially developing) countries.

The decisions made in 2010 were regarding France and the UK alone and there is no formal link to any NATO or European Security and Defence Policy. Both France and the UK agree that NATO remains the guarantor of European security and that their aim was to pursue even closer cooperation between the EU and NATO.

EUROPEAN RAPID REACTION FORCE

The current (late 2013) situation there is no standing European Rapid Reaction Force (other than the Franco – German Brigade or the EU Battlegroups) nor any EU agreement to create one. What has sometimes been referred to as a 'European Rapid Reaction Force' is, in fact, a catalogue of forces which member states could make available to the EU should they choose to participate in a particular EU-led operation. Any contribution to a particular EU-led operation would depend on the operation's requirements, the availability of forces at the time and the willingness of EU members to participate. However, it is likely that this will change during the next five years.

AFGHANISTAN (OPERATION HERRICK)

UK Forces are deployed to Afghanistan in support of the UN authorised, NATO led International Security Assistance Force (ISAF) mission and as part of the US-led Operation Enduring Freedom (OEF). UK operations in Afghanistan are being conducted under the name Operation HERRICK.

In mid 2013 the UK had approximately 8,000 personnel serving in Afghanistan as part of the international security Assistance Force (ISAF). The security situation varies across the country with over 70 per cent of violent incidents taking part in the southern provinces of Helmand, Kandahar and Kunar, areas where the population is about 11 per cent of the country's 28 million people. The UK's role is to assist the Afghan government to ensure security, governance, and development.

THE INTERNATIONAL SECURITY ASSISTANCE FORCE (ISAF)

The International Security Assistance Force (ISAF) is mandated under Chapter VII of the United Nations (UN) Charter (Peace Enforcing) by a number of UN Security Resolutions. ISAF exists to help the Afghan people, not to govern them. Additionally, under the UN mandate, the role of ISAF is to assist in the maintenance of security to help the Islamic Republic of Afghanistan and the UN in those areas it is responsible for.

NATO assumed command and control of the ISAF mission on August 11, 2003.

During mid 2013 there were approximately 97,800 troops in ISAF with contributions from 50 nations and with national contingent strengths changing on a regular basis. Major contributors include:

- ◆ United States   68,000
- ◆ United Kingdom   8,065
- ◆ Germany   4,400
- ◆ Italy   3,034
- ◆ Poland   1,740
- ◆ Georgia   1,560
- ◆ Romania   1,520
- ◆ Turkey   1,100
- ◆ Australia   1,030
- ◆ Canada   950
- ◆ Spain   860
- ◆ Denmark   520
- ◆ France   455

ISAF is supported by approximately 200,000 personnel from the Afghan National Army (ANA) and about 90,000 personnel from the Afghan National Police (ANP).

End of ISAF combat operations
The UK Government have announced that UK troop numbers in Afghanistan will reduce to approximately 5,200 by the end of 2013 with further significant reductions planned during 2014. ISAF combat operations in support of the Afghan Government are due to be completed by the end of 2014.

There is likely to be an International/NATO training mission in Afghanistan after combat operations cease at the end of 2014. This would be a 'train, advise and assist' mission and will not involve international troops being deployed in combat operations.

The UK is already committed to supporting this post 2014 NATO training mission and as yet (mid 2013) there is little more that speculation regarding the size and scope of this mission. Our belief is that the UK will continue to support the Afghan National Army Officer Academy and that the size of the UK contribution to the NATO training mission is unlikely to exceed 300 personnel.

The MoD is planning to recover about £4 billion of inventory previously deployed to Afghanistan – this would include all undamaged vehicles and major equipments. Totals could amount to the equivalent of about 6,500 twenty-foot containers of equipment, together with about 2,500 vehicles. Equipment and materiel identified as being surplus or beyond repair could be gifted locally or sold, as long as this would not comprise security and the end result would be the best value for money for the UK taxpayer.

AFGHANISTAN – COSTS

"When the army marches the treasury empties"

Sun Tzu – The Art of War (around 500 BC)

The additional costs for operations in Afghanistan (excluding salaries and ongoing costs that would have happened anyway) are paid for by the Governments Contingency Reserve fund. The next table shows annual costs from 2001.

Cost of Operations in Afghanistan 2002–2011

(in million of UK £)

FY 2001–2002	221	
FY 2002–2003	311	
FY 2003–2004	46	
FY 2004–2005	67	
FY 2005–2006	199	
FY 2006–2007	738	
FY 2007–2008	1,504	
FY 2008–2009	2,623	
FY 2009–2010	3,820	
FY 2010–2011	3,780	
FY 2011–2012	3,460	
FY 2012–2013	3,800	Estimate
FY 2013–2014	3,800	Estimate
FY 2014–2015	3,500	Estimate

Expenditure is expected to reduce due to smaller force levels in theatre towards the end of the mission.

THE FINANCES OF DEFENCE

"You need three things to win a war,
Money, money and more money".

Trivulzio (1441-1518)

In general terms defence is related to money, and a nation's ability to pay for its defence is linked to its GDP (Gross Domestic Product) as measured by the sum of all economic activity within a country. Estimates for the world's top eight GDP rankings for 2012 (in billions of US$) and the latest year for which accurate (International Monetary Fund) figures are available are as follows:

United States	$15.63 billion
China (PRC)	$12.32 billion
India	$4.71 billion
Japan	$4.61 billion
Germany	$3.19 billion
Russia	$2.51 billion
United Kingdom	$2.31 billion
France	$2.25 billion

Note: As an economic grouping the European Union has the world's largest GDP at $16.07 billion.

UK DEFENCE EXPENDITURE

In the 2014–2015 Financial Year (FY) the UK Government plans to spend £32.7 billion on defence.

For comparison purposes defence expenditure is often expressed as a percentage of GDP. Expenditure in FY 2013–2014 represented around 2.5 per cent of GDP. In 1985 UK defence expenditure represented 5.2 per cent of GDP.

The estimated total UK government expenditure for FY 2014–2015 is £363 billion.

Major spending departments include:

Department for Work and Pensions	£5.7 billion
Department of Health	£113 billion
Scotland	£28.4 billion
Education	£57.3 billion

Some interesting comparisons can be made when looking at estimates for the world's top eight defence budgets for 2012 (in billions of US$ and the latest year for which accurate figures are available) are as follows:

United States	US$ 682 billion
China (PRC)	US$ 166 billion
Russia	US$ 91 billion
United Kingdom	US$ 61 billion
Japan	US$ 59 billion
France	US$ 58 billion
Saudi Arabia	US$ 57 billion
India	US$ 46 billion

The figures in the above listing are figures derived from US$ exchange rates during mid 2012. Figures rounded to the nearest whole number (source SIPRI).

DEFENCE BUDGETS – NATO COMPARISON (2012 FIGURES)

The nations of the North Atlantic Treaty Organisation (NATO) spent some US$940 billion on defence during 2008.

It is probably worth noting that Canada and the European members of NATO spent approximately US$313 billion, while the US spent some US$682 billion. Collectively, Canada and the European members of NATO spent just over 31 per cent of the NATO expenditure..

For ease of conversions from national currencies, amounts are shown in US$.

Country	2012 Budget (billions of US$)
Albania	0.2
Belgium	5.3
Bulgaria	0.6
Canada	28.0
Czech Republic	2.5
Denmark	4.5
Estonia	0.3
France	58.9
Germany	43.4
Greece	7.5
Hungary	1.3
Italy	31.0
Latvia	0.2
Lithuania	0.4
Luxembourg	0.3
Netherlands	10.9
Norway	7.0
Poland	9.1

Portugal	5.2
Romania	2.1
Spain	13.9
Slovakia	1.0
Slovenia	0.7
Turkey	18.6
United Kingdom	61.0
Other NATO	**313.9**
United States	682.0
Final Total	**995.9**

Note: (1) Iceland has no military expenditure although it remains a member of NATO. (2) On 1 April 2009 Albania and Croatia were admitted into the NATO alliance.

An interesting comparison is made by the total national defence budget divided by the total number of full time personnel in all three services. 2012 figures for the top five world defence spending nations are as follows:

Nation	2012 Defence Budget US$	Total Active Service Personnel	Cost per serviceman US$
United States	US$ 682 billion	1,429,000	477,256
China (PRC)	US$ 166 billion	2,285,000	72,647
Russia	US$ 91 billion	1,040,000	87,500
United Kingdom	US$ 61 billion	177,700	344,632
Japan	US$ 59 billion	230,000	256,521
France	US$ 58 billion	228,000	254,385
India	US$ 46 billion	1,325,000	34,716
Germany	US$ 43 billion	188,000	228,723

UK MOD PERSONNEL FIGURES

During 2013 and 2014 Armed Forces redundancies will continue making really accurate personnel figures difficult to obtain.

Personnel Overview (as at 1 April 2013)

Total MoD Personnel	236,110
Military total	170,710
Officers	29,060
Other Ranks	141,650
Civilian total	65,400
Non Industrial	40,410
Industrial	7,660
Locally engaged (overseas)	8,250
Regular Forces stationed in the UK	150,310
MoD Civilian personnel stationed in the UK	53,050
Regular Forces stationed overseas	20,060
MoD Civilian personnel stationed overseas	10,000
Regular Forces stationed in Germany	14,840
MoD Civilian personnel stationed overseas	10,000

For comparison: Total Service and Civilian Personnel Strength (1990)

UK service personnel	305,700
UK civilian personnel	141,400
Total	447,100

Service Strengths (as at 1 April 2013 – Trained and Untrained)

	Total	Officers	Other Ranks
Royal Navy	33,960	6,940	27,020
Army	99,730	13,890	85,840
Royal Air Force	37,030	8,230	28,790

Trained Strengths and Requirements (as at 1 April 2013)

	Requirement	Strength	Surplus/Deficit
Royal Navy	30,530	31,420	+890
Officers	5,800	6,240	+430
Other Ranks	24,730	25,190	+460
Army	96,790	93,940	−2850
Officers	14,060	13,060	−1000
Other Ranks	82,730	80,880	−1850
Royal Air Force	35,620	35,350	−270
Officers	7,600	7,570	−30
Other Ranks	28,020	27,780	−240

Regular Forces by Gender (as at 1 April 2013)

Royal Navy	Strength	Females
Officers	6940	690
Other Ranks	27,020	2390
Army	Strength	Females
Officers	13,890	1,640
Other Ranks	85,840	6760
Royal Air Force	Strength	Females
Officers	8,230	1,340
Other Ranks	28,790	3,790

Intake to the Regular Forces (from 1 April 2012 to 1 April 2013)

Royal Navy	
Officers	280
Other Ranks	2,450
Army	
Officers	620
Other Ranks	9,440
Royal Air Force	
Officers	130
Other Ranks	1,170

Outflow from the Regular Forces (from 1 April 2012 to 1 April 2013)

Royal Navy	Trained	Untrained
Officers	530	60
Other Ranks	3,180	880

Army	Trained	Untrained
Officers	1,380	90
Other Ranks	10,990	2,440

Royal Air Force	Trained	Untrained
Officers	780	210
Other Ranks	3,160	140

Strength of the Volunteer Reserve Forces (at 1 April 2013)

Maritime Reserve Forces	
Trained	1,770
Untrained	850

Territorial Army	
Trained	19,230
Untrained	5,460

Royal Auxiliary Air Force	
Trained	1,040
Untrained	320

In the event of a national emergency, we believe that the UK MoD would be able to call on the following numbers of regular service personnel who had retired within the last five years. It would not be unrealistic to expect that such personnel would be capable of being absorbed into operational units with the minimum of training:

Royal Navy	12,000
Army	40,000
Royal Air Force	15,000

Regular Forces stationed Europe (outside UK)

	Total	Officers	Other Ranks
Cyprus	2,400	250	2,150
Belgium	330	170	160
Gibraltar	200	30	170
Italy	140	70	60
Netherlands	140	50	90
Portugal	30	20	10
Norway	40	20	10
France	40	20	10
Czech Rep	20	10	10
Germany	14,840	1,470	13,370

Regular forces stationed outside Europe

	Total	Officers	Other Ranks
Australia	50	40	10
Bahrain	10	10	–
Belize	10	10	–
Brunei	150	50	100 (figure excludes Gurkhas)
Canada	280	90	190 (figures excludes BATUS staff)
Indian Ocean	40	–	40
Kenya	180	40	140
Kuwait	40	30	10
Oman	90	50	40
Saudi Arabia	110	70	40
Sierra Leone	20	10	10
United States	560	370	190

Community Cadet Forces (at 1 April 2012)

Royal Navy

Sea Cadets	13,860
Adult Volunteers	5,190

Army Cadet Force

Army Cadets	45,110
Adult Volunteers	8,380

Air Training Corps

Air Cadets	35,750
Adult Volunteers	10,510

Totals: 94,730 cadets and 24,080 adult volunteers.

Combined Cadet Force (at 1 April 2012)

Royal Navy

Cadets	5,540
Adult Volunteers	320

Army

Cadets	30,250
Adult Volunteers	1,170

Royal Air Force

Cadets	9,220
Adult Volunteers	620

Totals: 45,020 cadets and 2,100 adult volunteers.

Note: Combined Cadet Force detachments are generally based at schools.

CHAPTER 2 – THE ROYAL NAVY

PERSONNEL SUMMARY (MID 2013)

Royal Navy		*Trained and Untrained Strength (mid 2013)*
Officers		6,940
	Males	6,250
	Females	690
Other Ranks		27,020
	Males	24,630
	Females	2,390
	Total	33,960

Note: The above figures include some 6,850 Royal Marines (including 760 officers) but do not include the approximate figure of 2,500 personnel from the Army attached to 3 Commando Brigade.

Not included in the above figures are approximately 2,000 civilian personnel manning support ships operated by the Royal Fleet Auxiliary (RFA).

	Personnel in training (mid 2013)
Officers	280
Other Ranks	2,450

FLEET STRENGTH OVERVIEW

Submarines
In service:
4 x Nuclear Powered Ballistic Missile firing (UK Strategic Deterrent)
7 x Nuclear Powered Attack type

New construction: 5 x Nuclear Powered Attack type.

Major surface vessels
In Service:
4 x Amphibious Assault Ships

New construction: 2 x Aircraft Carriers. Planned to enter service from 2018.

Destroyers and frigates
In Service:
6 x Destroyers
13 x Frigates

New Construction: 6 x Destroyers.

Minewarfare vessels
In Service:
15 x Minehunters and minesweepers. Deployable worldwide

Survey Ships
In Service:
4 x Ocean survey vessels

Patrol vessels
In service:
1 x Antartic patrol ship
2 x Fast patrol vessels. Gibraltar Squadron.
16 x Patrol craft

Fleet Support Ships
(Manned by Royal Fleet Auxiliary personnel. Supply fuel, stores and ammunition at sea to fleet units)

In Service:
2 x Fast fleet tankers
2 x Small fleet tankers
1 x Support tanker
3 x Replenishment ships
1 x Casualty receiving facility
3 x Landing Ships

Naval Aircraft (FAF – Forward Available Fleet)
21 x Merlin MK 1 Helicopters. Anti-submarine warfare
11 x Sea King MK 5. SAR and Utility
10 x Sea King Mk 7. Provides radar airborne early warning to fleet
4 x Lynx Mk 3 (training).
25 x Lynx Mk 8. Anti-submarine warfare and missile armed for surface ship attack
12 x Hawk. Fixed wing trainer
4 x King Air (training)

Note: Other naval aircraft are assigned to the Joint Force Harrier (JFH) and the Joint Helicopter Command (JHC). See Chapter 5.

Royal Marines Summary
1 x Commando Brigade Headquarters
3 x Royal Marine Commando (Battalion Size)
3 x Commando Assault Helicopter Squadrons
1 x Commando Light Helicopter Squadron
1 x Commando Regiment Royal Artillery
1 x Commando Regiment Royal Engineers
1 x Commando Logistic Regiment
4 Commando Assault Squadrons (Landing-Craft)
4 x Nuclear Security Guarding Squadrons
Royal Marines Training Establishment
Royal Marines Band Service
Reserve Units
4 x Special Boat Service Squadrons

Note: 1 x Army infantry battalion (1 Rifles) is assigned to 3 Commando Brigade.

COMPOSITION OF THE FLEET

Composition of the Fleet

Submarines			*In Refit*	*Home Base*
Strategic Trident Class	4	Vanguard, Victorious, Vigilant, Vengeance.	1	Faslane
Fleet Trafalgar Class	5	Tireless, Torbay, Trenchant, Talent, Triumph.		Devonport
Astute Class	2	Astute, Ambush.		
Under construction	5	Artful, Audacious, Anson, Agamemnom, Ajax.		Faslane
Type 23 Frigates	13	Sutherland, Monmouth, Northumberland, Somerset, Argyll, Montrose, Richmond, Lancaster, Iron Duke, Westminster, Kent, Portland, St Albans.	2	Devonport/ Portsmouth
Type 45 Destroyers	6	Daring, Dauntless, Diamond, Dragon, Defender, Duncan.		Portsmouth
Assault Ships	4	Albion, Bulwark, Invincible, Ocean.	1	Devonport
River Class	4	Tyne, Mersey, Severn, Clyde.	1	Portsmouth
Hunt Class Minehunters	8	Brocklesby, Chiddingfold, Ledbury, Middleton, Atherstone, Cattistock, Quorn, Hurworth.	2	Portsmouth
Sandown Class Minehunters	7	Penzance, Pembroke, Grimsby, Bangor, Blythe, Ramsay, Shoreham.	2	Faslane/ Portsmouth
Ice Patrol	1	Protector, Endurance (awaiting decision on future).		Portsmouth
Survey	4	Scott, Echo, Enterprise, Gleaner	2	Devonport
Scimitar Class Fast Patrol Boats	2	Scimitar, Sabre		Gibraltar
Archer Class Patrol Boats	16	Biter, Blazer, Archer, Charger, Dasher, Smiter, Puncher, Pursuer, Example, Explorer, Express, Exploit, Tracker, Raider, Ranger, Trumpeter.		

Two of the above craft (Raider and Tracker) act as the Faslane Patrol Boat Squadron. The remaining 14 are employed as University Naval Units (URNU) for training. The Gibraltar Squadron has 2 x 16 m patrol craft (Scimitar and Sabre).

Note: Numbers of surface ships and submarines worked up and fully operational can vary greatly, due to refit, repair or other problems. The Royal Navy has very high standards of both operational efficiency and safety. The Fleet is worked hard.

Royal Fleet Auxiliary

Fast Fleet Tankers	2	Wave Knight, Wave Ruler
Small Fleet Tankers	2	Black Rover, Gold Rover.
Support Tankers	1	Orangeleaf.
Replenishment Ships	3	Fort Austin, Fort Rosalie, Fort Victoria.
Casualty Receiving Facility	1	Argus.
Landing Ships	3	Lyme Bay, Mounts Bay, Cardigan Bay.
Forward Repair Ships	1	Diligence.

Strategic Sea Lift: The UK MoD has arrangements in place to take commercial vessels such as Ro-Ro ships and container vessels into service should the need arise. In 2013 the following appear to be available:

18 x passenger carriers; 8 x short-sea passenger carriers; 50 x petroleum tankers; 37 x roll on/roll off ferries; 3 x refrigerated cargo carriers; 14 x bulk carriers; 43 x cargo carriers; 19 x chemical tankers; 1 x combination ore/oil carrier; 4 x liquefied gas carriers; 1; livestock carrier; 1 x specialized tanker.

HIGHER MANAGEMENT OF THE ROYAL NAVY

The Ministry of Defence (MoD) is a Department of State, headed by the Secretary of State for Defence (SofS) who implements national defence policy and plans the expenditure of the defence budget. The MoD is the highest level of headquarters for the Armed Forces, both administrative and operational. All major issues of policy are referred to the SofS or to one of his Ministerial colleagues:

Minister of State for the Armed Forces
Minister of State for Defence Personnel, Welfare and Veterans
Parliamentary Under Secretary of State for Defence Equipment, Support and Technology
Parliamentary Under Secretary of State for International Security Strategy
Under Secretary of State and the House of Lords Spokesman for Defence

Under the direction of the Defence Council (described in Chapter 1) management of the Services is the responsibility of the Service Boards, in the case of the Royal Navy the Admiralty Board is the senior management directorate.

The Admiralty Board
The overall management of the Royal Navy is the responsibility of The Admiralty Board, the composition of which is as follows:

The Secretary of State for Defence
Minister of State for the Armed Forces
Minister of State for Defence Personnel, Welfare and Veterans
Parliamentary Under Secretary of State for Defence Equipment, Support and Technology
Parliamentary Under Secretary of State for International Security Strategy
Under Secretary of State and the House of Lords Spokesman for Defence
Chief of the Naval Staff and First Sea Lord
Commander-in-Chief Fleet
Second Sea Lord
Chief of Materiel
Controller of the Navy
Assistant Chief of Naval Staff

The Admiralty Board meets formally twice a year

The Navy Board

The First Sea Lord's responsibilities (delivery of naval capabilities, maintaining the strategic deterrent, planning and operational advice, management, overall efficiency and morale of the service) are exercised through the Service Executive Committee of the Admiralty Board, known as the Navy Board (NAVB). The First Sea Lord is the chairman of NAVB; its membership is similar to the Admiralty Board, but without Ministers. NAVB meets formally on a regular basis:

First Sea Lord
Fleet Commander & Deputy Chief of Naval Staff
Chief of Naval Personnel & Training and Second Sea Lord
Chief of Materiel
Commandant General Royal Marines
Controller of the Navy
Assistant Chief of Naval Staff (Policy)
2nd Permanent Secretary – the only member of the Civil Service
Non-Executive Director (Policy)

Meetings could also include: Executive Assistant to the First Sea Lord; Deputy Director Naval Staff (Meeting Secretary); Assistant Director of Defence Public Relations (Navy) and other staff officers as necessary.

Sub Navy Board Committee

Many pan Navy decisions are taken by the Sub Navy Board Committee (SNBC) which is chaired by the Assistant Chief of Naval Staff (ACNS) with the NAVB members' deputies; Deputy Commander in Chief Fleet (DCINCFLEET), COS/2SL/CNH, Chief of the Strategic Systems Executive (CSSE), Capability Manager (Strategic Deterrent CM(SD) and Director General Resources and Plans (DGRP).

FIRST SEA LORD AND CHIEF OF THE NAVAL STAFF

Admiral Sir George Zambellas KCB DSC

Admiral Sir George Zambellas was educated in Zimbabwe, at Stowe and Southampton University, graduating in Aeronautical and Astronautical Engineering. He joined the Royal Navy in 1980 from the aerospace industry and qualified as a pilot in 1982. He flew three tours in different helicopter types, serving in carriers and frigates. After staff training in 1990, and a brief spell as a corporate planner, he commanded the mine hunter HMS Cattistock. In 1993, he was posted to Northwood as a Fleet aviation operations officer before promotion in 1995 and command of the frigate HMS Argyll.

During the 1997/98 Strategic Defence Review, he served with the MoD Centre Staff, helping to shape the maritime case within Defence's tri-Service balance of investment. In 1999, as a Captain, he commanded HMS Chatham, which included Operation Palliser in Sierra Leone. In 2001 George Zambellas attended the Higher Command and Staff Course, and then became Deputy Flag Officer Sea Training, responsible for training Royal Navy and foreign warships and auxiliaries.

Between 2002 and 2004, as a Commodore, he was Principal Staff Officer to two Chiefs of the Defence Staff. In 2005 he commanded the Royal Navy's Amphibious Task Group, overseeing the introduction of two new amphibious classes of ships, and the Bowman radio and data system into amphibious operational use. He and his staff supported Operation Highbrow, the evacuation of civilians from the Lebanon , in July 2006.

In 2006, as a Rear Admiral, he was appointed as Chief of Staff (Transformation), leading the change programme to design and deliver the Fleet's new approach to the generation of maritime capability and support to operations. In 2007, he was Commander United Kingdom Maritime Force and, in October 2008, Chief of Staff (Operations) at the UK 's Permanent Joint Headquarters (PJHQ) at Northwood.

On promotion to Vice Admiral in January 2011, he was appointed Deputy Commander-in-Chief Fleet, Chief of Staff to the Navy Command Headquarters, and the Chief Naval Warfare Officer.

Following an appointment as the Commander Allied Maritime Command (Northwood) and the Royal Navy's Fleet Commander Admiral Zambellas was appointed First Sea Lord and Chief of Naval Staff in April 2013.

The First Sea Lord maintains effective command and control of the Royal Navy through the commander and staff of Fleet Headquarters.

Admiral Sir George Zambellas KCB DSC.
(MoD Crown Copyright 2013)

Commander-in-Chief Fleet
The Fleet Commander (and Deputy Chief of the Naval Staff) is Vice Admiral Philip Jones CB (appointed November 2012) Admiral Jones has full command of all deployable UK Fleet units, including the Royal Marines. His responsibilities include preparation of all aspects of The Fleet for participation in joint and combined operations with NATO allies including key maritime elements of the Standing NATO Response Force.

Navy Command Headquarters
This headquarters at Portsmouth has three major roles:

◆ The generation of maritime forces to match the operational requirement. Forces generated have to be manned, equipped and trained to the appropriate readiness states.
◆ Management of the resources provided to the Fleet and the monitoring of resources and assets thus employed to ensure operational effectiveness and value for money.
◆ The Commander-in-Chief Fleet manages maritime operations by delegating operational command and control to the Commander Operations (located at Northwood). Commander Operations has the majority of Fleet units under his direct command.

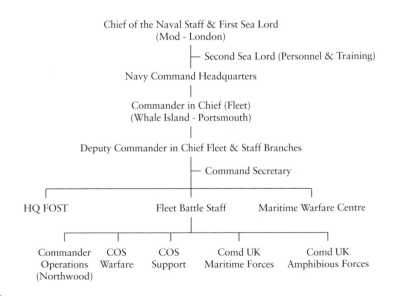

Fleet Battle Staff: Based in two locations (Portsmouth and Plymouth) the Fleet Battle Staff is the operational planning departments, capable of planning exercises and operations for large multinational naval and marine task groups across the globe. The actual conduct of naval operations is generally the responsibility of the Joint Forces Command.

Maritime Warfare Centre: The Maritime Warfare Centre provides the repository and focal point for 'Operational Knowledge Exploitation'. This is the ability to observe and process every aspect of operational experience to learn lessons from previous operations and enhance fighting power.

Flag Officer Sea Training: Is the officer responsible for training on all Royal Naval and Royal Fleet Auxiliary vessels.

Deputy Commander in Chief Fleet: Is the deputy for the Commander and is a member of the Sub Navy Board Committee. The Deputy Commander directs the staff work of Fleet Headquarters.

Commander (Operations): Is the officer who directs all maritime and amphibious forces and associated operations under the command of the CINCFLEET. In addition he is the commander of the submarine arm and is the NATO Commander Submarines East Atlantic and Commander Submarines Allied Naval Forces North.

Chief of Staff (Warfare): This officer and his staff are responsible for delivering the operational capability to match the perceived short and longer term requirement.

Chief of Staff (Support): Is responsible for sustaining the Fleet and ensuring that the required vessels and units are available for operations. His responsibilities include personnel administration, the Maritime Warfare Centre, communications systems, engineering and some aspects of the Fleet Air Arm support.

Commander UK Maritime Forces: Commander of the United Kingdom Task Group and Commander of the Amphibious Task Group.

Commander UK Amphibious Forces: Is the Head of Service for the Royal Marines, Commandant General Royal Marines and commander of 3 Commando Brigade.

The Command Secretary: Is the senior civilian in Fleet Headquarters responsible for civilian personnel, external accountability, resource management and some aspects of planning.

Navy Command HQ maintains Waterfront organisations at Devonport, Portsmouth and Faslane and is responsible for Naval Air Stations at Culdrose, Prestwick and Yeovilton.

The Chief of Naval Personnel & Training and Second Sea Lord is also based at Portsmouth.

LOGISTIC SUPPORT

In 2000 the three distinct separate service logistic functions were fused into one and the Defence Logistic Organisation was formed. In a further amalgamation, from 1 April 2007 the Defence Logistic Organisation (DLO) and the Defence Procurement Agency (DPA) were merged to form Defence Equipment and Support (DE&S).

The DE&S is the organisation that delivers 'Through Life' equipment and logistic support to the Royal Navy, attempting to ensure that the whole factory to front line process is seamless and properly integrated.

More detail regarding the DE&S is provided in Chapter 5.

MAJOR NAVAL BASES

HM Naval Base, Portsmouth
Home base to surface ships, notably Type 45 Destroyers and Type 23 Frigates. Currently the base for HMS Illustrious, it will be the home base for HMS Queen Elizabeth and HMS Prince of Wales when these vessels enter service. Portsmouth also hosts Navy Command Headquarters.

HM Naval Base, Devonport (Plymouth)
Largest naval base in Western Europe with five dry docks, 25 tidal berths, five basins and over 5,000 annual ship movements. Home port for Nuclear Attack Submarines (SSNs), Large Assault Ships, Some Type 23 Frigates, Hydrographic Ships. Also home to Flag Officer Sea Training and the RN Hydrographic School.

HM Naval Base, Clyde (Faslane)
Home base to UK's nuclear deterrent ballistic missile submarines (SSBNs). Also base to SSNs and minewarfare vessels. HMS Caledonia at Rosyth provides support for naval personnel standing by ships and submarines in refit at HM Naval Base, Clyde. All Royal Navy submarines will be based at Faslane by 2017.

RN Air Station, Yeovilton (HMS Heron)
Home base to RN, naval helicopter squadrons and other fixed wing aircraft. Yeovilton operates over 100 aircraft of different types that include Sea Kings, and Lynx (Wildcat in the future). Yeovilton also trains aircrew and engineers of resident aircraft types. RN Fighter Controller School trains ground and airborne AEW controllers. Nearly 4,000 uniformed and civilian personnel work at RNAS Yeovilton that also hosts the Royal Naval Historic Flight and the Fleet Air Arm Museum.

RN Air Station, Culdrose (HMS Seahawk)
RNAS Culdrose supports the Anti- Submarine Warfare and Airborne Early Warning helicopter squadrons of the Royal Navy equipped with both Merlin and Sea Kings. Eight Naval Air Squadrons are based at RNAS Culdrose, both front line and training Squadrons. The largest helicopter base in Europe with about 75 aircraft, Culdrose is responsible for the operational and advanced flying training of helicopter pilots, observers and aircrewmen.

HMS Caledonia
As a DE&S facility HMS Caledonia's role is to provide support services to both the Royal Navy and the MoD in the East of Scotland. As stated previously HMS Caledonia supports the requirements of personnel operating on RN vessels from HM Naval Base Clyde.

SHORE ESTABLISHMENTS

Britannia Royal Naval College (BRNC – Dartmouth)
The principal function of the College is the training of young officers for service in the Royal Navy, in addition a large number of students from foreign Navies are also receive their training at BRNC. A variety of other courses are undertaken including leadership and teambuilding programmes, seamanship, navigation and other naval subjects.

HMS Collingwood (Fareham)
HMS Collingwood is the lead establishment of the Maritime Warfare School (MWS) and the largest naval training centre in Western Europe . The MWS is a federated training establishment incorporating HMS Excellent, the Defence Diving School , the RN Physical Training School, the School of Hydrography and Meteorology in Plymouth and the Royal Marines School of Music at the Portsmouth

Naval Base. Other units at HMS Collingwood include the Royal Navy Leadership Academy, Fleet Intelligence Centre and the Maritime Warfare Centre.

At any one time the MWS is training about 10 per cent of the Royal Navy and has an annual throughput of about 3,000 Officers and Ratings, both regular and reserve.

HMS Excellent (Portsmouth)
HMS Excellent hosts the Navy Command Headquarters and delivers a range of different training functions under the direction of the MWS (HMS Collingwood). These include damage control and fire fighting and harbour training on board HMS Bristol (an obsolete destroyer permanently moored at Portsmouth) for RNR personnel, cadet forces and youth organisations.

HMS Raleigh (Torpoint)
HMS Raleigh is the initial entry training establishment for all junior ratings entering the Royal Navy and the Royal Naval Reserve. About 2,500 people work in the Establishment and a New Entry of around 80–90 ratings join most weeks of the year. New Entry rating generally undertake a ten week course before moving on to specialist training. HMS Raleigh is also the base for the Sea Cadet Training Centre and the Band of HM Royal Marines Plymouth.

HMS Raleigh also provides professional courses in military training, seamanship, logistics and submarine operations as well as vital training for ships' team preparing for operational deployments.

HMS Sultan (Gosport)
HMS Sultan is the home of Defence School of Marine Engineering (DSMarE) and the Royal Naval Air Engineering and Survival School (RNAESS) whose primary function is to supply the Fleet with engineering Officers and Ratings of the highest quality. Training of Marine and Air Engineers of Foreign and Commonwealth Navies is also undertaken. Large numbers of officer and rating students are trained annually e.g. the Ship Systems Group alone has a throughput of some 1,000 students per year.

HMS Temeraire (Portsmouth)
HMS Temeraire houses the staff of the Directorate of Naval Physical Development and hosts the Royal Naval School of Physical Training and the Fleet Recreation Centre.

HMS Gannet (Prestwick)
HMS Gannet hosts a flight of search and rescue Sea King helicopters from the Fleet Air Arm's 771 Naval Air Squadron.

Commando Training Centre Royal Marines (CTCRM)
All Royal Marines are required to undergo what is recognised as one of the longest and most demanding infantry training courses in the world. This is undertaken at the CTCRM at Lympstone in UK's West Country, not far from Dartmoor.

CTCRM selects and trains all Royal Marines Officers, recruits and reserves to deploy directly on operations world-wide. Between them the three training wings run more than 300 courses per year catering for over 3,000 students.

ROYAL NAVAL RESERVE (RNR) UNITS
The RNR is a part time organisation, which complements the Royal Navy in times of war, conflict and in peacetime when there is a requirement. Entry into the RNR is the same as for the regular service. Training takes place on evenings and at weekends at the units listed below:

HMS Calliope	Gateshead
HMS Cambria	Penarth
HMS Dalriada	Greenock
HMS Eaglet	Liverpool
HMS Ferret	Chicksands
HMS Hibernia	Lisburn
HMS Flying Fox	Bristol
HMS Forward	Birmingham
HMS King Alfred	Portsmouth
HMS President	London
HMS Scotia	Pitreavie
HMS Sherwood	Nottingham
HMS Vivid	Devonport
HMS Wildfire	Northwood

RNR numbers in mid 2013 were approximately 2,600 and are planned to be around 3,100 by 2018. Units of the Royal Marines Reserve (RMR) are listed in the Royal Marines entry later in this section.

University Royal Naval Units (URNU) are located as follows:

Aberdeen	HMS Archer
Oxford	HMS Smiter
Birmingham	HMS Exploit
London	HMS Puncher
Bristol	HMS Dasher
Manchester	HMS Biter
Cambridge	HMS Trumpeter
Northumbrian	HMS Example
Glasgow	HMS Pursuer
Sussex	HMS Ranger
Liverpool	HMS Charger
Southampton	HMS Blazer
Wales	HMS Express
Yorkshire	HMS Explorer

URNU ships are part of the 1st Patrol Boat Squadron.

PRINCIPAL WARSHIPS OF THE ROYAL NAVY

In the following paragraphs we comment briefly on the significant classes of warship currently in service with the Royal Navy, together with those under construction and projected. The most important units are those with which follow, the four submarines that carry the UK's strategic nuclear deterrent.

STRATEGIC DETERRENT

The United Kingdom's Strategic Deterrent is undertaken by the Royal Navy and submarine launched ballistic missiles (SLBM) have been installed in Royal Naval submarines since the late 1960s. Operational patrols commenced in 1969 with US Polaris missiles embarked. The first class of UK SSBN (Nuclear Powered Ballistic Missile Submarine) was the Resolution Class with four boats – this class has now been replaced by the larger Vanguard class armed with 16 x US Trident II D5 missiles. Each missile has the capability of carrying up to 12 x MIRV (Multiple Independently Targeted Re-entry Vehicles) warheads, making a possible total of 192 warheads per submarine. The UK is believed to have purchased 58 x Trident 2D-5 missile bodies from the United States and the range of the missile is believed to be in excess of 9,000 km with a CEP (Circular Error of Probability) of about 100 metres. It is believed that in UK service the Trident 2-D5 carry eight warheads per missile.

These large Vanguard Class submarines displace over 16,000 tonnes and have a length of 150 metres. The three decks offer accommodation for the crew of 130 which is unusually spacious for a submarine. Good domestic facilities are provided for the crew and the air purification system enables them to remain submerged for long periods without any outside support. Each submarine has two crews known as Port and Starboard – when one crew is away on patrol the other crew is training or taking leave.

HMS Vanguard leaving HMNB Clyde. (MoD Crown Copyright 2013)

Following the 1998 Strategic Defence Review (SDR), the UK MoD revealed that it was no longer necessary to have a stockpile of 300 warheads and that the stockpile was being reduced to 200 operationally available warheads. In addition, the 58 missile bodies already purchased would be sufficient to maintain a credible deterrent. The MoD confirmed that there would be one SSBN on patrol at any one time but carrying a reduced load of 48 warheads. In order to ensure one ship of a class to be available for operations, it is normally reckoned that three should be in service – one in repair or refit, one preparing for operations or working up and one fully operational. Four submarines provide a guarantee of one operational at all times. The four submarines of the Vanguard class commissioned as follows:

HMS Vanguard	1993
HMS Victorious	1995
HMS Vigilant	1996
HMS Vengeance	1999

In 2007 the UK Government stated that the current Vanguard Class submarines cannot last indefinitely and would begin to end their working lives sometime in the late 2020s (possibly 2028). A replacement submarine would need about 17 years of development and that early decisions on a replacement were required.

A number of studies are underway to determine the specifics of the solution that will replace the current Trident/Vanguard Class system, with a likely successor being a submarine launched ballistic arrangement (our interpretation of the evidence).

TRIDENT SUCCESSOR PROGRAMME

UK Government policy remains as set out in the Strategic Defence and Security Review 2010, in that a continuous submarine-based deterrent will be maintained and that work has begun on replacing the Vanguard class submarines. The UK MoD is continuing work on the assessment phase of the Successor submarine programme, to inform a Main Gate decision in 2016. Currently (2013) the Cabinet Office is leading a review into whether there are alternative systems and postures that could maintain a credible deterrent.

The Trident Successor programme will be funded from the MoD's core equipment budget and the MoD has also confirmed that once the new submarine comes into service, the in-service costs of the UK's nuclear deterrent, including the costs of the Atomic Weapons Establishment (AWE), will be similar to the current level of around 5–6 per cent of the defence budget.

An initial estimate is that the procurement costs for the complete new system will be in the range of £25 billion for a four-boat solution.

The replacement programme is currently in the Concept Phase and the costs will be refined as experts continue to engage in detailed discussion with industry.

During mid 2013 an Integrated Programme Management Team (IPMT) was in place to manage the delivery of the Successor submarine programme. It comprises about 50 personnel from the Ministry of Defence, BAE Systems Maritime-Submarines, Babcock Marine and Rolls-Royce.

The Integrated Master Schedule (IMS) is the consolidated plan linking all the activities required to deliver the Successor submarine programme and this plan is maintained on a continuous basis. If the Successor submarine programme goes ahead following Main Gate approval in 2016 and proceeds to production, it will sustain thousands of jobs across the UK submarine industry, including businesses at all levels of the submarine supply chain.

The current nuclear warheads will remain viable until the late 2030s and therefore, a decision on the replacement warhead will now be deferred until 2019.

Submarine Service personnel – The latest figures we have for the Submarine Service was 3,478 personnel (638 officers, 299 warrant officers and 2541 other ranks). This figure includes personnel assigned to the six crews for the four Vanguard submarines and submarine service personnel assigned to posts elsewhere in the MoD.

FLEET SUBMARINES

The Royal Navy operates a total of 7 Nuclear Powered Attack Submarines (SSNs) in two classes – the Trafalgar and Astute classes. Both classes are capable of continuous patrols at high underwater speed, independent of base support, and can circumnavigate the globe without surfacing. These submarines are capable of firing the Tomahawk Land Attack Cruise missile (TLAM).

All Royal Navy submarines will be based at Faslane by 2017.

TRAFALGAR CLASS

Dates of Service Entry:

Tireless	1984 (Planned out of service date 2013)
Torbay	1985 (Planned out of service date 2015)
Trenchant	1986 (Planned out of service date 2017)
Talent	1988 (Planned out of service date 2019)
Triumph	1991 (Planned out of service date 2022)

Key specifications are as follows:

Length 85.4 m; Displacement 4,700 tons surfaced and 5,200 tons dived; Max Speed 20 knots surfaced and 32 knots dived; Diving depth 400m (operational) and 600m maximum; Complement 12 officers and 85 ratings: Armament: a mix of the following; Submarine Launched Cruise Missiles (SLCM) – Tomahawk Block IIIC, range 1,700 km; Anti-Ship Missiles: UGM-84B Sub Harpoon Block 1C; range 130 km; Wire-guided Anti-ship/ submarine torpedoes; Range to 30 kms.

Trafalgar Class Submarine HMS Tireless off the North Pole in 2004. (Copyright US Navy)

The submarine refit facility at Devonport has the ability to defuel the Trafalgar class and Astute class submarines.

ASTUTE CLASS

Dates of Service Entry:

Astute	2010
Ambush	2013
Artful	2015
Audacious	2018
Anson	2020
Agamemnon	2022
Ajax	2024

Key specifications are as follows:

Length 97.0m; Beam 11.2 m; Displacement 6,500 tons surfaced and 7,800 tons dived; Max Speed 29 knots plus dived; Complement 12 officers and 86 ratings; Armament likely to be as for Trafalgar classes with 6 x torpedo tubes.

Astute Class Submarine HMS Ambush heads for open water.
(Copyright 2013 BAe Systems)

With its improved communications, a greater capacity for joint operations and the ability to carry more weaponry, the Astute-class submarines will become a cornerstone of UK defence capability until at least 2035. Astute will carry the Block IV Tomahawk long-range land attack missile with a range of over 1,000 miles and Spearfish long range torpedoes.

The first three boats of the Astute submarine programme is expected to have a total cost to the MoD of about £3.5 billion and about 5,500 people are believed to be employed on the project.

Astute Class submarines will have massively increased firepower compared with earlier attack submarines and can dive to depths in excess of 300 metres with a complement of 98 men. They are to be powered by a Pressurised Water Reactor 2, equipped with Core H, which will fuel the reactor for the submarine's full service life, ending the need for costly reactor refuelling.

This will be the first class of Royal Navy submarines to use electro-optics for 360 degree surface images replacing the traditional periscope. The boat manufactures its own drinking water and oxygen and from sea water and could in theory remain submerged for up to 25 years.

In December 2012 a £1.2 billion contract was awarded for the construction of Audacious, the fourth boat of the class with an in-service date of 2018.

Astute class submarines will be based at Faslane on the Clyde and will undergo refits at Devonport.

SURFACE FLEET

The Royal Navy's surface fleet comprises of two flotillas, one based at Portsmouth and the other at Devonport. There are four major fleet elements:

Assault ships – the largest ships in the fleet and capable of mounting amphibious/heliborne operations in support of the UK's Response Task Group. Of the four vessels in the group, HMS Illustrious is based at Portsmouth and HMS Albion, Bulwark and Ocean at Devonport.

Destroyers and frigates – as always these vessels are the workhorses of the fleet. Destroyers concentrate on air defence and frigates concentrate on surface and sub-surface warfare. The MoD's longer term intention is to operate a fleet of 19 destroyers and frigates.

Smaller fighting vessels – which include include mine countermeasures vessels (MCM). Neutralisation of mines is a vital task if sea lanes are to be kept open and the Royal Navy is an acknowledged world leader in mine countermeasures operations.

Offshore patrol vessels – these continue to play an important role in UK home waters by enforcing fishery laws and providing protection to UK oil and gas facilities.

ASSAULT SHIPS

Albion Class (LPD)

Dates of Service Entry:

Albion	2003 (Planned out of service date 2033)
Bulwark	2004 (Planned out of service date 2034)

The contract (worth £449 million) to build the two LPDs (Landing Platform Docks) was awarded on 18 July 1996 and first steel was cut 17 November 1997. Each vessel has two helicopter landing spots and the configuration includes a well dock and stern gate together with side ramp access. Substantial command and control facilities are included within a large combined Operations Room and the vessels are a good fit with the UK governments concept of expeditionary activities worldwide.

Both vessels are capable of carrying 305 troops, with an overload of a further 405 for short periods. There is a vehicle deck capacity for up to 6 x main battle tanks or up to 30 x armoured all-terrain vehicles. In addition, there is a floodable well dock, with the capacity to take either four utility landing craft (each capable of carrying a main battle tank or shelter a hovercraft landing craft). There are 4 x smaller landing craft on davits, each capable of carrying 35 troops.

HMS Bulwark is also the Royal Navy's flagship.

Key specifications are as follows: Length: 176 m; Displacement: 19,560 tons full load; Max Speed: 20 knots; Range 8,000 n.miles at 15 knots; Complement: 325; Military lift: 305 x troops; 67 x support vehicles; 4 x LCU Mk 10 or 2 x LCAC (dock); 4 x LCVP Mk 5 (davits). Armament – Guns: 2–20 mm (twin); 2 Goalkeeper Close-in Weapon Systems (CIWS); Helicopters – Platform for 3 x Merlin EH 101; Chinook capable.

HMS Albion operating with Chinook helicopters. (MoD Crown Copyright 2013)

Ocean (LPH)

Date of Service Entry:

Ocean	1998 (Planned out of service date 2022)

HMS Ocean, an LPH (Landing Platform Helicopter) was built by Kvaerner Govan, on the Clyde, taking advantage of commercial build methods and facilities, before sailing for Barrow-in-Furness for fitting out prior to acceptance into service with the Royal Navy. The hull of the ship was built to Merchant Navy standards at a cost of some £170 million. The ship is capable of carrying an air group of 12 x Sea King troop lift helicopters, 6 x Lynx/Wildcat attack helicopters and 4 x Landing Craft Vehicle Personnel (LCVP). The vessel's secondary roles include afloat training, with a limited anti-submarine warfare capability, and the possibility of being used as an afloat base for anti-terrorist operations.

During the 2012 Olympic Games HMS Ocean was moored on the Thames and provided essential command and security support to the security services. Currently the Royal Navy's largest warship, in late 2012 it was announced that HMS Ocean would undergoing a comprehensive upgrade at Devonport Royal Dockyard. This upgrade will take about 15 months and cost approximately £65 million.

Key specifications are as follows:

Length: 203.4 m; Displacement: 21,758 tons full load; Max Speed: 19 knots; Range 8,000 n.miles at 15 knots; Complement: 285, 206 Air Group, plus up to 830 marines (Marine Commando Group); Military lift: 4 LCVP

Army Air Corps Apache takes off from HMS Ocean during Operation Ellamy (Libya). (MoD Crown Copyright 2013)

Mk 5 (on davits); 2 Griffon hovercraft; 40 vehicles; Armament – Aircraft. Helicopters; 12 Sea King HC Mk 4 / Merlin plus 6 Lynx (or navalised variants of WAH-64 Apache); Guns: 8 x Oerlikon / BMARC 20 mm GAM-B03 (4 twin); 3 x Vulcan Phalanx Mk 15 Close-in Weapon Systems.

Illustrious

Date of Service Entry:

Illustrious   1982 (Planned out of service date 2014)

Illustrious is the last of the Invincible Class carriers with the other two, HMS Invincible and HMS Ark Royal having been withdrawn from service.

The primary task of this class of ship was to act as the command ship for a small task force and provide organic air power against limited opposition. Since entering service in the early 1970s, the ships of this class proved vital in projecting UK interests overseas from the Falklands conflict of 1982 through to the amphibious assault on Iraq in the spring of 2003.

HMS Illustrious is currently the UK's High Readiness Helicopter and Commando Carrier means and the vessel is capable of mounting operations using Merlin, Sea King, Lynx / Wildcat or Apache helicopters.

Key specifications are as follows:

Length: 209.1m; Displacement: 20,600 tons full load; Max Speed: 28 knots; Range 7,000 n.miles at 19 knots; Complement: 685 (60 officers) plus 366 (80 officers) air group plus up to 600 marines if required; Guns: 3 x Close-in Weapon Systems (Goalkeeper or Vulcan Phalanx) anti-aircraft or anti-missile.

The Royal Navy Invincible-class aircraft carrier HMS Illustrious, and Nimitz-class aircraft carriers USS Harry S Truman and USS Dwight D Eisenhower transit in formation during a multi-ship maneuvering exercise in the Atlantic Ocean. (Photograph US Navy)

DESTROYERS

Type 45 – Daring Class.

The first Type 45 Destroyer (HMS Daring) entered service during 2009 with five subsequent vessels following at regular intervals until 2013. The current estimated unit production cost of each Type 45 is £561.6 million, based on the approved programme of six ships. This estimate includes the cost of the principal surface to air missile system Sea Viper (PAAMS), which is the primary weapons system for the Type 45 destroyer. Within the figure of £561.6 million overall budget, the cost of the Sea Viper system is approximately one third or about £187 million.

Type 45 Destroyer HMS Daring. (Copyright 2013 BAe Systems)

In addition to its role as an air defence vessel, the Type 45 destroyer is a versatile platform that is planned to deliver a number of capabilities. These include naval gunfire support and, through its embarked helicopter, anti-submarine and anti-surface warfare. It is capable of employment in a full range of tasks including maritime force protection, interdiction and peace support operations.

The vessel is powered by the WR21 Gas Turbine enabling her to reach speeds of up to 29 knots.

By mid 2013 HMS Daring, Dauntless and Diamond had already completed operational tours to the Mediterranean, the Gulf and the Atlantic Ocean.

Portsmouth is the home port for Type 45 vessels.

Key specifications are as follows:

Length: 152.4 m; Displacement; 7,350 tons full load; Max Speed; 29 knots; Range 7,000 n miles at 18 knots; Complement; 190; Armament (Estimated) – Missiles: SSM; 8 x Harpoon (2 quad); Surface to Air (SAM); 6 x DCN Sylver A 50 VLS Sea Viper (principal anti-air missile system); 16 x Aster 15 and 32 Aster 30 weapons or combination; Guns – 1 x Vickers 4.5 in (114 mm)/55 Mk 8 Mod 1; 2 x 20 mm Vulcan Phalanx Close-in Weapon Systems; Helicopter: Merlin.

FRIGATES

Outline Organisation of a Frigate Crew

The organisation of a typical RN frigate is the result of hundreds of years of evolution and above all, the ship is organised to fight. The six major departments in a modern frigate are the following:

Executive Department – The Executive Department is responsible for the command of the ship with the First Lieutenant (Executive Officer) having overall responsibility for the Department. The Executive Department has the overall responsibility for the medical, chaplaincy, physical training and seamanship aspects of the ship. In addition discipline and routines in the ship are maintained by the Master At Arms and Leading Regulator.

Warfare Department – This department basically "fights" the ship and is the direct descendant of the Seaman Branch which manned the guns in earlier generations.

Marine Engineering Department – Runs the machinery of the ship ie. the main propulsion units that drive the vessel (gas turbines or diesels), the electrical power supplies and all of the ancillary machinery required.

Weapons Engineering Department – Responsible for the efficient functioning of all of the ship's highly complex sensors and weapons.

Supply Department and Logistics Department – Responsible for the logistic arrangements in the ship ie. catering, spares for all of the weapons, general stores, sensors and machinery spares and for all pay and accounting matters.

Flight – The ship's helicopter is arguably the most potent weapon platform available and can generally carry Stingray torpedoes and depth charges for use against submarines, and Sea Skua missiles for engaging surface targets. The Flight Team is usually composed of a small group of aircrew supported by a team of skilled flight engineers.

Departments – All of the departments are inter-dependent and each has a head of department – known collectively as "the HODs". These HODs meet at regular intervals and agree such matters as programmes, training and the efficient administration of everything on board. Whilst each HOD is responsible directly to the commanding officer for the efficiency of his department. HODs are likely to be Lieutenant Commanders and, even if senior to the First Lieutenant, are subordinate to him – the First Lieutenant is the man who takes over if the Commanding Officer is unable to perform his duties.

The cleaning of the ship and all of the general tasks are shared by the departments, and the HODs would discuss these matters at their meetings – for example, they would agree how many sailors would be required from each department for a storing at sea operation. A recent development is the presence on board many RN ships of female personnel. These females share all the duties of their male counterparts but, of course, have separate living quarters.

The Commanding Officer is usually a Commander RN (with a background in the Warfare/Operations Department) and he is known as "The Captain". In command of a squadron of frigates an officer with the rank of Captain RN will be found who doubles the duties both of "Captain" of his ship and Captain (F) to whom the "Captains" of the frigates in his squadron report.

The complement of a frigate relates to the requirement to man the ship for battle. A Type 23 has a total of 181 (13 officers).

Type 23 (Duke Class)
The first of class was ordered from Yarrows on 29 October 1984 at the height of the Cold War. Further batches of three were ordered in September 1986, July 1988, December 1989, January 1992 and February 1996. There were some early problems, e.g. the Command System was not operational as quickly as had been planned, but these have been overcome and the RN has made steady improvements to weapons and sensors in the ships over the years since first introduction. From 1999, the Lynx helicopter was replaced on some of the vessels by the EH 101 Merlin helicopter. These ships are powered by a CODLAG system (Combined diesel-electric and gas-turbine propulsion) and the diesel-electric is used for minimum underwater noise during ASW operations

Key specifications are as follows: Length:133.0 m; Displacement; 4,200 tons full load; Max Speed; 28 knots. Range 7,800 n.miles at 15 knots; Complement; 181 (13 officers); Armament – Missiles: Surface-to-Surface (SSM); 8 x Harpoon (130km range); Surface-to-Air (SAM) Sea Wolf (Range 6 kms); Guns: 1 x 4.5 in (25 rounds/min; Range 22kms); 2 x 30mm twins (Range 10kms); Modern above and under water sensors and decoys; Helicopter: Lynx/Wildcat or Merlin (Missile and Torpedo armed)

Date of Service Entry:

Argyll	1989	(Planned out of service date 2023)
Lancaster	1990	(Planned out of service date 2024)
Monmouth	1991	(Planned out of service date 2026)
Iron Duke	1991	(Planned out of service date 2025)
Westminster	1992	(Planned out of service date 2028)
Northumberland	1992	(Planned out of service date 2029)
Montrose	1992	(Planned out of service date 2027)
Richmond	1993	(Planned out of service date 2030)
Somerset	1994	(Planned out of service date 2031)
Sutherland	1996	(Planned out of service date 2033)
Kent	1998	(Planned out of service date 2034)
Portland	1999	(Planned out of service date 2035)
St Albans	2000	(Planned out of service date 2036)

Type 23 Frigate HMS Lancaster. (MoD Crown Copyright 2013)

FUTURE SURFACE COMBATANT – TYPE 26 GLOBAL COMBAT SHIP (GCS)

During January 2013 details of the Royal Navy's Type 26 GCS were unveiled. The first of these multi-mission ships should enter service in the early 2020s (to replace Type 23 Frigates in UK service) and will be capable of supporting a range of tasks from low to high intensity operations. Type 26 GCSs may operate as part of a joint or multi-national task force or could operate independently for significant periods.

Current planning assumptions suggest the construction of about 13 vessels and the programme is currently in the assessment phase. A build announcement is expected in 2015 and it is likely that each vessel will cost between £250 and £350 million.

First indications are that the Type 26 GCS might have the following characteristics:

Length: 148 m
Displacement: 5,400 tonnes
Armament: medium calibre gun (127 mm?); Phalanx CIWS
Helicopters: Merlin or Wildcat
Capable of launching unmanned air, underwater or surface vehicles

Type 26 – Global Combat Ship (GCS). (Copyright 2013 BAe Systems)

THE FUTURE CARRIER STRIKE CAPABILITY

The platform element of the Carrier Strike capability will be provided by the Queen Elizabeth Class Aircraft Carriers, and the aircraft element by the short take-off and vertical landing (STOVL) variant of the JSF (Joint Strike Fighter – F-35B – Lightning II).

Queen Elizabeth Class Aircraft Carriers (CVF)

Following the 2007 contract award, two vessels of this type are being built in various locations across the UK with final assembly at Rosyth. The first, HMS Queen Elizabeth should begin sea trials in 2017 and construction of the second, HMS Prince of Wales is underway, with a decision to operate expected in 2015. Current plans are for the CVF to be based at Portsmouth.

Queen Elizabeth Class Aircraft Carriers. (Copyright 2013 BAe Systems)

Each 65,000 ton vessel with a length of 280 metres is expected to be able to embark up to 40 aircraft. With a complement of about 680 officers and ratings (1,600 for air operations) the vessels will have a range of about 10,000 nautical miles and a top speed of 25 knots (46 km/h). We would expect the vessels to be armed for local defence with CIWS type weapons.

Both HMS Queen Elizabeth and her sister ship HMS Prince of Wales will have two island sections that will provide independent control of navigation (forward) and air traffic control operations (aft). The hangar deck measures 155 x 33 metres, with two large lifts capable of lifting two aircraft onto the flight deck simultaneously in about 60 seconds.

The vessels are powered by two Rolls Royce MT30 gas turbine units each generating about 36MW and two Wartsila diesel generators producing enough power to support a town of over 200,000 people.

Projections of the costs of the programme vary, but most analysts agree on a total cost for the two carriers of between £3.5 and £4 billion. Both vessels are expected to have a 50 year service life.

The CVF project will provide the Royal Navy with the largest and most powerful warships ever constructed in the UK and should create or sustain over 10,000 UK jobs.

JOINT STRIKE FIGHTER – F-35B (LIGHTNING II)

Crew 1; Max speed Mach 1.6 (1,200 mph/1,900 km/h); Length 15.6 m; Span 10.67 m; Max altitude 50,000 feet; Weight (loaded) 22,400 kg; Max take off weight 31,800 kg; Range 2,220 kms); Combat radius 1,080 kms on internal fuel); Armament – Gun – 1 x GAU-22/A Equalizer 25 mm cannon with 180 rounds; Missiles – Paveway IV, AMRAAM, ASRAAM, Brimstone, Storm Shadow

In May 2012 the UK MoD announced its decision to deliver its carrier strike capability using the short take-off and vertical landing (STOVL) variant of the US Joint Strike Fighter (JSF) as opposed to the Carrier Variant (CV) of the JSF. This decision was made in light of revelations that the CV aircraft would delay the introduction into service by up to three years, and that fitting catapults and arrestor gear could cost up to £2 billion more than originally planned.

First operational aircraft are due to arrive in 2016 and first STOVL aircraft flight trials should commence off HMS Queen Elizabeth during 2018.

The UK version of the JSF, the F35B, will be a stealthy, multi-role, all-weather, day and night, fighter/attack air system, designed to operate as a STOVL aircraft from land bases and from the Queen Elizabeth Class aircraft carriers. Once in service we would expect the F35B to be capable of undertaking air interdiction operations, making low or medium level attacks using precision-guided, freefall or retarded bombs. Close air support

Carrier variant of the F-35B Lightening II. (Copyright 2013 BAe Systems)

missions against targets in the forward edge of the battle area and fleet air defence patrols in the area of vessels that require protection from enemy air attack.

An announcement in July 2012 confirmed that the UK would initially order 48 aircraft and later reports suggested that the overall cost of the programme is forecast at being in the region of £2.5 billion. The aircraft should remain in service until 2040.

Although the US Company Lockheed Martin is the prime contractor, the UK is a Level 1 partner with the US and a number of British companies, including BAE Systems and Rolls-Royce are involved in building and developing the aircraft.

The F35B will be based at RAF Marham in Norfolk and by 2018 the only offensive aircraft in the UK inventory should be the F-35B and the Typhoon. The aircraft will be operated by both RAF and Fleet Air Arm personnel.

The US Marine Corps intends to buy 340 F-35Bs and the Italian Navy 22.

RESPONSE FORCE TASK GROUP (RFTG)

The RFTG was created following the 2010 defence review and is a rapid reaction force held at high readiness, that deals with unexpected world events that require military intervention.

During late 2012 the RFTG took part in a major multi-national exercise in the Mediterranean (Cougar 12) and was structured around the following units:

HMS Bulwark
HMS Illustrious
HMS Northumberland
HMS Montrose
RFA Mounts Bay
MV Hartland Point

Headquarters of 3 Commando Brigade
45 Commando
30 Commando IX Group
539 Assault Squadron Royal Marines

814 Naval Air Squadron (Merlins)
815 Naval Air Squadron (Lynx)
829 Naval Air Squadron (Merlins)
845 Naval Air Squadron (Commando-carrying Sea Kings)

846 Naval Air Squadron (Commando-carrying Sea Kings)
854 Naval Air Squadron (airborne surveillance and control Sea Kings)

656 Squadron Army Air Corps (Apache gunships)
659 Squadron Army Air Corps (Lynx)

WARFARE TRAINING FACILITY (MCTS)

During 2012 the Royal Navy unveiled its new state-of-the-art warfare training facility. MCTS (the Maritime Composite Training Facility). Representing the most radical change to Royal Naval training for over 40 years, MCTS provides shore-based training for Warfare teams. The system allows crews of Type 45 Destroyers, Type 23 Frigates, Assault ships and Carriers to prepare for service.

Based across two sites at Fareham and Plymouth , the MCTS features banks of flat panel LCD screens faithfully replicating equipment used at sea. The system that has cost around £108 million will be used by around 1,000 new trainees a year and will allow existing personnel to maintain their warfare skills.

The two major MCTS sites are about 200 miles apart but are connected by a fibre optic link. At HMS Collingwood in Fareham, Hampshire there are three reconfigurable Warfare Team Trainers (WTT) and eight Electronic Classroom Trainers (ECT) with a similar facility at Devonport in Plymouth consisting of two WTTs and one ECT.

Preparations are underway to consider training for sailors who will join the Queen Elizabeth Class Carriers later in the decade and the Type 26 Global Combat Ship after 2020.

BAE Systems Mission Systems is the prime contractor, systems integrator and supplier of major elements of the MCTS. The following companies are also involved in the programme: Aerosystems International, Hewlett Packard, Flagship Training, MacDonald Dettwiler and Associates, Serco and Pennant.

MINE COUNTER MEASURES (MCM) VESSELS

Hunt Class (Minesweepers/Minehunters – Coastal)

The first of this class of GRP-built mine countermeasures vessels, HMS Brecon (now decommissioned) entered service in 1979. The Royal Navy has a small but highly efficient mine warfare force and the Hunts were regarded as very costly when first entering service. However they have proved their value repeatedly and modernisation proceeds. Hunt Class vessels have recently been fitted with Sonar 2193 which has replaced the older Sonar 193M. In addition, the

Hunt Class Minehunter HMS Ledbury at Portsmouth. (Free Software Foundation)

command system has been replaced with a newer system developed from the NAUTIS system already fitted in Sandown class vessels.

When deployed operationally Hunt Class vessels are fitted with additional weapon systems and communications. Also used for Fishery Protection duties.

Key specifications are as follows:
Length: 57.0 m; Displacement: 750 tons full load; Max Speed: 15 knots. Range 1,500 n.miles at 12 knots; Complement: 45 (5 officers); Armament – 1 x 30 mm (650 rounds/min. Range 10 km); For operational deployments also fitted with 2 x 20 mm (900 rounds/min to 2 km) and 2 x 7.62 mm MGs; Full range of sensors and systems for dealing with all types of ground and moored mines.

Dates of Service Entry:

Ledbury	1979
Cattistock	1981
Brocklesby	1982
Middleton	1983
Chiddingfold	1983
Hurworth	1984
Atherstone	1986
Quorn	1988

SANDOWN CLASS (MINEHUNTERS)

HMS Sandown, the first of the class, entered service in 1988 (since decommissioned), and HMS Blythe, the latest, entered service in January 2001. Of Glass Reinforced Plastic (GRP) construction, they are capable of operating in deep and exposed waters, e.g. the approaches to the Clyde where the ballistic missile armed submarines are based. Sandown Class vessels are equipped with a mine-hunting sonar and mine-disposal equipment, making them capable of dealing with mines at depths of up to 200 m.

Key specifications are as follows:
Length: 52.2m; Displacement 450 tons full load; Max Speed 13 knots; Range 2,500 n.miles at 12 knots; Complement 34 (5 officers); Armament 1 x 30mm (650 rounds/min. Range 10km); Full range of sensors and systems for undertaking any mine hunting task.

Dates of Service Entry:

Penzance	1997
Pembroke	1997
Grimsby	1998
Bangor	1999
Ramsey	1999
Shoreham	2001
Blythe	2001

Sandown Class Minehunter. (Copyright VT Group)

REPLACEMENT MCM VESSELS

It would appear that a replacement programme for both the Hunt and Sandown MCM vessels is in the concept phase but it is unlikely that replacements will be available until at least the mid 2020s. There may be an update (capability insertion) to the current vessels around 2018 that could consist of unmanned surface/underwater vehicles that would provide a 'stand off' capability.

The 2010 SDR suggested that replacement vessels would have a common hull and a modular design. This would result in major cost savings for a new class that would support MCM, hydrographic and patrol operations – the Mine Counter Measures (MCM, Hydrography and Patrol Capability (MHPC) Programme.

ANTARCTIC PATROL SHIPS

Endurance

HMS Endurance (previously MV Polar Circle) entered service with the Royal Navy in 1991 and supported British interests in the South Atlantic and Antarctic waters. The ship worked alongside members of the British Antarctic Survey Team, carrying out hydrographic surveying, meteorological work and research programmes.

Following an incident that resulted in severe damage to the ship in 2009, HMS Endurance is currently berthed at Portsmouth awaiting a decision on its future.

Key specifications are as follows:
Length: 57.0m; Displacement: 6,500 tons full load; Max Speed: 15 knots; Range 6,500 n.miles at 12 knots; Complement: 112 (15 officers) plus 14 Royal Marines; Helicopters: 2 x Westland Lynx HAS 3; Range of Sensors.

HMS PROTECTOR

In March 2011 the UK Government replaced HMS Endurance with a Norwegian ship (MV Polarbjørn) on a three-year loan basis. The new, 6,000 tonnes ship, renamed HMS Protector has a similar mission to that of HMS Endurance in patrolling and surveying the Antarctic and South Atlantic

The hull is painted red for easy recognition in ice and the vessel has importance as a political presence in the Southern Ocean and Antarctica.

HMS Protector in the Antartic. (MoD Crown Copyright 2013)

SURVEY SHIPS

Scott

This ship was ordered in January 1995 and entered service in June 1997. She is equipped with an integrated navigation suite for surveying operations, together with a Sonar Array Sounding System (SASS) and data processing equipment.

She also has gravimeters, a towed proton magnetometer and the Sonar 2090 ocean environment sensor. The ship is planned to remain at sea for 300 days per year with a crew of 42, 20 personnel being rotated from shore to allow leave and recreation.

Key specifications are as follows:
Length: 131.1m; Displacement: 13,500 tons full load; Max Speed: 17.5 knots; Complement: 62 (12 officers); Hydrographic sensor fit (See above); Helicopters: Platform for 1 x light helicopter.

HMS Scott in New York. (Free Software Foundation)

Echo Class

An order placed with Vosper Thorneycroft in 2000 for two new hydrographic vessels resulted in a 'through life contract' covering support for 25 years. The ships work with the fleet worldwide, supporting mine warfare and amphibious tasks besides carrying out specialist hydrographic activities. As with Scott (see previous entry) the ships work over 300 days per year at sea.

Key specifications are as follows: Displacement, tons: 3,470 full load; Dimensions, feet (metres): 295.3 x 55.1 x 18 (90 x 16.8 x 5.5); Main machinery: Diesel electric; 4 MW; 2 azimuth thrusters; Speed 15 knots; Range 9,000 at 12kt; Complement 46 with accommodation for 81; Hydrographic Sensor fit.

HMS Echo and an RAF Sea King helicopter assisting in a rescue in the Irish Sea. (MoD Crown Copyright 2013)

Dates of Service Entry:

Echo	2003
Enterprise	2004

Gleaner

Commissioned in 1983 HMS Gleaner is the smallest commissioned vessel in the Royal Navy and has been designed to conduct inshore surveys around the coast of the United Kingdom.

Key specifications are as follows: Length: 16 m; Complement: 8

PATROL VESSELS

Patrol Vessels are used for fishery protection and patrolling Britain's offshore gas and oilfield installations. In addition these useful ships can be used further afield, e.g. Castle class vessels (now decommissioned) have been used in the Falklands patrol role.

River Class

Vosper Thorneycroft contracted in May 2001 for the construction, lease and support of four vessels over an initial ten -year period to replace the ships of the Island Class. Each vessel has a large working cargo deck that allows the vessel to be equipped for a specific role such as disaster relief, anti-pollution, fire fighting, rescue work or interception of other vessels. Standard containers can be handled using a fitted 25 ton crane.

HMS Clyde. (Copyright VT Group)

In late 2012 the MoD announced the outright purchase of the vessels for £39 million. The average annual running cost of a River Class patrol vessel (including maintenance) is approximately £20 million.

Dates of Service Entry:

Tyne	2003
Severn	2003
Mersey	2004
Clyde	2006

Key specifications are as follows:

Length: 79.75m; Displacement: 1,700 tons full load; Max Speed 20 knots; Range 5,500 n.miles at 15 knots; Complement: 30 (plus 18 Boarding Party); Armament: 1 x 20mm Gun; Sensors and Combat Data System; Small helicopter deck.

SHIPS NAMES

The Ships Names and Badges Committee has the task of assessing all the possible names for new ships before making their recommendations through the First Sea Lord and the Secretary of State for Defence before final approval by Her Majesty the Queen.

A new class of Royal Navy warships will have a theme as advised by the First Sea Lord in consultation with the Controller of the Navy. Names of individual ships will be informed by a number of guiding principles including: names associated with a long and illustrious heritage, tradition, Battle Honours and names classically associated with a type of vessel. The naming of Royal Navy warships associated with an illustrious heritage instils a sense of pride, tradition and esteem in today's Royal Navy personnel.

THE ROYAL FLEET AUXILIARY SERVICE

The Royal Fleet Auxiliary Service (RFA) is a civilian manned fleet, owned by the Ministry of Defence. Its main task is to replenish the warships of the Royal Navy at sea with fuel, food, stores and ammunition. Thus it fills a vital role that is becoming increasingly important as the current UK government has worldwide ambitions which demand the services of the Royal Navy across the globe. Other RFA tasks include amphibious support and sea transport for the Army. The RFA is managed by the Commodore RFA who is directly responsible to Commander in Chief Fleet for the administration and operation of the organisation.

The RFA employs about 2,000 (2013 figure) civilian officers and ratings, and is one of the larger employers in the UK shipping industry. Replenishment of warships at sea requires specialist knowledge and training, and RFA personnel are on terms of service that take account of both of these activities and of being directed to possible operational areas. Many RFA ships carry naval or military parties for tasks such as the operation and maintenance of helicopters.

The RFA boasts a significant number of large ships, especially in comparison with the warships it supports. The largest ship in the present Royal Navy is HMS Ocean, displacing 21,758 tons full load. In the RFA there are 10 vessels (the largest at 49,000 tons) that are larger. Though many of these ships are ageing, there is fair provision for realistic support of a Royal Naval reach.

The UK MoD believes that the RFA average cost of maintenance is estimated at £3.5 million per annum for each vessel. This includes maintenance on operational vessels, defect rectification, post design work, stock consumption and small packages of upkeep. In addition an element has been included to reflect the cost of scheduled refits, which are generally undertaken on a five yearly basis for each vessel.

TANKERS

Wave Class (Large Fleet Tankers)

Following a tendering process, contracts to build two ships were placed with VSEL (BAE Systems) on 12 March 1997. There were many delays in the construction of the two vessels but the first, Wave Knight, entered service in March 2003, two years later than originally planned. Wave Ruler entered service in 2004. The ships have a one spot flight deck with full hangar facilities for a Merlin helicopter. There are three replenishment rigs and one crane.

RFA Wave Knight is able to operate in support of amphibious forces, anti-surface and anti-submarine warfare operations and protection of vital sea areas and shipping.

Key specifications are as follows:
Length: 196.5m; Displacement 31,500 tons full load; Max Speed 18 knots; Range 10,000 n miles at 15 knots; Complement 80 plus 22 helicopter personnel; Cargo capacity 16,000 metric tons; Helicopters 1 x Merlin helicopter; Guns Fitted for 2 x Phalanx Close-in Weapon Systems; 2 x BMARC 30mm.

Date of Service Entry:
Wave Knight	2003
Wave Ruler	2004

Appleleaf Class (Support Tankers)

Support Tankers have the dual role of both replenishing warships and fleet tankers at sea and undertaking the bulk movement of fuels between naval supply depots. Specifications for each ship differ somewhat, therefore figures below are illustrative.

Key specifications are as follows: Length: 170.0m; Displacement: 38,000 tons full load; Speed: 15.5 knots; Complement: 56 (19 officers); Cargo capacity 25,000 metric tons; Guns: 2 x 20mm Oerlikon. 4 x 7.62mm MGs.

Date of Service Entry:
Orangeleaf	1982

Rover class (Small Fleet Tankers)

These small tankers have proved most valuable over many years in supplying HM ships at sea with fuel, fresh water, limited dry cargo and refrigerated stores in all parts of the world. There is no hangar but a helicopter platform is served by a stores lift, to enable stores to be transferred at sea. Three of the class (five originally constructed) have been sold on.

Key specifications are as follows:
Length: 140.6m; Displacement: 11,522 tons full load; Speed: 19 knots; Range 15,000 at 15 knots; Complement: 50 (17 officers); Cargo capacity 6,600 metric tons; Guns: 2 x 20mm Oerlikon; 4 x 7.62mm MGs.

Dates of Service Entry:
Gold Rover	1974
Black Rover	1974

FLEET REPLENISHMENT SHIPS

Fort Victoria Class (Fleet Replenishment Ships)

These ships provide fuel and stores support to the Fleet at sea. The original plan was to build six of the class but the diminishing requirement and undoubted budget problems has meant that only two of these large and excellent ships have been constructed. There are four dual-purpose abeam replenishment rigs for simultaneous transfer of liquids and solids, besides stern refuelling. There are repair facilities for Merlin helicopters.

Key specifications are as follows: Length: 203.5 m; Displacement: 36,580 tons full load; Speed 20 knots; Complement: Ships crew 134 (95 RFA plus 15 RN plus 24 civilian stores staff); Embarked Air Group up to 150 personnel (includes 28 officer air crew); Cargo capacity 12,500 metric tons liquids. 6,200 metric tons solids; Helicopters: 5 x Sea King or Merlin helicopters; Guns: 2 x 30mm. 2 x Phalanx Close-in Weapon Systems; Sensor fit appropriate for aircraft control.

Date of Service Entry:
Fort Victoria   1994

Fort Grange Class (Fleet Replenishment Ships)
These ships were ordered in 1971 and after valuable service are over 25 years old. Usually a single helicopter is embarked and ASW armaments for helicopters are carried on board. There are six cranes, three of 10 tons lift and three of 5 tons.

Key specifications are as follows:
Length: 183.9m; Displacement: 23,384 tons full load; Speed: 22 knots; Range 10,000 at 20 knots; Complement: 114 (31 officers) plus 36 RNSTS (civilian supply staff) plus 45 RN aircrew; Cargo capacity 3,500 tons ammunition and stores; Helicopters: Up to 4 x Sea King; Guns: 2 x 20mm.

Dates of Service Entry:
Fort Rosalie   1978
Fort Austin   1979

LANDING SHIPS

Bay Class – Landing Ship Dock (Auxiliary)
These ships will displace over double the figure of the class they are replacing Two ships were ordered in 2000 and contracts for two further ships of the class were placed in November 2001. The design is based on the Dutch LPD Rotterdam and Bay Class vessels are designed to transport troops, vehicles, ammunition and stores as a follow-up to an amphibious assault. Offload is carried out by a flight deck capable of operating heavy helicopters, an amphibious dock capable of operating one LCU and mexeflotes which can be hung on the ships' sides. There is no beaching capability.

Key specifications are as follows:
Length: 176.0m; Displacement: 16,160 tons full load; Speed: 18 knots; Range 8,000 n.miles at 15 knots; Complement: 60, plus 356 troops; Military Lift: Space for vehicles equating to 36 Challenger MBTs or 150 light trucks plus 200 tons ammunition; Helicopters: Platform capable of operating Chinook. Armament: 1 x 30mm cannon; CIWS Phalanx.

Dates of Service Entry:
Lyme Bay   2007
Mounts Bay   2007
Cardigan Bay   2008

Note: RFA Largs Bay was sold to the Royal Australian Navy in 2011 and renamed HMAS Choules.

MISCELLANEOUS RFA VESSELS

Argus – Casualty Receiving Facility and Aviation Training Ship
Argus was initially procured as a helicopter training role. This former Ro-Ro container ship was converted for her new task by Harland and Wolf, completing in 1988. The former Ro-Ro deck is used as a hangar with four sliding WT doors able to operate at a speed of 10 m/min. Argus can replenish other ships underway. There is one lift port midships and one abaft the funnel. Domestic facilities are somewhat limited if she is used in the Command support role. She was the first RFA to be fitted with a command system

Argus now has a primary role as a Primary Casualty Receiving Ship having been upgraded with state of the art medical equipment in an extensive refit worth over £23M, that provides hospital facilities to troops in war zones. Medical equipment installed includes the latest advances in CT scanning equipment, used to assess casualties by 3D X-ray imagery, as well as new sterilising kit. As a Primary Casualty Receiving Facility, Argus can accommodate 100 casualties at any time ensuring wounded service personnel can receive swift primary care.

Studies are underway relating to a Joint Casualty Treatment Ship (JCTS) programme intended to replace the capability currently provided by RFA Argus in a 2020 timeframe. This programme would aim to deliver a ship-borne medical facility broadly similar in scope to a field hospital, capable of treating a full range of casualties, whether from sea, land or air environments.

Argus started a refit at Falmouth in early 2013 that should be completed by September 2013.

Key specifications are as follows:
Length: 175.1m; Displacement: 26,421 tons full load; Speed: 18 knots. Range 20,000 n.mile at 15 knots; Complement: 80 (22 officers) plus 35 permanent RN plus 137 RN Aviation personnel; Military lift: 3,300 tons dieso; 1,100 tons aviation fuel; 138 x 4 ton vehicles in lieu of aircraft; Guns: 4 x 30mm. 4 x 7.62mm MG; Combat Data System and Sensor fit appropriate for aircraft control; Fixed-wing aircraft: Provision to transport 12 x BAe Harrier; Helicopters: 6 Westland Sea King HAS 5/6 or similar.

Diligence – Forward Repair Ship
This ship was originally the Stena Inspector, designed as a Multipurpose Support Vessel for North Sea oil operations, and completed in 1981. She was chartered on 25 May 1982 for use as a fleet repair ship during the Falklands War and purchased from Stena (UK) Line in October 1983. She was then converted in 1984 for use as Forward Repair Ship in the South Atlantic (Falkland Islands).

The vessel has four 5 ton anchors for a four-point mooring system and is strengthened for operations in ice. In addition to supporting the Royal Navy in the Falklands and the Balkans she has also been used as a support ship in the Gulf.

Following an overhaul in 2007 we would expect this vessel to remain in service until at least 2016.

Key specifications are as follows:
Length: 112.0m; Displacement: 10,765 tons full load; Speed: 12 knots. Range: 5,000 n.mile at 12 knots; Complement: 38 (15 officers) plus accommodation for 147 plus 55 temporary; Cargo capacity: Long-jib crane SWL 5 tons; maximum lift, 40 tons; Guns: 4 x 20mm. 4 x 7.62mm MGs.

RFA decommissioning programme
Current plans for the decommissioning of RFA vessels are as follows: Orangeleaf 2015; Gold Rover 2016; Black Rover 2017; Fort Rosalie 2021; Fort Austin 2021; Argus 2020; Wave Ruler 2028; Wave Knight 2028.

MILITARY AFLOAT REACH AND SUSTAINABILITY PROJECT (MARS)

As part of the MARS project, in early 2012 the UK MoD announced a £432 million contract to build four new 37,000 ton tankers, each over 200 metres in length.

With the first vessels entering service in 2016, these tankers will maintain the RFA's ability to refuel Royal Navy ships at sea for the next 25 years. MARS tankers will be capable of supporting all types of maritime and expeditionary operations and will be compatible with the aircraft carriers HMS Queen Elizabeth and HMS Prince of Wales.

The MARS vessels that will replace the existing Royal Fleet Auxiliary (RFA) single hulled tankers will enter service at yearly intervals following the introduction into service of the first vessel in 2016.

Daewoo Shipbuilding and Marine Engineering (DSME) is the Government's preferred bidder for the contract. UK companies will however benefit from £150 million of associated contracts.

HARBOUR SERVICES

Historically, all waterborne harbour services and some others (e.g. Mooring and Salvage Vessels) were operated by the personnel of the Royal Maritime Auxiliary Service (RMAS) under the direction of the local Captain of the Port or Queen's Harbourmaster. However in 1996 the majority of harbour services, particularly in the Dockyard ports of Devonport, Portsmouth and The Clyde, were awarded to Serco Denholm Ltd under a Government Owned/Commercially Operated (GOCO) contract.

FLEET AIR ARM

The Fleet Air Arm numbers just over 5,200 personnel and operates about 200 aircraft of various types. Operating Merlin, Sea King and Lynx helicopters from ships at sea and two main Naval Air Stations at Yeovilton and Culdrose, the Fleet Air Arm provides the Royal Navy with the aviation support required to conduct maritime operations.

During late 2012 Fleet Air Arm personnel numbers included 635 pilots of whom 123 were under training, 38 were fixed wing pilots and 597 were helicopter pilots.

NAVAL AIRCRAFT (FAF – FORWARD AVAILABLE FLEET)

21 x Merlin MK 1 Helicopters. Anti-submarine warfare
11 x Sea King MK 5. SAR and Utility
10 x Sea King Mk 7. Provides radar airborne early warning to fleet
4 x Lynx Mk 3. Anti-submarine warfare and missile armed for surface ship attack
25 x Lynx Mk 8. Anti-submarine warfare and missile armed for surface ship attack
4 x King Air. Fixed wing trainer
12 x Hawk – Fleet training and support

(1) There are 28 x Lynx Wildcat on order and deliveries of the first aircraft commenced in early 2013 with final aircraft being delivered in 2017. Lynx Wildcat should be available for operational deployment from 2015.
(2) Lynx Mk 3 are expected to leave operational service during 2013.
(3) Other Royal Naval helicopters (22 x Sea King HC4 – Commando Helicopter Force) are assigned to the Joint Helicopter Command (JHC). See Chapter 5.

NAVAL AIR SQUADRONS

Squadron	Location	Aircraft	Role
702W	Yeovilton	Lynx Wildcat	Trials/training
702	Yeovilton	Lynx Mk 8	Training
815	Yeovilton	Lynx Mk3/Mk8	Onboard HM ships
845	Yeovilton	Sea King Mk 4	Commando Helicopter Force
846	Yeovilton	Sea King Mk 4	Commando Helicopter Force
847	Yeovilton	Lynx Mk 7/9	Commando Helicopter Force support
848	Yeovilton	Sea King Mk 4	Commando Helicopter Force training
771	Culdrose	Sea King Mk 5	Search and rescue
814	Culdrose	Merlin Mk 1	Anti-submarine
820	Culdrose	Merlin Mk 1	Anti-submarine
824	Culdrose	Merlin Mk 1	Operational conversion unit

829	Culdrose	Merlin Mk 1	Onboard HM ships
849	Culdrose	Sea King Mk 7	Airborne surveillance training
854	Culdrose	Sea King Mk 7	Airborne surveillance training
857	Culdrose	Sea King Mk 7	Airborne surveillance training

(1) There are other training squadrons such as: 703 Sqn at Yeovilton (Grob Tutor gliders – air experience); 705 Sqn at Barkstone Heath (Squirrel Mk 1/2 – single engine helicopter training); 750 Sqn at Culdrose (King Air – pilot and observer training); 792 Sqn at Culdrose (aerial targets); HMS Gannet SAR Flight at Prestwick (Sea King Mk 5).

(2) The 12 x Hawk used for fleet training and support are based at Culdrose.

(3) The programme to transfer the RAF's Merlin Mk 3 helicopters to the Royal Navy Commando Helicopter Force, to replace the Sea King Mk 4, has begun, and should be complete by the end of 2015.

JOINT HELICOPTER COMMAND

As from 1 October 1999 the Commando Helicopter Force joined with the support and battlefield helicopters of the Army Air Corps and the Royal Air Force in a new Joint Helicopter Command (JHC). The JHC is a single authority under Commander-in-Chief Land. The Fleet Air Arm contribution consisted of all the aircraft (plus about 1,000 personnel) of 845, 846, 847 and 848 Naval Air Squadrons plus 9 further aircraft from an attrition reserve.

More details relating to the JHC are given in Chapter 5.

NAVAL AIRCRAFT

Sea King
Principal Characteristics:
HC4: Crew: 1 x pilot and 1 x aircrewman: Fuselage Length 22m: Width 3.78m: Height 4.72m: Weight (empty) 6201kg: Max Take-Off Weight 9525kg: Rotor Diameter 18.9m: Cruising Speed 208km h (129mph) at sea level: Service Ceiling 1,220m.

The Westland Sea King is a licence-built version of the US Sikorsky S-61. The Royal Navy's HAS Mark 1 aircraft's first flight was in 1969. Since that time, the aircraft has been extensively upgraded and passed through a series of Marks.

Royal Navy Westland Sea King HC 4 prepares to land aboard the U.S. Military Sealift Command (MSC) ship USNS Pecos. (Photograph US Navy)

The Sea King Mk 7 is used for airborne surveillance and control and has Search Water 2000 Radar carried in a radardome that can be swivelled down underneath the aircraft for operational air and sea searches. In addition, there is an Orange Crop Electronic Support Measures system fitted. A detachment of 3 x AEW 2 aircraft generally deploys with each assault ship. The newly upgraded Merlin Mk 2 will replace the Sea King Mark 7 and is capable of fulfilling several roles, including provision of the Airborne Surveillance and Control capability.

The Sea King HC4 (Commando) is a tactical military helicopter capable of transporting 28 fully equipped troops or 6,000 lbs (2,720 kg) as an internal load. Carrying 28 troops the aircraft has a range of about 246 miles (396 km). The first HC4 deliveries were made to the Royal Navy in 1979.

By the end of 2015 20 x Merlin Mk 3 medium support helicopters will be transferred from the RAF to the Commando Helicopter Force.

The Mk 5 aircraft in service with 771 Sqn are SAR aircraft (Search & Rescue). RN SAR aircraft are stationed at Prestwick and Culdrose. From 2016 10 x Sikorsky S92s and 10 x AgustaWestland AW189s operated by Bristow Helicopters will replace the Sea Kings Mk 5.

Current plans suggest that the last Sea Kings will retire from service at the end of March 2016.

EH101 Merlin HM Mk1

Principal Characteristics:
Service Ceiling 4,572m: Range 550 n miles (1,019km): Top Speed 167 knots: All Up Weight 14,600kg: Sensors: GEC-Marconi Blue Kestrel 5000 radar, Thomson Marconi Flash AQS 960 dipping sonar, GEC-Marconi sonobuoy acoustic processor AQS-903,

Royal Navy Merlin HM 1. (Photograph Adrian Pingstone PD)

Racal Orange Reaper ESM: Weapons: ASW 4 x Stingray torpedoes or Mk 11 Mod 3 depth bombs plus anti-ship missiles.

Merlin was ordered in the early 1990s in a contract worth £1.5 billion and the first of 44 production aircraft appeared in 1996. Merlin was accepted into service in 1999. The Royal Navy currently operates 21 x aircraft (with four in reserve) in the anti-submarine and anti-surface warfare role in 4 x squadrons (814, 820, 824 and 829 Sqns). All are based at RNAS Culdrose. When embarked, the aircraft can operate from almost any capable flight deck.

The aircraft has a state-of-the-art mission system, which processes data from an extensive array of on-board sensors, giving Merlin an independent capability to search for, locate and attack submarine targets. It is this autonomous capability which makes Merlin almost unique among Anti Submarine Warfare helicopters.

Merlin's operational debut came during operations in the Northern Gulf and Southern Iraq during 2003. The planned out of service date for the Merlin Mk 1 is 2029.

A 2010 contract confirmed the award of a £1.1 billion contract for an upgrade under the Merlin Sustainment Programme (MCSP). The MCSP is for technological enhancements to 30 aircraft with an option for a further eight. All upgraded Merlins should be returned to service by the end of 2013.

Another 20 x Merlin Mk 3 medium support helicopters will be transferred from the RAF to the Commando Helicopter Force. This transfer should be complete by the end of 2015.

LYNX

Principal Characteristics: Crew 2 on the flight-deck and up to 2 mission crew in the fuselage; Length Fuselage 11.92m; Height 3.2m; Rotor Diameter 12.8m; Max Speed 144mph (232km h) at sea level; Ferry Range 1,046km (650 miles) with max internal and external fuel tanks; Weight (max take-off) 4,876kg (10,750lbs).

Lynx aircraft are at sea with all frigates and destroyers, to provide anti-surface surveillance, anti-submarine warfare (ASW) capabilities and anti-ship attack capabilities. From the introduction into service of the first of the upgraded 44 x HAS 3, HMA 8 aircraft in late 1994, the Lynx in Royal Naval service was turned from an anti-submarine helicopter into a dedicated maritime attack aircraft. Capable of carrying anti-submarine torpedoes (range 10km) and anti-ship Sea Skua missiles (range 20km), the HMA 8 is capable of integrating its navigational, communications and fighting systems through a 1553B databus.

Typical combat mission profiles in the anti-submarine role could be a patrol out to 60 miles, a two-hour loiter in the search area carrying torpedoes and smoke markers etc and return.

Wildcat (AW159)

Crew 2 pilots and a door gunner; Length 15.2 m; Height 3.7 m; Main rotor diameter 12.8 m; Max take off weight 6,000 kg; Engine 2 x LHTEC CTS800-4N turboshaft, 1,015 kW (1,361 hp); Max speed 290 km/h (180 mph); Range: 770 km (480 miles).

The MoD has ordered 62 x Wildcat helicopters, 28 in the naval version (to replace Lynx Mk 8) and 34 in the army version.

During January 2013 the first Wildcat delivered to the Royal Navy's 702W Squadron made its maiden flight from RNAS Yeovilton. With a more powerful

AW159 Wildcat. (Copyright AgustaWestland)

engine than its Lynx predecessor, a new radar system with 360 degree coverage, state of the art sensors and a more robust fuselage, the Wildcat will be capable of operating in more extreme weather conditions.

As a maritime attack helicopter, capable of a wide range of operational tasks including anti-submarine warfare, Wildcat will carry Sting Ray torpedoes and the light and heavy variants of the future Anti-Surface Guided Weapon (Missiles). Direct fire capability will be provided by a door mounted .50 heavy machine gun and the aircraft can carry 6 x passengers.

The in-service date for the naval variant is January 2015.

The prime contractor for the Wildcat contract is Agusta Westland who have subcontracted elements of the project to other companies. The most recent estimate of the cost of the project is £1.644 billion.

NAVAL MISSILES

Trident D-5

The UK Strategic deterrent (US Trident D-5) is deployed in the four Vanguard class Ballistic Missile Nuclear-Powered Submarines (SSBNs). The Trident D-5 missile is a three-stage, solid propellant Submarine Launched Ballistic Missile (SLBM) – it is 13.42 m long and has a body diameter of 2.11 m. The launch weight is 59,090 kg and the missile has a maximum range of 12,000 km. The minimum range is believed to be about 2,500 km and the current cost of each D-5 missile is believed to be in the region of £8.8 billion.

It has been stated that although the UK missiles are capable of carrying up to 12 warheads, they are currently carrying three warheads each making a total of 48 warheads each per Vanguard Class submarine. Each D-5 missile has a multiple independently targetable re-entry vehicle (MIRV) capability which allows the D-5 missile to engage multiple targets simultaneously.

There appear to be some UK plans to use some Trident D-5 missiles in a `sub-strategic' role, with a single warhead set to produce a smaller yield, believed to be around 10 kT.

The UK Government expects the Trident D5 missile to remain in service until about 2040 with a main gate decision on the replacement missile due in 2016. The estimated cost of the replacement missile system is between £2 billion and £3 billion (at 2006 prices).

Trident D5 missile during test firing from HMS Vanguard in 2005.
(MoD Crown Copyright 2013)

The Defence Equipment Plan for 2012 suggests an expenditure of £12.7 billion over the next 10 years to maintain the Trident strategic weapons system.

SLCM: Hughes Tomahawk Block IIIC/Block IV

US-built Tomahawk is deployed in all RN Attack submarines. In 1995, the first export order for Tomahawk missiles was announced, with the UK ordering 65 missiles, an Advanced Tomahawk Weapon Control Systems for seven boats, and a shore-based mission planning system. The missiles were UGM-109C TLAM-C versions to the Block 3/4 build standard, to be launched from standard torpedo tubes in attack submarines. The UK fired 20 missiles

Tomahawk Block IV cruise missile during a flight test (US Navy).
(MoD Crown Copyright 2013)

against targets in Serbia in early 1999, with more missiles fired against Afghanistan in 2001 and Iraq in 2003 and Libya (at least 12) in 2011.

In February 2006 it was disclosed that Tomahawk missiles had been purchased as follows: 1997 – 48; 1998 – 17; 1999 – 0; 2000 – 0; 2001 – 20; 2002 – 0; 2003 – 22; 2006 – 64 x Block IV.

The Block IV missiles have a range of up to 1200 kms (780) miles, can be retargeted in flight and can loiter above a target for more than two hours. Average cost of a Block IV Missile is believed to be in the region of £800,000.

Harpoon

Harpoon, manufactured by McDonnell Douglas of the USA, is an extremely powerful anti-shipping missile that is fitted to Type 23 Frigates and Type 45 Destroyers. The Sub Harpoon (UGM-84A) is also deployed in Astute and Trafalgar Class submarines. The latest versions of this missile have extremely sophisticated electronic counter measures (ECM), and the ability to fly a sea-skimming course on a dog-leg path through three pre-programmed

HMS Argyle firing Harpoon. (MoD Crown Copyright 2013)

way points. The warhead is extremely powerful and a hit from Harpoon is almost certain to result in the destruction or disablement of a major surface vessel.

Principal Characteristics: Length 3.84m: Diameter 0.343m: Total Weight 526kg: Warhead Weight 225kg: Range 110kms.

In the longer term we would expect Harpoon to be replaced by the Thales Lightweight Multi-Role Missile (LMM).

Sea Viper (PAAMS – Aster)

Aster 15 – Principal characteristics: Range 30kms (in excess of): Weight 310kg: Length: 4.2m: Diameter 0.18m: Speed Mach 3: Aster 30 – Principal characteristics: Range 100kms (in excess of): Weight 450 kg: Length 4.9m: Diameter 0.18m: Speed Mach 4.5.

The Sea Viper (PAAMS – Principal Anti Air Missile System) is the surface to air missile system that is found on the Type 45 Destroyers. Two versions will be in service, the Aster 15 (short range) and the Aster 30 (long range). Sea Viper is the only available system that can integrate three operational naval missions: self-defence, local area defence of nearby vessels and fleet area defence. The complete system consists of the missiles, missile launchers, command and control (C2) system and the associated radars.

Within the figure of £561.6 million overall cost for a Type 45 Destroyer, the cost of the Sea Viper system is approximately one third or about £187 million.

Sea Viper is also being purchased by France and Italy.

Sea Viper launching. (Photograph MBDA)

Sea Wolf

Principal Characteristics: Length 1.91m; Diameter 0.18m; Total Weight 79.8kgs; Range 20 kms (approx); Altitude 3/4000m.

Sea Wolf is a ship-based, surface-to-air missile designed for the defence of point targets. This is a highly efficient system thought to be capable of dealing with aircraft, missiles and even artillery rounds.

The missile is fired from a vertical silo on Type 23 frigates, and guided on to its target by means of a close in target engagement radar on the vessel under attack.

The guidance system is semi-automatic command to line of sight with radar and/or infra-red missile and target tracking.

The range of the original Sea Wolf was limited to about 10 kms but recent missile and radar upgrades are believed to have doubled the range of the system.

Current plans suggest that the Sea Wolf system will reach its out of service date in 2020.

Sea Skua
Length 2.85m; Diameter 0.22m; Total Weight 147kg
Range 20 kms approx.

Sea Wolf Block 2 firing. (Photograph MBDA)

Sea Skua is a short-range, anti-ship missile that has been in Royal Naval service since 1982. The missile is currently carried as the main armament of the Lynx aircraft flying from RN destroyers/frigates. The guidance system is semi-active terminal homing.

Sea Skua is currently planned to leave service from around the latter part of the decade when it is intended to be replaced by the Future Anti Surface Guided Weapon (Light) that could be carried by Wildcat helicopters.

Future Anti-Surface Guided Weapons (FASGW)
The Future Anti-Surface Guided Weapon (FASGW) is intended to meet the requirement for the Royal Navy to maintains its Anti-Surface Warfare (ASuW) attack capability well into the middle part of the next century.

FASGW will provide the most cost-effective ASuW delivery system to meet the perceived threat of missile firing Fast Attack Craft (FAC) and to help establish sea control/sea denial within the area of operations (including the littoral) and on relatively undefended coastal targets.

Sea Skua firing from a Royal Navy Lynx helicopter. (Photograph MBDA)

The MoD has a requirement for two types of missile, a light version and a heavy version:

Future Anti-Surface Guided Weapon (Light) – (FASGW(L))
This requirement is to be met with a Thales Lightweight Multi-Role Missile System (LMM), a derivative of the Starstreak missile. LMM will be used to attack smaller surface targets at sea and unprotected targets on land.

In 2011 Thales received a production contract for 1,000 LMM that provided for final testing and qualification and integration of the LMM on helicopter platforms. The LMM includes beam riding or semi-active laser guidance where the missile homes in on reflected energy with differing warhead options.

The LMM is believed to have a weight of under 14 kg and a range of up to 9,000 m (about 5.5 miles). The main LMM investment decision is expected in 2014 after which series production could start. We would expect the Wildcat maritime attack helicopter would initially be armed with LMM, and in the longer term the Type 26 Global Combat Ship.

Future Anti-Surface Guided Weapon (Heavy) – (FASGW(H))
MBDA is leading the Assessment Phase for the FASGW(H)) requirement and it is likely that the design will include a system that incorporates a new 100 kg modular, infrared-guided weapon system derived from the Sea Skua. FASGW (H) is expected to be available from around 2013.

There is a chance that FASGW(H)) could be part of a cooperative development signed by the governments of France and the UK, both governments having a similar requirement. The French are believed to requirement for an FASGW(H)) type system for their Panther and NH90 helicopters.

The MoD has spent about £1.7 million (end of 2012) on the FASGW(H)) assessment and the in-service date has yet to be finalised. Our estimate is that an in-service date of 2016–2017 would not be unrealistic.

Future Local Area Air Defence System (FLAADS(M)) – Sea Ceptor
The MoD has confirmed that a new Royal Navy missile air defence system named Sea Ceptor that will be able to intercept and destroy enemy missiles travelling at supersonic speeds is planned to be in service by late 2016. A £483 million contract to develop the system was announced in early 2012.

It is believed that the Sea Ceptor concept, that uses a new UK-developed missile capable of reaching speeds of up to Mach 3 and with a range of over 30 kms (19 miles), will have the ability to deal with multiple targets simultaneously, protecting an area of around 500 square miles over land or sea.

The Sea Ceptor air defence system has been designed for initial use on the Type 23 frigates to replace Sea Wolf air defence system when it is retired later later in the decade. In the longer term it is planned to be used on the Type 26 Global Combat Ship when it enters service early in the 2020s.

Sea Ceptor will be developed under a contract with MBDA (UK) that is expected to last for about five years. In the longer term Sea Ceptor could be adapted for both Army and RAF requirements.

THE ROYAL MARINES

The Royal Marines (RM) are an elite Corps and specialists in Amphibious Warfare – and wherever there is action, the Royal Marines are likely to be involved. They were prominent, for example, in the Falklands campaign, and they can be found wherever the UK Armed Services are actively involved e.g. Northern Ireland, the Balkans, Sierra Leone, Iraq and Afghanistan. The Royal Marines number approximately 6,850 (including 760 officers) and, since the end of the Cold War, and especially in recent years, the Corps appears to have reverted to its traditional role of being ready for operations anywhere in the world.

Royal Marine Major Units

Headquarters Royal Marines	(Portsmouth)
HQ 3 Commando Brigade Plymouth	(Stonehouse)
3 Commando Bde HQ & Signal Squadron	(Stonehouse)
3 Commando Bde Air Sqn	(Yeovilton)
30 Commando	(Stonehouse)
40 Commando	(Taunton)
42 Commando	(Plymouth)
43 Commando	(Clyde)
45 Commando	(Arbroath)
Commando Logistic Regiment	(Barnstaple))
539 Assault Sqn Plymouth	(Barnstaple)
Commando Training Centre	(Lympstone)
Royal Marines Stonehouse	(Plymouth)
1 Assault Group	(Poole)

All Royal Marines, except those in the Royal Marines Band Service, are first and foremost, commando soldiers. They are required to undergo a 32 week initial training course recognised as one of the longest and most demanding infantry training courses in the world. This is undertaken at the Commando Training Centre Royal Marines at Lympstone in UK's West Country, not far from Dartmoor.

The titular head of the Royal Marines is always a Major General – Commandant General Royal Marines (CGRM). There have been significant recent structural changes in the higher management of the Royal Navy recently and this has added to the responsibilities and raised the profile of CGRM.

The Royal Marines have small detachments in ships at sea and other units worldwide with widely differing tasks. However, the bulk of the manpower of the Royal Marines is grouped in battalion-sized organisations known as Commandos (Cdo). There are 4 Commando Groups and they are part of a larger formation known as 3 Commando Brigade (3 Cdo Bde).

3 Cdo Bde Commando Organisation

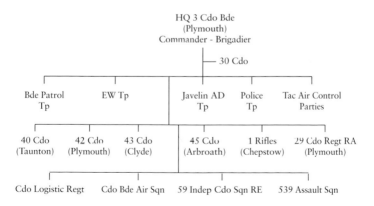

Notes:

(1) For operations expect 3 Commando Brigade to come under the command of the Joint Forces Command (JFC).

(2) **30 Commando** – Information Exploitation Group is the organisation that provides command, communications, reconnaissance and intelligence capabilities to 3 Commando Brigade.

(3) **1st Battalion The Rifles** – 3 Commando Brigade's Fourth Manoeuvre Unit
From 1 April 2008 1 Rifles has been attached to 3 Commando Brigade as a fourth manoeuvre unit. 3 Commando Brigade is now capable of providing a both a brigade at high readiness for operations anywhere in the world and also has the ability to support programmed operations.
1 Rifles will remain on the Army list under the Full Command of the Chief of the General Staff but serve under the direction of the Commander in Chief Fleet and the Commander of 3 Commando Brigade Royal Marines. The battalion has been structured as a Light Role Battalion and personnel will continue to wear the Rifles cap-badge. For normal tri-service operations.

(4) **539 Assault Squadron** has the personnel that allows troops and equipment from 3 Commando Brigade to land from vessels at sea to the operational areas (mainly beaches) where operations are to be conducted. 539 Assault Squadron is equipped with hovercraft, landing craft, raiding craft and Viking vehicles.

(5) **29 Cdo Regt RA** has one battery stationed at Arbroath with 45 Cdo.

(7) 1st Bn The Royal Netherlands Marine Corps can be part of 3 Cdo Bde for NATO assigned tasks.

(8) There are three regular Tactical Air Control Parties and one reserve.

Commando Organisation

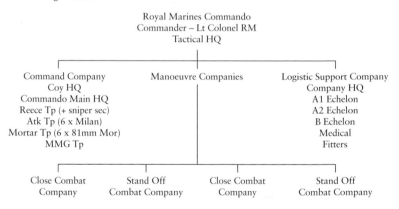

Note: There are 4 x Manoeuvre Companies:

2 x Close Combat Companies each with 3 x Fighting Troops (5 x officers and 98 other ranks).

2 x Stand Off Combat Companies one of which is tracked (Viking armoured vehicle) and the other wheeled. Each Stand Off Combat Company has 1 x Heavy Machine Gun Troop with 6 x 0.5 HMG, 1 x Anti-Tank Troop with 6 x Milan and 1 x Close Combat Fighting Troop (5 x officers and 78 other ranks).

Total personnel strength is approximately 690 all ranks. A troop (Tp) roughly equates to an army platoon and consists of about 30 men.

43 Commando (Fleet Protection Group)

This specialist Commando group was originally formed in 1980 as Comacchio Group and has the task of guarding the UK's nuclear weapons, and other associated installations from a variety of threats, plus the security of UK oil rigs against terrorist attacks. Personnel are also deployed world-wide on specialist tasks.

During 2001 Comacchio Group was renamed as the Fleet Protection Group Royal Marines (FPGRM) and the unit moved from RM Condor to HMNB Clyde. In 2012 the unit adopted its current name and became part of 3 Commando Brigade.

43 Commando is structured around 3 x rifle squadrons and 1 x headquarters squadron. Personnel strength is in the region of 533 personnel.

1 Assault Group Royal Marines (1 AGRM)

1 AGRM provides the central expertise and training support for Amphibious Warfare and Royal Navy Board and Search Training and is located at Plymouth. A secondary role is the provision of training and advise to allied nations. 1 AGRM has 3 x sub-units:

10 Landing Craft Training Squadron (Poole).
11 Amphibious Trials and Training Squadron (Instow).
School of Board and Search (Torpoint).

Special Boat Service

This organisation is the Naval equivalent of the Army's SAS (Special Air Service). Personnel are all volunteers from the mainstream Royal Marines and vacancies are few with competition for entry fierce.

Generally speaking only about 30 per cent of volunteers manage to complete the entry course and qualify. The SBS specialises in mounting clandestine operations against targets at sea, in rivers or harbours and against occupied coastlines.

The SBS are a part of the UK Special Forces Group – see Chapter 5.

Royal Marines Reserve (RMR)

The RMR consists of about 750 personnel based around the following locations:

RMR London: The detachment is in London and is located alongside the HQ. The remaining detachments are based in Cambridge, Chatham, Henley and Portsmouth.

RMR Merseyside: The Headquarters is in Liverpool where there is a detachment. The other detachments are based in Birmingham, Nottingham and Manchester.

RMR Scotland: HQ is in Glasgow with the remaining detachments based in Greenock, Edinburgh, Dundee, Aberdeen, Inverness and Belfast.

RMR Tyne: Location at Newcastle-on-Tyne. Hartlepool and Leeds.

RMR Bristol: The main detachment is in Bristol which is located alongside the HQ. The four remaining detachments are based in Poole, Plymouth, Cardiff and Lympstone.

CHAPTER 3 – THE BRITISH ARMY

PERSONNEL SUMMARY (MID 2013)

Army		Trained and Untrained Strength (mid 2013)
Officers		13,890
	Males	12,250
	Females	1,640
Other Ranks		85,840
	Males	79,080
	Females	6.760
	Total	99,730

Figures in the table above including approximately 3,700 Gurkha officers and soldiers.

Current plans appear to call for an Army of 112,000 by 2020. This would result in a Regular Army strength of 82,000 and a Reserve strength of 30,000.

Personnel in training (mid 2013)

	Personnel in training
Officers	620
Other Ranks	9,440

BRITISH ARMY STATISTICS

Strength of The Regular Army (early 2014)

Armour	9 x Regiments (1)
Royal Artillery	13 x Regiments (2)
Royal Engineers	16 x Regiments (3)
Regular Infantry Battalions	32 x Battalions (4)
Army Air Corps	4 x Regiments
Signals	12 x Regiments
Equipment Support	7 x Battalions (5)
Logistics	12 x Regiments
Medical	10 x Major Units (6)
Military Police	3 x Regiments

Notes: (1) Excludes Household Cavalry Mounted Regiment. (2) Includes 1 x Training Regiment and 29 Commando Regiment. (3) Includes 4 x Works Groups. (4) Excludes 1 x battalion of the Royal Gibraltar Regiment. (5) Includes 1 x Equipment Support (Aviation) Battalion; (6) Includes 6 x Medical Regiments, 3 x Hospitals and 1 x RAVC Regiment.

In general these Battalions/Regiments are commanded by Lieutenant Colonels and have a strength of between 500 and 800 personnel.

Strength of the Territorial Army as identified in late 2013

Arm or Corps	*Number of regiments or battalions*
Infantry	14
Armour	**4** (1)
Royal Artillery	7(2)
Royal Engineers	5
Special Air Service	2
Royal Signals	5
Equipment Support	2
Logistics	16
Intelligence Corps	2
Aviation	1
Medical	15 (3)
Total	73

Notes: (1) 4 x Regional National Defence Reconnaissance Regiments; (2) Includes Honourable Artillery Company (HAC). (3) Total includes Medical Regiments and Field Hospitals.

Notes: (1) 4 x Regional National Defence Reconnaissance Regiments; (2) Includes Honourable Artillery Company (HAC).

UK MoD figures show that in mid 2013 the overall Territorial Army strength was 24,690 (19,230 trained and 5,460 untrained).

FORMATIONS

HQ ARRC (NATO Deployable HQ)	1 x Corps Headquarters
Reaction Force Divisional HQ	1 x Headquarters plus 5 x Brigades
Adaptable Force Divisional HQ	1 x Headquarters plus 8 x Brigades
Force Troops Grouping	1 x Headquarters plus 8 Brigades
Regional HQ	8 x Headquarters
District HQ	1 (London District)

Armoured Infantry Brigades	3
Air Assault Brigade	1
Regional Infantry Brigades	7
Logistics Brigades	3
Artillery Brigade	1
Engineer Brigade	1
Signal Brigades	2
Medical Brigades	1
Intelligence & Surveillance Brigade	1
Military Police Brigade	1

Special Forces

Special Air Service	1 x Regular Regiment
Special Air Service	2 x Territorial Army Regiments
Special Forces Support Group	1 x Regiment (based on 1 Para)
Special Reconnaissance Regiment	1 x Regiment
Special Boat Service (Royal Marines)	4 x Squadrons

Joint Helicopter Command

Regular Army Air Corps Regiments	4 x Regiments
Territorial Army Aviation	1 x Regiment

BRITISH ARMY EQUIPMENT SUMMARY

Armour: 345 x Challenger 2 (probably about 220 in service); 320 x Scimitar; 720 x FV 432 and Bulldog; 793 x MCV 80 Warrior (probably about 365 in service); 450 x Spartan (includes about 60 x Stormer); 200 x Sultan; 300 x Mastiff; 400 x Jackal; 400 x Panther; 200 x Foxhound;166 x Vector (plus 12 x ambulance); 161 x Viking; 155 x Ridgeback; 115 x Warthog; 73 x Wolfhound; 250 x Husky.

Artillery and Mortars: 116 x AS 90 (in service); 36 x 227mm (G)MLRS ; 125 x 105mm Light Gun; 215 x 60 mm Mortar; 500 x 81 mm Mortar (including some SP); 2,000 x 51mm Light Mortar.

Air Defence: 32 x SP Rapier Fire Units; 145 x Starstreak LML; 60 x HVM (SP).

Army Aviation: 20 x Gazelle; 38 x Wildcat; 7 x BN-2; 67 x Apache AH Mk 1; Helicopters available from RAF – 38 x Chinook; 24 x Puma; 25 x Merlin.

HIGHER MANAGEMENT OF THE ARMY

The Ministry of Defence (MoD) is a Department of State, headed by the Secretary of State for Defence (SofS) who implements national defence policy and plans the expenditure of the defence budget. The MoD is the highest level of headquarters for the Armed Forces, both administrative and operational. All major issues of policy are referred to the SofS or to one of his Ministerial colleagues:

Minister of State for the Armed Forces
Minister of State for Defence Personnel, Welfare and Veterans
Parliamentary Under Secretary of State for Defence Equipment, Support and Technology
Parliamentary Under Secretary of State for International Security Strategy
Under Secretary of State and the House of Lords Spokesman for Defence

Under the direction of the Defence Council (described in Chapter 1) management of Armed Forces is the responsibility of the Service Boards, in the case of the Army, the Army Board is the senior management directorate.

THE ARMY BOARD

The routine management of the Army is the responsibility of The Army Board the composition of which is as follows:

Secretary of State for Defence
Minister of State for the Armed Forces
Minister of State for Defence Personnel, Welfare and Veterans
Parliamentary Under Secretary of State for Defence Equipment and Support
Parliamentary Under Secretary of State for International Security Strategy
Permanent Under Secretary
Chief of the General Staff
Second Permanent Under-Secretary of State (Secretary of the Army Board)
Assistant Chief of the General Staff
Adjutant General
Quartermaster General
Master General of the Ordnance
Commander-in-Chief Land Forces

The Army Board generally meets formally twice a year

Executive Committee of the Army Board (ECAB)

Attended by senior UK Army commanders, ECAB dictates the policy required for the Army to function efficiently and meet the aims required by the Defence Council and government. The Chief of the General Staff is the chairman of the Executive Committee of the Army Board.

Army Board and ECAB decisions are acted upon by the military staff at the various headquarters worldwide.

The Chief of the General Staff (CGS) is the officer responsible for the Army's contribution to the national defence effort and he maintains command and control through the commanders and the staff branches of each of the various army headquarters organisations.

CHIEF OF THE GENERAL STAFF – GENERAL SIR PETER WALL

Educated at Whitgift School (Croydon), General Peter Wall was commissioned into the Royal Engineers in 1974. After a short period of military duties he studied engineering at Cambridge University, before joining airborne forces and going on to serve with the Royal Engineers in Belize and Rhodesia. He was appointed Chief of Staff of 5 Airborne Brigade, before commanding 9 Parachute Squadron, Royal Engineers. He was then appointed Commanding Officer of 32 Engineer Regiment in Germany, deploying on operations to Bosnia.

General Wall was promoted to Brigadier and assumed command of 24 Airmobile Brigade in 1999 where he was responsible for converting the formation into 16 Air Assault Brigade later that year. In 2001 he became Chief of Joint Force Operations at Permanent Joint Headquarters Northwood, and went on to serve as Chief of Staff of the National Contingent HQ in Qatar, overseeing UK operations in Iraq, from January 2003.

General Sir Peter Wall GCB, CBE, ADC Gen.
(MoD Crown Copyright 2013)

In May 2003 General Wall was appointed General Officer Commanding 1st (UK) Armoured Division in which capacity he was responsible for security in Basra in Iraq. In 2005 he became Deputy Chief of Joint Operations at the Permanent Joint Headquarters Northwood and in 2007 he was appointed Deputy Chief of Defence Staff (Commitments).

He was appointed as Commander-in-Chief, Land Forces in August 2009 and appointed Knight Commander of the Order of the Bath (KCB) in the 2009 Birthday Honours.

In September 2010 General Wall succeeded General Sir David Richards as Chief of the General Staff (CGS).

Note: General Wall's predecessor as CGS was General Sir David Richards.

CHAIN OF COMMAND

The Chief of the General Staff (CGS) commands the Army through three subordinate commanders (Commander Land Forces (CLF), Adjutant General (AG) and Commander Force Development and Training (Comd FDT)). The Assistant Chief of the General Staff (ACGS) supported by the General Staff (GS) provides control and coordination.

CLF is the CGS's deputy and the 'supported commander' delivering the Army's principal outputs. AG and Comd FDT are supporting, but they are responsible to the CGS, with direct access on high level policy issues.

AG and Comd FDT support the CLF by providing the resources that he requires to achieve his mission. CLF has Operational Control of the Field Army, Army Reserves and the Army Firm Base.

The Adjutant General is responsible for bringing together personnel policies, plans and services to support the generation of military operational capability. Some of his subordinates include the Military Secretary, Director Personnel, Director Army Medical Services, Director Army Legal Services and the Comptroller and Auditor General.

Commander Force Development and Training is responsible for recruiting training and educating the Army's officers and soldiers; designing, developing and integrating capabilities and doctrine plus providing realistic and focused training. One of his major responsibilities is the Royal Military Academy (RMAS) Sandhurst.

Joint Forces Command (JFC) at Northwood in Middlesex has an important input into command at the operational level, and it is almost certain that any major operation involving Land Forces will be under the overall operational command of Commander JFC.

The following diagram illustrates this chain of command as at early 2014.

ARMY HEADQUARTERS (ARMY HQ)

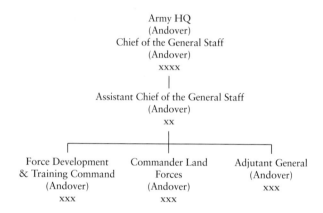

The Chief of the General Staff keeps a small 'forward headquarters' at the MoD in London.

Note: Stars denote the rank of the incumbent: xxxx General; xxx Lieutenant General; xx Major General; x Brigadier.

COMMANDER LAND FORCES (CLF)

CLF's role is to deliver and sustain the Army's operational capability, whenever required throughout the world and CLF is responsible for all of the Army's fighting troops . These are organised into three formations (plus London District) and are commanded by Major Generals.

CLF is one of the largest single service Top Level Budget (TLB) Holder, with a budget of almost £6 billion. CLF's command contains almost all the Army's fighting equipment, including attack helicopters, Challenger 2 tanks, Warrior Infantry Fighting Vehicles and AS90 artillery guns.

CLF Structure

CLF has Operational Control of the Joint Helicopter Command (JHC).

CLF is also responsible fpr the drawdown and return to the UK of units from British Forces Germany (BFG). The majority of combat units will be in the UK by the end of 2015.

3 (UK) DIVISION

This division provides the high readiness force (Reaction Force) that will undertake short notice contingency tasks and provide the conventional deterrence for Defence. Trained and equipped to undertake the full spectrum of operational tasks, this force, based upon three Armoured Infantry Brigades, and Air Assault Brigade and associated enablers, will provide the basis for any future enduring operation. Given the high readiness status of this Division it will be comprised of predominantly Regular personnel with approximately 10 per cent coming from the Reserve Force.

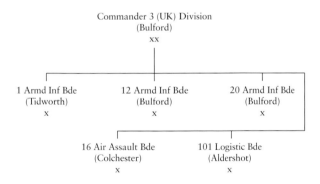

Note: The Royal Marines 3 Commando Brigade (under command of the Royal Navy) could be assigned to 3 (UK) Division for operations.

1 (UK) DIVISION

This division comprises a pool of Regular and Reserve Forces (the Adaptable Force) organised during peace, under seven regionally based Infantry Brigade Headquarters for training and administrative purposes. For a specific operation a force package could be selected from the range of divisional units based on the requirements for that specific task. Although 2 (UK) Division will be at a lower state of readiness than 3 (UK) Division it will be able to undertake a wide variety of challenging tasks, some of which are listed below:

◆ Follow-on forces for any future enduring operation. This means that the units of this division will be required to achieve appropriate levels of training and operational institutional awareness.
◆ Military support to homeland resilience. This includes maintaining a contingent capability to deal with natural disasters and other tasks in support of the civilian community.
◆ Where necessary building overseas military capability. This could mean training and developing indigenous armies in order to strengthen their national institutions and prevent future conflict.

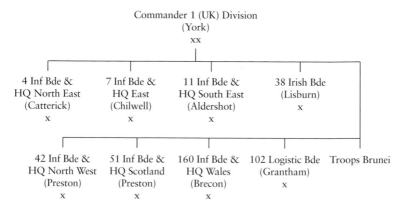

FORCE TROOPS

The third major element in the new structure are the Force Troop Brigades that provide the wide range of support (Artillery, Engineers, Logistics, Medical, Signals etc) required to ensure that operational requirements of every type are properly supported. Some of these Brigades that have a mix of Regular and Reserve personnel also provide a Regional Administrative Headquarters.

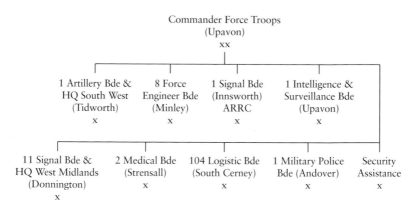

LONDON DISTRICT

This Headquarters is responsible for all Army units within the M25 boundary. The activity for which the Headquarters and the District is most well known is State Ceremonial and Public Duties in the Capital. The district insignia shows the Sword of St Paul representing the City of London and the Mural Crown representing the County of London. The District has its Headquarters in Horse Guards and is commanded by a Major General.

Between 500 and 600 troops are involved at any one time in MoD-sponsored equipment trials, demonstrations and exhibitions. Public Duties in London also take up two/three battalions at any one time. All troops not otherwise operationally committed are also available to provide Military Aid to the Civil Authorities in the United Kingdom.

Expect London District to consist of:

Kings Troop RHA
Household Cavalry Mounted Regiment
2 x Guards Battalions
3 x Guards Public Duties Companies
1 x Military Police Company
Logistic Support Units
Other Command Support Units

JOINT HELICOPTER COMMAND (JHC)

CLF has Operational Control of the JHC.

The primary role of the JHC is to deliver and sustain effective Battlefield Helicopter and Air Assault assets, operationally capable under all environmental conditions, in order to support the UK's defence missions and tasks.

Major formations that can be assigned to the JHC are as follows:

◆ All Army Aviation Units
◆ RAF Support Helicopter Force
◆ Commando Helicopter Force
◆ 16 Air Assault Brigade
◆ Combat Support Units
◆ Combat Service Support Units
◆ Joint Helicopter Command and Standards Wing

HQ JHC is at Andover and there is more detail relating to the JHC in Chapter 6.

ARMOURED BRIGADE

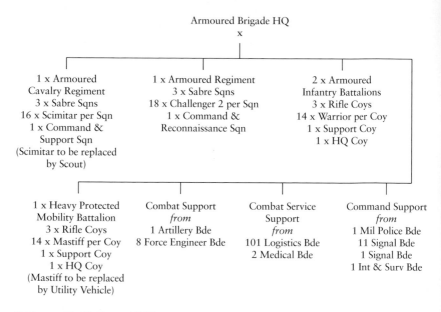

Armoured Brigade HQ

x

1 x Armoured Cavalry Regiment
3 x Sabre Sqns
16 x Scimitar per Sqn
1 x Command & Support Sqn
(Scimitar to be replaced by Scout)

1 x Armoured Regiment
3 x Sabre Sqns
18 x Challenger 2 per Sqn
1 x Command & Reconnaissance Sqn

2 x Armoured Infantry Battalions
3 x Rifle Coys
14 x Warrior per Coy
1 x Support Coy
1 x HQ Coy

1 x Heavy Protected Mobility Battalion
3 x Rifle Coys
14 x Mastiff per Coy
1 x Support Coy
1 x HQ Coy
(Mastiff to be replaced by Utility Vehicle)

Combat Support
from
1 Artillery Bde
8 Force Engineer Bde

Combat Service Support
from
101 Logistics Bde
2 Medical Bde

Command Support
from
1 Mil Police Bde
11 Signal Bde
1 Signal Bde
1 Int & Surv Bde

Totals:
56 x Challenger 2 MBT
48 x Scimitar
84 x Warrior
42 x Mastiff
200 x Other Armoured Vehicles
24 x AS 90 SP Gun (from 1 Artillery Brigade)
Approx 5,000–6,000 personnel

There are 3 x Armoured Brigades in 3 (UK) Division.

16 AIR ASSAULT BRIGADE

Almost 10,000 personnel form the personnel component of 16 Air Assault Brigade. Using everything from Apache helicopter to air-mobile artillery equipment and high velocity air defence missiles, this Brigade has marked a considerable leap forward in Britain's defence capability.

Support helicopters are provided by the RAF (from the Joint Helicopter Command) and the Brigade would normally expect to operate with 18 x Chinook and 18 x Puma. An air assault infantry battalion can be moved by 20 x Chinook equivalents lifts. Each air assault infantry battalion has a personnel strength of 687 and a battalion has 12 x ATGW firing posts.

The following diagram shows a possible configuration for 16 Air Assault Brigade during significant operations:

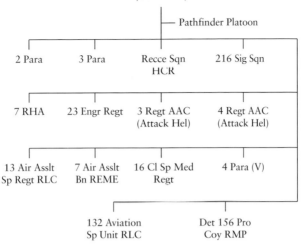

HQ 16 Air Assault Bde
(Colchester)

Pathfinder Platoon

| 2 Para | 3 Para | Recce Sqn HCR | 216 Sig Sqn |

| 7 RHA | 23 Engr Regt | 3 Regt AAC (Attack Hel) | 4 Regt AAC (Attack Hel) |

| 13 Air Asslt Sp Regt RLC | 7 Air Asslt Bn REME | 16 Cl Sp Med Regt | 4 Para (V) |

| 132 Aviation Sp Unit RLC | Det 156 Pro Coy RMP |

Note: This Brigade is under the command of 3 (UK) Division.

LIGHT BRIGADE – 1 (UK) DIVISION

A Light Brigade of the type assigned to 1 (UK) Division could have the following configuration:

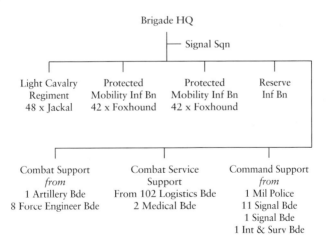

Brigade HQ

Signal Sqn

| Light Cavalry Regiment 48 x Jackal | Protected Mobility Inf Bn 42 x Foxhound | Protected Mobility Inf Bn 42 x Foxhound | Reserve Inf Bn |

| Combat Support *from* 1 Artillery Bde 8 Force Engineer Bde | Combat Service Support From 102 Logistics Bde 2 Medical Bde | Command Support *from* 1 Mil Police 11 Signal Bde 1 Signal Bde 1 Int & Surv Bde |

Note: (1) Vehicle types and numbers are provisional. (2) Support from Force Troops would be on an 'as required' basis.

LOGISTICS BRIGADES

There are three Logistic Brigades – 101 Logistic Brigade, 102 Logistic Brigade and 104 Logistic Brigade.

The operational role of a Logistic Brigade is to receive both troops and equipment into the theatre of operations, and be responsible for movement to the forward areas, ensuring that the combat formations have the combat supplies necessary to achieve their aim. 102 Logistics Brigade is also responsible for the establishment of Field Hospitals and the evacuation of casualties to the UK.

As an example 101 Logistics Brigade (Aldershot) has the following structure:

3 x Close Support Regiments RLC
3 x Theatre Support Regiments RLC
3 x Armoured Medical Regiments
3 x REME Close Support Regiments
2 x REME Force Support Regiments
3 x Transport Regiments RLC (V)

THE BATTLEGROUP

A division usually consists of 3 x brigades. These brigades are further sub divided into smaller formations known as Battlegroups. The Battlegroup is the basic building brick of the fighting formations.

A Battlegroup is commanded by a Lieutenant Colonel, and the infantry battalion or armoured regiment that he commands provides the command and staff element of the formation. The Battlegroup is then structured according to task, with the correct mix of infantry, armour and supporting arms.

The Battlegroup organisation is very flexible and the units assigned can be quickly regrouped to cope with a change in the threat. A typical battlegroup fighting a defensive battle might be composed of one armoured squadron and two armoured infantry companies, containing about 600 men, 12 tanks and about 80 other armoured vehicles.

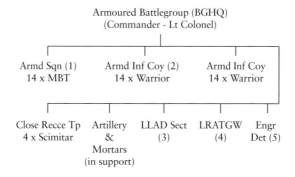

Notes:
(1) Armoured Squadron; (2) Armoured Infantry Company; (3) LLAD-Low Level Air Defence – HVM; (4) LRATGW – Long Range Anti Tank Guided Weapon; (5) Engineer Detachment.

The number of Battlegroups in a division and a brigade could vary according to the task the formation has been given. As a general rule you could expect a division to have as many as 9 x Battlegroups and a brigade to have up to 3. The above diagram shows a possible organisation for an Armoured Battlegroup in 3 (UK) Division.

UNITS OF THE ARMY (SITUATION DURING EARLY- 2014)

Armour

The Household Cavalry and the RAC is composed of 10 regular regiments (including the two regiments of the Household Cavalry, discussed below) and the four reserve Yeomanry Regiments with the TA. Apart from the Royal Tank Regiment, which was formed in the First World War with the specific task of fighting in armoured vehicles, the regular element of the RAC is provided by the successors of those regiments that formed the mounted units of the pre-mechanised era. The Yeomanry Regiments are tasked with providing a variety of operational reinforcement tasks in support of the regular RAC.

Although very much part of the RAC as an 'Arm', the Household Cavalry (HCav) is a discrete corps consisting of two regiments. The Household Cavalry Mounted Regiment (HCMR), which is permanently stationed in London has the task of providing mounted troops for state ceremonial functions. The Household Cavalry Regiment (HCR) is stationed in Windsor and is a Force Reconnaissance (FR) Regiment that plays a full role in operational and training activity within the Field Army. Officers and soldiers from the Household Cavalry are posted between the two regiments as needs dictate (For general purposes, in this publication, the term RAC includes the HCav).

Regimental Titles are as follows:

The Household Cavalry

The Household Cavalry Regiment	HCR
The Household Cavalry Mounted Regiment	HCMRD

The Royal Armoured Corps

1st The Queen's Dragoon Guards	QDG
The Royal Scots Dragoon Guards	SCOTS DG
The Royal Dragoon Guards	RDG
The Queen's Royal Hussars	QRH
The King's Royal Hussars	KRH
The Light Dragoons	LD
The Royal Tank Regiment	RTR
The Royal Lancers	RL

Locations

Household Cavalry and Armoured Regiment Locations (from late 2014)

The Household Cavalry Mounted Regiment	Hyde Park	
The Household Cavalry Regiment	Windsor	AC
1st The Queen's Dragoon Guards	Swanton Morley (from 2016)	LC
The Royal Scots Dragoon Guards	Leuchars (from 2015)	LC
The Royal Dragoon Guards	Catterick	AC
The Queen's Royal Hussars	Tidworth (from 2017)	CR
The King's Royal Hussars	Tidworth	CR
The Light Dragoons	Catterick (from 2016)	LC
The Royal Tank Regiment	Tidworth	CR
The Royal Lancers	Catterick	AC
The Heavy Cavalry Band	Catterick	
The Light Cavalry Band	Bovington	

Note: Abbreviations in the third column relate to the role: AC – Armoured Cavalry Regiment; LC – Light Cavalry Regiment; CR – Challenger 2 Main Battle Tank (MBT) Regiment.

Territorial Army (TA)

The Royal Yeomanry	London (RHQ)	LC
The Queen's own Yeomanry	Newcastle (RHQ	LC
The Royal Wessex Yeomanry	Bovington (RHQ)	
Royal Mercian and Lancastrian Yeomanry	Dudley (RHQ)	LC

ARMOURED REGIMENT

The following diagram shows the current structure of an Armoured Regiment equipped with Challenger 2 main battle tanks. A Challenger 2 Regiment with three Squadrons of main battle tanks would have an all up total of 56 tanks when deployed for war.

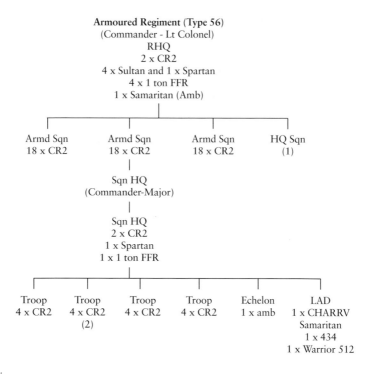

Armoured Regiment (Type 56)
(Commander - Lt Colonel)
RHQ
2 x CR2
4 x Sultan and 1 x Spartan
4 x 1 ton FFR
1 x Samaritan (Amb)

Armd Sqn 18 x CR2 | Armd Sqn 18 x CR2 | Armd Sqn 18 x CR2 | HQ Sqn (1)

Sqn HQ
(Commander-Major)

Sqn HQ
2 x CR2
1 x Spartan
1 x 1 ton FFR

Troop 4 x CR2 | Troop 4 x CR2 (2) | Troop 4 x CR2 | Troop 4 x CR2 | Echelon 1 x amb | LAD 1 x CHARRV Samaritan 1 x 434 1 x Warrior 512

Notes:

(1) HQ Sqn may have a Reconnaissance Troop with 8 x Scimitar which is under direct control of the CO in the field.

(2) Tank Troop commanded by 2Lt/Lt with Troop Sergeant as 2ic in own tank. The third tank is commanded by a Corporal.

(3) Totals: 56 x CR2, 8 x SCIMITAR, 4 x CHARRV. Total strength for war is approx 550.

(4) A Challenger 2 has a crew of 4 – Commander, Driver, Gunner and Loader/Operator.

ARMOURED RECONNAISSANCE

Armoured Reconnaissance is major responsibility for the RAC. Following the latest restructuring Armoured Reconnaissance is the responsibility of 3 x Armoured Cavalry Regiments (tracked) and 6 x Light Cavalry Regiments (wheeled) of which three are Regular and three TA.

Reconnaissance regiments are usually under the direct command of a formation Headquarters (generally a brigade). Their more usual task in a defensive scenario is to identify the direction and strength of the enemy thrusts, impose maximum delay and damage to the enemy's reconnaissance forces while allowing main forces to manoeuvre to combat the threat. They would be assisted in such a task by using their own organic long range anti-tank guided weapons and other assets that might be attached such as anti-tank helicopters (Lynx with TOW and perhaps Apache Longbow (WAH64D). In support would be the indirect fire guns (AS90) and Multiple Launch Rocket System (MLRS) of the assigned artillery, and an air defended area (ADA) maintained by Rapier and Stormer HVM air defence missiles.

The basic task of Armoured Reconnaissance is to obtain accurate information about the enemy and develop an intelligence picture in their areas of responsibility for their superior commanders in the chain-of-command, as quickly as possible. However during recent operations in Afghanistan, reconnaissance regiments have proved capable of providing armour support to infantry.

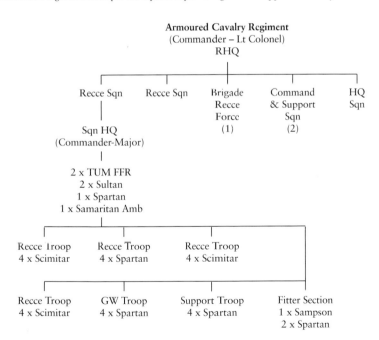

A regiment usually operates with 48 x Scimitar – in the longer term we expect Scimitar to be replaced by Scout (towards the end of the decade).

Notes:

(1) The Brigade Reconnaissance Force (BRF) operates as squadron sized unit using protected vehicles to identify and if necessary strike hostile elements.

(2) Expect the Command and Support Squadron to include a ground surveillance troop, a TACP/FAC party and an NBC protection troop in addition to the normal command and control elements.

(3) Full wartime establishment is approximately 600 all ranks.

(4) In war, each Regiment could receive an additional reconnaissance squadron from the TA Yeomanry.

(5) Expect a Light Cavalry Regiment to have a similar structure but equipped with 16 x Jackal in each Sabre Squadron.

THE INFANTRY

The British Infantry is based on the well tried and tested Regimental System, which has proved to be repeatedly successful on operations over the years. It is based on Regiments, most of which have one or more regular Battalion and all have associated TA Battalions. The esprit de corps of the Regimental system is maintained in the names and titles of British Infantry Regiments handed down through history, with a tradition of courage in battle. The repeated changing size of the British Army, dictated by history and politics, is reflected in the fact that many of the most illustrious Regiments still have a number of Regular and Territorial Reserve Battalions. For manning purposes, in a number of cases Infantry Regiments are grouped within administrative 'Divisions'. These 'Divisions' are no longer field formations but represent original historical groupings based on recruiting geography.

The 'Division' of Infantry is an organisation that is responsible for all aspects of military administration, from recruiting, manning and promotions for individuals in the Regiments under its wing, to the longer term planning required to ensure continuity and cohesion. Divisions of Infantry have no operational command over their regiments, and should not be confused with the remaining operational divisions, such as 1 (UK) Division and 3 (UK) Division.

By the end of 2014 it would appear that the 32 battalions of infantry will be located as follows:

United Kingdom	29 battalions
Cyprus	2 battalions
Brunei	1 battalion (Gurkha)
Falkland Islands	1 company group on detachment

During early 2014 the trained strength of the infantry was approximately 23,000.

Infantry Structure during mid 2014

The Guards Division	5 regular battalions
The Scottish Division	4 regular battalions (plus 1 x public duties company)
The Queen's Division	5 regular battalions
The King's Division	4 regular battalions
The Prince of Wales Division	4 regular battalions

Not administered by 'Divisions' of Infantry but operating under their own similar administrative arrangements are the following:

The Rifles	5 regular battalions
The Parachute Regiment	3 regular battalions
The Brigade of Gurkhas	2 regular battalions

Note: 1st Bn The Parachute Regiment form the core element of the Special Forces Support Group and are not always counted in the infantry battalion total.

TA battalions were under the administrative command of the following:

The Guards Division	1 TA battalion
The Scottish Division	2 TA battalions
The Queen's Division	3 TA battalions

The King's Division	2 TA battalions
The Prince of Wales Division	2 TA battalions
The Rifles	2 TA battalions
The Parachute Regiment	1 TA battalion
The Royal Irish Regiment	1 TA battalion
The Royal Gibraltar Regiment	1 composite battalion

INFANTRY BATTALIONS

The Guards Division
Regular Bns
1st Bn Grenadier Guards	1 GREN GDS
1st Bn Coldstream Guards	1 COLDM GDS
1st Bn Scots Guards	1 SG
1st Bn Irish Guards	1 IG
1st Bn Welsh Guards	1 WG

Note: The Guards Division has 3 x Public Duties Companies: Nijmegen Company – Grenadier Guards; No 7 Company – Coldstream Guards; F Company – Scots Guards.

Territorial Army Bn
| The London Regiment | LONDONS |

The Scottish Division
Regular Bns
1st Bn The Royal Regiment of Scotland	1 SCOTS
2nd Bn The Royal Regiment of Scotland	2 SCOTS
3rd Bn The Royal Regiment of Scotland	3 SCOTS
4th Bn The Royal Regiment of Scotland	4 SCOTS

Note: The Scottish Division has 1 x Public Duties Company: Balaclava Company – 5 Scots.

Territorial Army Bns
| 6th Bn The Royal Regiment of Scotland | 6 SCOTS |
| 7th Bn The Royal Regiment of Scotland | 7 SCOTS |

The Queen's Division
The Princess of Wales's Royal Regiment (Queen's and Royal Hampshires) Regular Bns
| 1st Bn The Princess of Wales's Royal Regiment | 1 PWRR |
| 2nd Bn The Princess of Wales's Royal Regiment | 2 PWRR |

Territorial Army Bn
| 3rd Bn The Princess of Wales's Royal Regiment | 3 PWRR |

The Royal Regiment of Fusiliers
Regular Bns
| 1st Bn The Royal Regiment of Fusiliers | 1 RRF |

Territorial Army Bn
| 5th Bn The Royal Regiment of Fusiliers | 5 RRF |

The Royal Anglian Regiment
Regular Bns

1st Bn The Royal Anglian Regiment	1 R ANGLIAN
2nd Bn The Royal Anglian Regiment	2 R ANGLIAN

Territorial Army Bn

3rd Bn The Royal Anglian Regiment	3 R ANGLIAN

The King's Division
The Duke of Lancaster's Regiment (King's, Lancashire and Border) Regular Bns

1st Bn The Duke of Lancaster's Regiment	1 LANCS
2nd Bn The Duke of Lancaster's Regiment	2 LANCS

Territorial Army Bn

4th Bn The Duke of Lancaster's Regiment	3 LANCS

The Yorkshire Regiment
Regular Bns

1st Bn The Yorkshire Regiment	1 YORKS
2nd Bn The Yorkshire Regiment	2 YORKS

Territorial Army Bn

4th Bn The Yorkshire Regiment	4 YORKS

The Prince of Wales's Division

The Mercian Regiment
Regular Bns

1st Bn The Mercian Regiment	1 MERCIAN
2nd Bn The Mercian Regiment	2 MERCIAN

Territorial Army Bn

4th Bn The Mercian Regiment	4 MERCIAN

The Royal Welsh
Regular Bns

1st Bn The Royal Welsh	1 R WELSH

Territorial Army Bn

3rd Bn The Royal Welsh	3 R WELSH

The Royal Irish Regiment
Regular Bn

1st Bn The Royal Irish Regiment	1 R IRISH

Territorial Army Bn

2nd Bn The Royal Irish Regiment	2 R IRISH

The Rifles
Regular Bns

1st Bn The Rifles	1 RIFLES
2nd Bn The Rifles	2 RIFLES

3rd Bn The Rifles	3 RIFLES
4th Bn The Rifles	4 RIFLES
5th Bn The Rifles	5 RIFLES

Territorial Army Bns

| 6th Bn The Rifles | 6 RIFLES |
| 7th Bn The Rifles | 7 RIFLES |

The Parachute Regiment
Regular Bns

1st Bn The Parachute Regiment	1 PARA
2nd Bn The Parachute Regiment	2 PARA
3rd Bn The Parachute Regiment	3 PARA

Territorial Army Bn

| 4th Bn The Parachute Regiment | 4 PARA |

Note: 1 PARA have formed the core element of the new Special Forces Support Group and as such have been removed from the formal Infantry structure

The Brigade of Gurkhas
Regular Bns

| 1st Bn The Royal Gurkha Rifles | 1 RGR |
| 2nd Bn The Royal Gurkha Rifles | 2 RGR |

ARMOURED INFANTRY BATTALION ORGANISATION

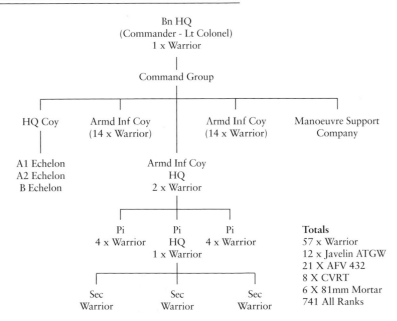

Note: Expect the Manoeuvre Support Company to have a Reconnaissance Platoon, a Mortar Platoon, an Anti Tank Guided Weapons (ATGW) Platoon and in some cases an Assault Pioneer Platoon.

HEAVY PROTECTED MOBILITY BATTALION ORGANISATION

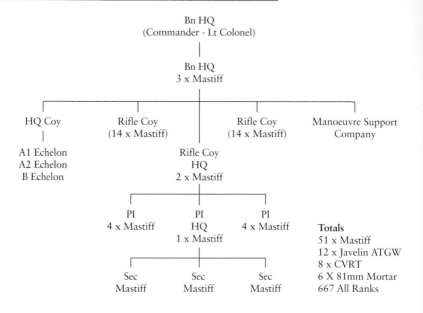

Bn HQ
(Commander - Lt Colonel)

Bn HQ
3 x Mastiff

HQ Coy | Rifle Coy (14 x Mastiff) | Rifle Coy (14 x Mastiff) | Manoeuvre Support Company

A1 Echelon
A2 Echelon
B Echelon

Rifle Coy
HQ
2 x Mastiff

PI
4 x Mastiff

PI
HQ
1 x Mastiff

PI
4 x Mastiff

Sec Mastiff | Sec Mastiff | Sec Mastiff

Totals
51 x Mastiff
12 x Javelin ATGW
8 x CVRT
6 X 81mm Mortar
667 All Ranks

Note: The Heavy Protected Mobility Battalion (above) is found in 3 (UK) Division. In 1 (UK) Division there are 4 x Protected Mobility Infantry Battalions with a similar structure but equipped with Foxhound vehicles.

Both 1 (UK) Division and the Territorial Army have a number of Light Role Infantry Battalions:

LIGHT ROLE INFANTRY BATTALION ORGANISATION

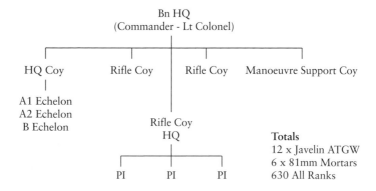

Bn HQ
(Commander - Lt Colonel)

HQ Coy | Rifle Coy | Rifle Coy | Manoeuvre Support Coy

A1 Echelon
A2 Echelon
B Echelon

Rifle Coy
HQ

PI | PI | PI

Totals
12 x Javelin ATGW
6 x 81mm Mortars
630 All Ranks

Note:
(1) A battalion of this type will usually be equipped with a range of both light and protected vehicles.
(2) Many battalions now have sniper platoons equipped with the Long Range Rifle that has an effective range of up to 1,100 m plus.
(3) Air Assault Bns have an HMG Pl with 6 x .50 Calibre Machine Guns mounted on TUM.

PLATOON ORGANISATION

The basic building bricks of the Infantry Battalion are the platoon and the section.

Under normal circumstances, the whole platoon with the exception of the LMG (Light Machine Gun) gunners are armed with IW – SA80 (Individual Weapon).

In an armoured or mechanised battalion, the platoon vehicles could be either Warrior or Mastiff.

Under normal circumstances expect a British infantry platoon to resemble the organisation in the following diagram:

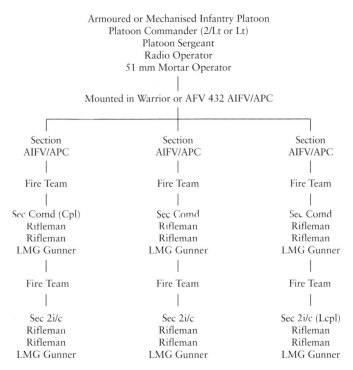

Armoured or Mechanised Infantry Platoon
Platoon Commander (2/Lt or Lt)
Platoon Sergeant
Radio Operator
51 mm Mortar Operator

Mounted in Warrior or AFV 432 AIFV/APC

Section AIFV/APC	Section AIFV/APC	Section AIFV/APC
Fire Team	Fire Team	Fire Team
Sec Comd (Cpl) Rifleman Rifleman LMG Gunner	Sec Comd Rifleman Rifleman LMG Gunner	Sec Comd Rifleman Rifleman LMG Gunner
Fire Team	Fire Team	Fire Team
Sec 2i/c Rifleman Rifleman LMG Gunner	Sec 2i/c Rifleman Rifleman LMG Gunner	Sec 2i/c (Lcpl) Rifleman Rifleman LMG Gunner

Note: In addition to the above, infantry platoons deploying to Afghanistan have a range of other weapons and systems available to them. It would almost certainly be unwise to list these enhancements here while operations continue.

INFANTRY LOCATIONS

Regular Infantry Battalion Locations (from late 2014)

1st Bn Grenadier Guards	Aldershot (from 2015)
1st Bn Coldstream Guards	Windsor
1st Bn Scots Guards	Aldershot (from 2015)
1st Bn Irish Guards	Hounslow (from 2015)
1st Bn Welsh Guards	Pirbright (from 2015)

1st Bn The Royal Regiment of Scotland	Belfast
2nd Bn The Royal Regiment of Scotland	Edinburgh
3rd Bn The Royal Regiment of Scotland	Fort George
4th Bn The Royal Regiment of Scotland*	Catterick (from 2015)
5th Bn The Royal Regiment of Scotland	Edinburgh (public duties coy)
1st Bn The Princess of Wales Royal Regiment	Bulford (from 2017)
2nd Bn The Princess of Wales Royal Regiment	Cyprus
1st Bn The Royal Regiment of Fusiliers	Tidworth
1st Bn The Royal Anglian Regiment	Woolwich
2nd Bn The Royal Anglian Regiment	Cottesmore
1st Bn The Duke of Lancaster's Regiment	Catterick
2nd Bn The Duke of Lancaster's Regiment	Weaton
1st Bn The Yorkshire Regiment	Warminster
2nd Bn The Yorkshire Regiment	Cyprus
1st Bn The Mercian Regiment	Bulford
2nd Bn The Mercian Regiment	Chester
1st Bn The Royal Welsh Regiment	Tidworth
1st Bn The Rifles	Chepstow
2nd Bn The Rifles	Abercorn Bks, Ballykinler
3rd Bn The Rifles	Edinburgh
4th Bn The Rifles	Aldershot (from 2015)
5th Bn The Rifles	Bulford (from 2016)
1st Bn The Royal Irish Regiment	Tern Hill
2nd Bn The Parachute Regiment	Colchester
3rd Bn The Parachute Regiment	Colchester
1st Bn The Royal Gurkha Rifles	Brunei
2nd Bn The Royal Gurkha Rifles	Shorncliffe

ARMY AIR CORPS

The Army obtains its aviation support from Army Air Corps (AAC), which is an organisation with four separate operational regiments and a number of independent squadrons and flights. The AAC is the smallest of the combat arms.

AAC manpower is believed to number around 2,000 personnel of all ranks, including about 400 officers (early 2014). Unlike the all-officer Navy and Air Force helicopter pilot establishments, almost two-thirds of AAC aircrew are non-commissioned officers. The AAC is supported by REME and RLC personnel numbering around 2,000 all ranks. Total AAC-related personnel strength is believed to be about 4,000.

With certain exceptions, during peace, all battlefield helicopters come under the authority of the Joint Helicopter Command (JHC).

The introduction into AAC service of the WAH-64D Apache Longbow attack helicopter is transforming AAC doctrine, organisation, and order of battle. The British Army designation of the type is Apache

AH Mk1 and approximately 48 aircraft are concentrated in two Attack Regiments. Theses are 3 and 4 Regts at Wattisham in Suffolk.

Each attack regiment is believed to have 3 x attack squadrons equipped with 8 x Apache AH Mk1. Deliveries of some 34 x Wildcat helicopters to the AAC are underway and by 2015 they should all have been delivered.

The Army Air Corps battlefield helicopter fleet has accumulated a vast amount of operational experience in recent years, and is arguably a more capable force than that possessed by any other European nation.

The current (2014) AAC Regimental and Squadron locations are shown below.

Army Air Corps force structure and helicopters during early 2014

Regiment	Location	Helicopter/aircraft	Fleet (estimate)
1 Regiment	Yeovilton	Lynx/Wildcat	24
2 (Training) Regiment	Middle Wallop	Apache, Lynx/Wildcat Gazelle	36 (variable)
3 Attack Regiment	Wattisham	Apache	24
4 Attack Regiment	Wattisham	Apache	24
5 Regiment	Aldergrove	Gazelle	8
6 Regiment (V)	Bury St Edmunds	Support	n/a
7 (Trg) Regiment (V)	Middle Wallop	Gazelle	12
Independent units			
Joint Special Forces Aviation Wing	Odiham	Lynx/Wildcat/Various	12
Development & Trials	Middle Wallop	All types	Variable
Initial Training	Shawbury	Squirrel HT 1	12

Note: (1) Flights include 7 Flight (Brunei), 8 Flight (Hereford), 12 Flight (Germany), 29 BATUS Flight (Canada). (2) Current plans are for Gazelle helicopters to be withdrawn in 2018.

The AAC Centre at Middle Wallop in Hampshire acts as a focal point for all Army Aviation, and it is here that the majority of corps training is carried out. Although the AAC operates some fixed-wing aircraft for training and liaison flying, the main effort goes into providing helicopter support for the land forces. About 160 AAC helicopters were believed to be in operational service during early 2014.

7 x Britten-Norman Defender (fixed wing aircraft) are used for reconnaissance and airborne command. The Defender has a top speed of about 320 km/h (200 mph) and a range of around 1,500 kms (990 miles). Currently flown by 651 Squadron.

THE ROYAL REGIMENT OF ARTILLERY

Background

The Royal Regiment of Artillery (RA) provides the battlefield fire support and air defence for the British Army in the field. Its various regiments are equipped for conventional fire support using field guns, for area and point air defence using air defence missiles and for specialised artillery locating tasks.

The RA remains one of the larger organisations in the British Army with 12 Regiments included in its regular Order of Battle. By the end of 2014 our estimate is that the Royal Artillery personnel strength will be in the region of 6,500 officers and soldiers.

The Royal Artillery provides the modern British armoured formation with a protective covering. The air defence covers the immediate airspace above and around the formation, with the field artillery reaching out to approximately 30 km in front and across the flanks of the formation supported by the

70 km range of GLMRS. An armoured formation that moves out of this protective covering is open to immediate destruction by an intelligent enemy.

By the end of 2014 and following the reorganisation demanded during the recent SDSR the Royal Artillery should have the following structure

Field Regiments (155 mm AS 90 SP Guns)	3
Field Regiments (105 mm Light Guns)	4 (1)
Air Defence Regiments (Rapier)	1
Air Defence Regiment (HVM)	1
Surveillance & Target Acquisition Regiment	1
UAS Regiment	2
Training Regiment (School Assets Regt)	1
The Kings Troop (Ceremonial)	1

Note:

(1) Of these four Regiments, one is a Commando Regiment (29 Cdo Regt) and another is an Air Assault Regiment (7 PARA RHA). Either of these Regiments can be called upon to provide Manoeuvre Support Artillery to the AMF (Allied Command Europe Military Force).

(2) Although the artillery is organised into Regiments, much of the 'Gunner's' loyalty is directed towards the battery in which they serve. The guns represent the Regimental Colours of the Artillery and it is around the batteries where the guns are held that history has gathered. A Regiment will generally have three or four gun batteries under command.

(3) The Royal Horse Artillery (RHA) is an important part of the Royal Regiment of Artillery and its regiments have been included in the totals above. There is considerable cross posting of officers and soldiers from the RA to the RHA, and some consider service with the RHA to be a career advancement.

(4) Artillery training is carried out at the Royal School of Artillery at Larkhill in Wiltshire. After initial training officers and gunners are posted to Regular RA units.

Current Organisation

During early 2014 the Regular and Territorial Army Regiments of the Royal Artillery were as follows:

Royal Artillery Regiment Locations (from late 2014)

The Kings Troop RHA	Woolwich	Ceremonial
1 Regiment RHA	Larkhill	AS90
3 Regiment RHA	Hexam	Light Gun
4 Regiment RA	Topcliffe	Light Gun
5 Regiment RA	Catterick	STA & Special Ops
7 Parachute Regiment RHA	Colchester	Light Gun
12 Regiment RA	Thorney Island	HVM
14 Regiment RA	Larkhill	Phase 2 training
16 Regiment RA	Thorney Island	Rapier
19 Regiment RA	Larkhill	AS90
26 Regiment RA	Larkhill	AS90
29 Commando Regiment RA	Plymouth	Light Gun
32 Regiment RA	Larkhill	UAS
47 Regiment RA	Larkhill	UAS

Note: Abbreviations: STA – Surveillance and Target Acquisition; HVM – Hyper Velocity Missile UAS – Unmanned Air Systems.

Territorial Army (TA) (Late 2013)

Honourable Artillery Company	London	STA & Special Ops
100 Regiment RA (V)	RHQ Luton	Light Gun
101 Regiment RA (V)	RHQ, Gateshead	STA/GMLRS
103 Regiment RA (V)	RHQ, St Helens	Light Gun
104 Regiment RA (V)	Newport, South Wales	UAS
105 Regiment RA (V)	RHQ, Edinburgh	Light Gun
106 Regiment RA (V)	Grove Park, London	HVM

Notes:

(1) The Regimental HQ of 29 Commando Regiment with one battery is at Plymouth. The other two batteries are at Arbroath and Poole. Those at Poole provide the amphibious warfare Naval Gunfire Support Officers (NGSFO).

(2) All Regiments equipped mainly with 155 mm AS 90 now have the ability to deploy on operations using the 105 mm Light Gun.

HQ 1 Artillery Brigade (HQ 1 Arty Bde)

The following units are under the command of Tidworth based HQ 1 Arty Bde: 1 RHA; 3 RHA; 4 Regiment; 19 Regiment; 26 Regiment; 3 x TA Light Gun Regiments.

Joint Ground Based Air Defence (JGBAD)

12 Regiment; 16 Regiment and 1 x TA HVM Regiment are under the command of the RAF's JGBAD organisation based at High Wycombe.

DIVISIONAL ARTILLERY GROUP (DAG)

An armoured formation in the field will be allocated artillery support under command that relates to the operational requirement. In the following example we show what could be allocated to an armoured division in a high intensity combat situation (the most extreme case). This artillery might consist of 3 x Close Support Regiments, with a number of units detached from the Artillery Brigade. Reserve reinforcements would be allocated as required.

Armoured Divisional Artillery Group (DAG) – Possible Organisation for War

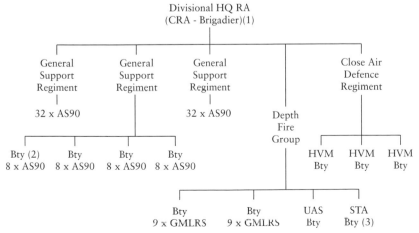

Notes:

(1) In an operation where a complete Armoured Division is required, expect each of the three brigades to have one Close Support Regiment with AS 90 indirect support.

(2) For planning purposes we assume that and AS90 Regiment has four batteries each with eight guns. The exact number of guns per battery may change from Regiment to Regiment.

(3) The Locating Batteries may have a metrological troop with BMETS, a radar troop with Cobra and a UAV troop with Phoenix.

(4) Area Air Defence (AAD) is provided by Rapier.

(5) Artillery regiments are commanded by a Lieutenant Colonel and a battery is commanded by a Major.

CORPS OF ROYAL ENGINEERS

Background

The engineer support for the Army is provided by the Corps of Royal Engineers (RE). Known as Sappers, the Royal Engineers are one of the Army's six combat arms, and are trained as fighting soldiers as well as specialist combat engineers. The Corps of Royal Engineers performs highly specialised combat and non-combat, and is active all over the world in conflict and peacetime. The Corps has no battle honours, its motto 'ubique' (everywhere), signifies that it has taken part in every battle fought by the British Army in all parts of the world.

Role

The Royal Engineers provide specialist support to the combat formations and engineer detachments can be found at all levels from the Combat Team / Company Group upwards. Combat Engineers tasks are amongst the following:

♦ **Defence**: Construction of field defences; laying anti-tank mines; improvement and construction of obstacles.

♦ **Attack**: Obstacle crossing; demolition of enemy defences (bunkers etc); mine clearance; bridge or ferry construction.

♦ **Advance**: Building or strengthening roads and bridges; removal of booby traps; mine clearance; airfield construction; supply of water; survey.

♦ **Withdrawal**: Demolition – of airfields, roads and bridges, fuel, ammunition and food dumps, railway tracks and rolling stock, industrial plant and facilities such as power stations; route clearance; laying anti-tank mines; booby trapping likely enemy future positions and items that might be attractive to the enemy. Often amongst the first soldiers into battle, and still involved in dangerous tasks such as mine clearance in the former Yugoslavia, the Sappers can turn their hands to almost any engineering task.

Recent military operations have once again highlighted the importance of combat engineers. Tasks for which engineer support was requested stretched the resources of the Corps to its limit and the first priority in almost any operational call for support is for engineers. Tracks have to be improved, roads must be built, water and power provided, mines lifted and where necessary accommodation constructed. All of these are engineer tasks that soak up large amounts of manpower.

Force structure

As of early 2012, the RE had a regular Army establishment of some 9,700 personnel. This large corps is presently organised as follows:

Armoured Engineer Regiments	3
Field Engineer Regiments	3
Air Assault Regiment	1
Commando Regiment	1
Air Support Regiments	1

EOD Regiments	2
Geographic Regiment	1
Training Regiments	2
Specialist Work Groups	6
TA Engineer Regiments	4

Royal Engineers: Regular Army units and locations during 2014

Unit	Location	Notes
21 Engineer Regiment	Catterick	Germany until 2017
22 Engineer Regiment	Perham Down	Armoured Engineers
23 Engineer Regiment	Woodbridge	16 Air Assault Brigade
26 Engineer Regiment	Perham Down	Armoured Engineers
32 Engineer Regiment	Catterick	Germany until 2015
33 Engineer Regiment	Wimbish	Explosive Ordnance Disposal
35 Engineer Regiment	Perham Down	Armoured Engineers (UK from 2017)
36 Engineer Regiment	Maidstone	Force Support
39 Engineer Regiment	Kinloss	Air Support
42 Engineer Regiment	RAF Wyton	Geographic survey
101 Engineer Regiment	Wimbish	Explosive Ordnance Disposal
20 Works Group RE	RAF Wittering	Air Support
62 Works Group RE	Chilwell	Water
63 Works Group RE	Chilwell	Electrical
64 Works Group RE	Chilwell	Fuel
64 Works Group RE	Chilwell	Ports and Railways
66 Works Group RE	Chilwell	Geotechnical
59 Commando Sqn RE	Chivenor	3 Commando Brigade
Royal Engineer Band	Chatham	

Note: The majority of the units listed above are under the command of 8 Force Engineer Brigade (Minley).

The former Gurkha Engineer Regiment QGE (Queen's Gurkha Engineers) now forms part of 36 Engineer Regiment, comprising 50 Headquarters Squadron, two wheeled field squadrons (20 Field Squadron and 69 Gurkha Field Squadron) and an engineer logistic squadron (70 Gurkha Field Support Squadron).

There are also a number of independent engineer squadrons in the UK.

Territorial Army Royal Engineer Regiments and independent units are shown below:

Royal Engineers: Territorial Army units and locations in late 2015

Unit	Location
71 Engineer Regiment (V)	Leuchars
72 Engineer Regiment (V)	Newcastle
73 Engineer Regiment (V)	Nottingham
75 Engineer Regiment (V)	Warrington
Royal Monmouthshire RE (Militia)	Monmouth
131 Independent Commando Squadron (V)	London
135 Independent Geographic Squadron (V)	Ewell
591 Independent Field Squadron (Volunteers)	Bangor (N Ireland)

Contingents of Royal Engineers (including Volunteer Reservists) are likely to be deployed in all combat zones, including most recently Afghanistan, Iraq, Balkans, Democratic Republic of Congo, Georgia, Liberia and Sierra Leone.

Training

For both officers and other ranks, specialist engineer training is mainly conducted by 1 and 3 Royal School of Military Engineer (RSME) Regiments based at Chatham and Blackwater. 1 RSME Regiment is the support regiment for training. During a year, some 8000 students may pass through 1 RSME Regiment, many of whom have recently joined the army and who have arrived at Chatham for a long engineering course lasting, in some cases, up to 44 weeks. 1 RSME Regiment incorporates the Construction Engineer School at Chatham, where civil and mechanical engineering skills are taught.

3 RSME Regiment is responsible for combat engineer training. The Combat Engineer School is located at Minley. 55 and 57 Training Squadrons are responsible for Combat Engineer and Assault Pioneer training, and the Driver Training Troop. 63 Training Support Squadron, is responsible for ABLE and RE Module Driver training.

Engineer Organisations

The smallest engineer unit is the field troop which is usually commanded by a Lieutenant and consists of approximately 44 men. In an armoured division a field troop can be expected to have up to four sections and each section is mounted in an APC. Engineer Regiments in the UK may have only three sections and may be mounted in wheeled vehicles such as Land Rovers and 4 Ton Trucks. An engineer troop will carry equipment, stores and explosives to enable it to carry out its immediate battlefield tasks.

There are generally 3 x Field Troops and 1 x Support Troop in each Field Squadron. An Engineer Regiment could be expected to have 3 x Field Squadrons, a Field Support Squadron, a Headquarters Squadron and a REME LAD. An Engineer Regiment generally has between 600 and 700 all ranks (depending upon role and task).

THE ROYAL CORPS OF SIGNALS

Overview

Royal Signals is the Combat Command Support Arm (CCS) that provides the Communications and Information Systems (CIS – the bearer network) and Information Communication Services (ICS – infrastructure and applications) used throughout the command structure of the Army, as well as supporting the other armed services and coalition partners. Traditionally this has been concentrated at Brigade level and above, but with the increasing hunger for information at the tactical level, this now stretches down to battle group level and below in direct support of the combat arms.

In addition to these tasks the Royal Signals also provide Electronic Warfare (EW) and Signals Intelligence (SIGINT). Life support and force protection duties also fall to Royal Signals units supporting certain formations.

Information is the lifeblood of any military formation in battle and it is the responsibility of the Royal Signals to ensure the speedy and accurate passage of information that enables commanders to make informed and timely decisions, and to ensure that those decisions are passed to the fighting troops in contact with the enemy. The rapid, accurate and secure employment of command, control and communications systems maximises the effect of the military force available and consequently the Royal Signals act as an extremely significant 'Force Multiplier'. The Corps motto is 'Certa Cito' (Swift and Sure) and its soldiers are usually some of the first to be deployed and last to be withdrawn during any operation. The Corps possesses a large Special Forces element as well as air assault, air support and special communications units.

As a sign of the changing times, in order to deliver the increasingly sophisticated and complex communications requirements at battle group level and below, some battle groups now deploy with a Royal Signals Regimental Signals Officer (RSO) and a highly trained multi-discipline Royal Signals Infantry Support Team (RSIST).

The overarching mission of the Royal Corps of Signals is to deliver elements of deployable integrated Combat Command Support, Electronic Warfare and Force Protection in order to enable decisive command.

Force structure

Royal Signals provides about 9 per cent of the Army's manpower with eleven regular regiments, one training regiment, and four Territorial Army regiments, each generally consisting of between three and six squadrons with between 400 and 600 personnel. There are also independent troops and detachments supporting various units around the world. Following the Strategic Defence and Security Review (SDSR), the Corps has been restructuring to make most efficient use of its capabilities.

Royal Signals personnel are found wherever the Army is deployed including every UK and NATO headquarters in the world. The Headquarters and 'Home' of the Corps is at Blandford Camp in Dorset.

Royal Signals units based in the United Kingdom provide command and control communications for forces that have operational roles providing the necessary command support and Electronic Warfare (EW) support for both the British Army and other NATO forces. Royal Signals personnel are also based in several other locations including Cyprus, the Falkland Islands, Kenya, Canada, and Gibraltar.

During early 2014 we believe that the personnel strength of the Royal Corps of Signals is in the region of 7,000.

From 2014 onwards the Royal Signals will have the following structure:

5 x Multirole Signal Regiments
1 x ARRC Signal Regiment
1 x JRRF Signal Regiment
1 x ECM / Force Protection Regiment
1 x UKSF Signal Regiment
1 x Information Support Signal Regiment
1 x Electronic Warfare Signal Regiment
1 x Air Assault Signal Squadron

Regular Army Royal Signals units are shown in the following table:

Royal Signals: Regular Army units and locations during 2014

Unit	Location	Notes
HQ 1 Signal Brigade	Innsworth	
HQ 11 Signal Brigade	Donnington	
1 Signal Regiment	Stafford	Multirole Regiment
2 Signal Regiment	York	Multirole Regiment
3 Signal Regiment	Bulford	Multirole Regiment
10 Signal Regiment	Corsham	Electronic Countermeasures
14 Signal Regiment	Brawdy	Electronic Warfare
15 Signal Regiment	Blandford	Information Systems
16 Signal Regiment	Stafford	Multirole Regiment
18 Signal Regiment	Hereford	UK Special Forces Support

21 Signal Regiment	Colerne	Multirole Regiment (JHC)
22 Signal Regiment	Stafford	ARRC Communications
30 Signal Regiment	Bramcote	JRRF Communications
JSSU	Cyprus	Joint Service Signals Unit
216 Air Assault Signal Squadron	Colchester	16 Air Assault Brigade
299 Signal Squadron		Special communications
11 Signal Regiment	Blandford	Royal School of Signals Training Regiment

Royal Signals TA units are shown in the next table:

Royal Signals : Territorial Army units during late 2013

Unit	Notes
32 Sig Regt (V)	Scotland, North of England and Northern Ireland
37 Sig Regt (V)	Wales, West Midlands and East Anglia
38 Sig Regt (V)	Yorkshire, Nottinghamshire, Buckinghamshire
39 Sig Regt (V)	Home Counties and the West
71 Sig Regt (V)	London and Essex
43 Sig Sqn (V)	JHC Support with 21 Sig Regt
63 (SAS) Sqn (V)	UK SF Support with 18 Sig Regt
81 Sig Sqn (V)	Corsham

Royal Signals TA provides individual reinforcements to regular regiments on operations.

Functions of Military Communications
Military communications roles undertaken by the Royal Signals may be divided into three separate functions:

Strategic communications: Communications between the political leadership, military high command, and military administrative and field commands at the divisional level. In terms of capability as opposed to function, modern communications systems increasingly blur the distinction between strategic and tactical systems as a consequence of technological advance.

Tactical communications: Communications between field formations from corps to division through brigade down to battalion level.

Electronic Warfare: The security of own forces and friendly forces communications, and the penetration, compromise and degradation of hostile communications.

Training
All Royal Signals officers undergo officer training at RMA Sandhurst (44 weeks) before taking the Royal Signals Troop Commanders Course at 11th (Royal School of Signals) Signal Regiment, Blandford Camp. Many Royal Signals officers have on entry, or obtain through the course of their careers, university degree-level engineering qualifications.

Recruit training for other ranks involves two phases:

Phase 1 – Soldier training (14 to 23 weeks)
Phase 2 – Trade training (7 to 50 weeks)

All Royal Signals soldiers, whether arriving from the Army Training Regiments at Pirbright, Winchester or Harrogate also complete trade, leadership, ethos and additional military training at

11 (Royal School of Signals) Signal Regiment. The length of the course depends on the trade chosen, varying from 7 weeks up to 50. Electronic Warfare operators also attend additional modules at the Defence Intelligence and Security Centre, Chicksands.

11 Signal Regiment is responsible for the special to arm training for both officers and other ranks.

The Royal School of Signals at Blandford Camp conducts over 140 different types of courses per year. There are in excess of 5,000 students completing courses throughout the year with as many as 1,000 students on courses at any one time. These figures equate to around some 450,000 Man Training Days a year.

THE ROYAL LOGISTIC CORPS

The Royal Logistic Corps RLC is the youngest Corps in the Army and was formed in April 1993 as a result of the recommendations of the MoD's Logistic Support Review. The RLC results from the amalgamation of the Royal Corps of Transport (RCT), the Royal Army Ordnance Corps (RAOC), the Army Catering Corps (ACC), the Royal Pioneer Corps (RPC) and elements of the Royal Engineers (RE). During early 2014 we believe that the RLC had a Regular Army personnel strength of about 14,000.

Role

The RLC has very broad responsibilities throughout the Army, these include operational re-supply, the movement of personnel throughout the world, the Army's air despatch service, maritime and rail transport, and explosive ordnance disposal that includes the hazardous bomb disposal in operational areas such as Iraq or Afghanistan and the mainland UK Other roles include the operation of numerous very large vehicle and stores depots both in the UK and overseas, the training and provision of cooks to virtually all units in the Army, the provision of pioneer labour and the Army's postal and courier service.

Force Structure

There are 12 Regular RLC Regiments (plus 2 training regiments) and 11 TA Regiments including the Catering Support Regiment RLC (V).

3 x Close Support Logistic Regiments
3 x Theatre Logistic Regiments
2 x Force Logistic Regiments
1 x Air Assault Support Regiment
1 x Port and Maritime Regiment
1 x Regular Postal Courier and Movement Regiment
1 x Ordnance Disposal Regiment

The principal field elements of the RLC are the Close Support and the General Support Regiments whose primary role is to supply the fighting units with ammunition, fuel and rations (Combat Supplies).

Expect a formation such as 1 (UK) Division on operations to have the support of at least one Close Support Regiment, responsible for manning and operating the supply chain to Brigades and Divisional units. This Close Support Regiment will have large sections holding stores both on wheels and on the ground. A Division will typically require about 1,000 tons of Combat Supplies a day but demand can easily exceed that amount in high intensity operations.

Royal Logistic Corps: Regular Army units and locations during 2014

Unit	Location	Notes
HQ 101 Logistic Brigade	Aldershot	
HQ 102 Logistic Brigade	Grantham	
HQ 104 Logistic Support Brigade	South Cerney	
1 Close Support Logistic Regiment	Bicester	Germany until 2016
3 Close Support Logistic Regiment	Aldershot	Germany until mid-2014
4 Close Support logistic Regiment	Abingdon	Oh
6 Force Logistic Regiment	Dishforth	Germany until 2016.
7 Force Logistic Regiment	Cottesmore	
9 Theatre Logistic Regiment	Hullavington	
10 The Queen's Own Gurkha Logistic Regiment	Aldershot	
11 Explosive Ordnance Disposal Regiment	Didcot	Detachments dispersed throughout the UK
13 Air Assault Support Regiment	Colchester	Supports 16 Air Assault Brigade.
17 Port and Maritime Regiment	Southampton	Port and Maritime capability
23 Pioneer Regiment	Bicester	Commands 47 (Air Despatch) Squadron
27 Theatre Logistic Regiment	Abingdon	
29 Postal, Courier and movements Regiment	South Cerney	Detachments dispersed throughout the UK
5 Training Regiment RLC	Grantham	Phase 1 and 2 training regiment for TA
25 Training Regiment RLC	Deepcut	Training regiment for RLC

Royal Logistic Corps : Territorial Army units during late 2013

Postal, Courier and movements Regiment (V)	Grantham	
150 (Yorkshire) Transport Regiment (V)	Hull	Transport function
151 (London) Transport Regiment (V)	London	Transport function
152 (Ulster) Transport Regiment (V)	Ulster	Transport function
155 Transport Regiment (V)	Plymouth	Transport function
156 Transport Regiment (V)	Liverpool	Transport function
158 Transport Regiment (V)	Peterborough	Transport function
159 Supply Regiment (V)	West Bromwich	Supply function
160 Transport Regiment (V)	Grantham	Transport function
165 Port Regiment (V)	Grantham	Port and Maritime function
166 Supply Regiment (V)	Grantham	Supply function
168 Pioneer Regiment (V)	Grantham	Pioneer function
Scottish Transport Regiment (V)	Dunfermline	Transport function
Welsh Transport Regiment (V)	Cardiff	Transport function
Catering Support Regiment (V)	Grantham	

THE ROYAL ELECTRICAL & MECHANICAL ENGINEERS

Equipment Support remains separate from the other logistic pillar of Service Support and consequently the Royal Electrical & Mechanical Engineers (REME) has retained not only its own identity but expanded its responsibilities. Equipment Support encompasses equipment management, engineering support, supply management, provisioning for vehicle and technical spares and financial management responsibilities for in-service equipment. During early 2014 we believe the REME has a Regular Army personnel strength of about 9,000.

Role

The aim of the REME is 'To keep operationally fit equipment in the hands of the troops' and in the current financial environment it is important that this is carried out at the minimum possible cost. The equipment that REME is responsible for ranges from small arms and trucks to helicopters and main battle tanks. All field force units have some integral REME support (1st line support) which will vary, depending on the size of the unit and the equipment held, from a few attached tradesmen up to a large Regimental Workshop of over 200 men. In war REME is responsible for the recovery and repair of battle damaged and unserviceable equipment.

The development of highly technical weapon systems and other equipment has meant that REME has had to balance engineering and tactical considerations. On the one hand the increased scope for forward repair of equipment reduces the time out of action, but on the other hand engineering stability is required for the repair of complex systems.

Force Structure

Seven REME Support Battalions have been established. Six of these battalions provide second line support for the British contribution to the ACE Rapid Reaction Corps (ARRC) and UK formations. An Aviation Support Battalion supports the Army Air Corps and units assigned to the Joint Helicopter Command.

There are currently four TA REME Equipment Support Battalions.

Royal Electrical and Mechanical Engineers: Regular Army units and locations during 2014

Unit	Location	Notes
1 Close Support Battalion	Catterick	102 Logistic Brigade
2 Close Support Battalion	Leuchars	101 Logistic Brigade (From Germany 2015)
3 Armoured Close Support Battalion	Tidworth	101 Logistic Brigade (From Germany 2017)
4 Armoured Close Support Battalion	Tidworth	101 Logistic Brigade
5 Force Support Battalion	Cottesmore	101 Logistic Brigade (From Tidworth 2015)
6 Armoured Close Support Battalion	Tidworth	101 Logistic Brigade
7 Air Assault Battalion	Wattisham	16 Air Assault Brigade

ARMY MEDICAL SERVICES

Royal Army Medical Corps (RAMC)

In peace, the personnel of the RAMC are based at the various medical installations throughout the world or in field force units and they are responsible for the health of the Army during peace and war.

During early 2014 we believe that the overall RAMC regular personnel strength is in region of 2,400.

Role

The primary role of the Corps is the maintenance of health and the prevention of disease. On operations, the RAMC is responsible for the care of the sick and wounded, with the subsequent evacuation of the wounded to hospitals in the rear areas. Each Brigade has a medical squadron attached which is a regular unit that operates in direct support of the forward Battlegroups. These units are either armoured, airmobile or parachute trained. In addition, each division has Medical Regiments under command that provide medical support for the divisional troops and can act as manoeuvre units for the forward brigades when required.

Force Structure
All Medical Regiments and Squadrons have medical sections that consist of a medical officer and eight Combat Medical Technicians. These sub-units are located with the Battlegroup or units being supported and they provide the necessary first line medical support. In addition, the Medical Regiments provides a dressing station where casualties are treated and may be resuscitated or stabilised before transfer to a field hospital. These units have the necessary integral ambulance support, both armoured and wheeled to transfer casualties from the first to second line medical units.

Field hospitals may be regular or TA and all are 200 bed facilities with a maximum of 8 surgical teams capable of carrying out life-saving operations on some of the most difficult surgical cases. Since 1990, most regular medical units have been deployed on operations either in Iraq, Afghanistan or the former Yugoslavia.

Casualty Evacuation (CASEVAC) is by ambulance either armoured or wheeled and driven by RLC personnel or by helicopter when such aircraft are available. A Chinook helicopter is capable of carrying 44 stretcher cases and a Puma can carry 6 stretcher cases and 6 sitting cases.

During early 2014 the Regular element of the RAMC was capable of providing 9 x major units (6 x Medical Regiments and 3 x Field Hospitals). The TA provides up to 10 x Field Hospitals and 5 x Medical Squadrons and 3 x Medical Regiments.

The Queen Alexandra's Royal Army Nursing Corps (QARANC)
On 1 April 1992 the QARANC became an all-nursing and totally professionally qualified Corps. Its male and female, officer and other rank personnel, provide the necessary qualified nursing support at all levels and covering a wide variety of nursing specialities. QARANC personnel can be found anywhere in the world where Army Medical services are required. During early 2014 we estimate the QARANC personnel strength as approximately 750 all ranks.

Royal Army Dental Corps (RADC)
The RADC fulfils the essential role of maintaining the dental health of the Army in peace and war, both at home and overseas. Qualified dentists and oral surgeons, hygienists, technicians and support ancillaries work in a wide variety of military units – from static and mobile dental clinics to field medical units, military hospitals and dental laboratories. Strength in early 2014 posssibly in the region of 350 (about 100 officers).

THE ADJUTANT GENERAL'S CORPS

The Adjutant General's Corps (AGC) was formed on 1 April 1992 and its sole task is the management of the Army's most precious resource, its soldiers. The Corps absorbed the functions of six existing smaller corps; the Royal Military Police, the Royal Army Pay Corps, the Royal Army Educational Corps, the Royal Army Chaplain's Department, the Army Legal Corps and the Military Provost Staff Corps.

The Corps is organised into four branches, Staff and Personnel Support (SPS), Provost (PRP), Educational and Training Services (ETS) and Army Legal Services (ALS). During early 2014 we believe the AGC consisted of approximately 5,000 officers and soldiers allocated as follows:

Provost (Royal Military Police)	1,500
Staff and Personnel Support	3,100
Educational and Training Services	300
Army Legal Services	100

The Role of the Provost Branch

The Provost Branch was formed from the formerly independent Corps of Royal Military Police (RMP) and the Military Provost Staff Corps (MPSC). Although they are no longer independent they are still known as the AGC (PRO) and AGC (MPS) thus forming the two parts of the Provost Branch.

Royal Military Police

To provide the police support the Army requires the RMP has the following functions:

◆ Providing operational support to units in the field
◆ Preventing crime
◆ Enforcement of the law within the community and assistance with the maintenance of discipline
◆ Providing a 24 hour response service of assistance, advice and information.

Operational support includes advising commanders and the staff who produce the operational movement plans. RMP traffic posts are deployed along the main operational movement routes and provide a constant flow of traffic information regarding the progress of front line troops and the logistical resupply. RMP units with a vehicle to man ratio of 1:3 are also a valuable force for the security of rear areas. In addition, there is a highly trained RMP close protection group that specialises in the protection of high risk VIPs.

The RMP provides the day to day police support for both the army in the UK and dependents and MoD civilians overseas. RMP units are trained and equipped to deal with the most serious crimes. The Special Investigation Branch (SIB) operates in a similar fashion to the civilian CID.

The Military Provost Staff

AGC(MPS) staff recruited from within the Army are carefully selected for the leadership, management and training skills necessary to motivate the predominantly young offenders with whom they work. The majority of AGC(MPS) personnel are located in the Military Corrective Training Centre (MCTC) at Colchester where offenders sentenced by military courts are confined.

The Role of SPS Branch

The role of SPS Branch is to ensure the efficient and smooth delivery of Personnel Administration to the Army. This includes support to individual officers and soldiers in units by processing pay and Service documentation, first line provision of financial, welfare, education and resettlement guidance to individuals and the provision of clerical skills and information management to ensure the smooth day to day running of the unit or department.

AGC (SPS) officers are employed throughout the Army, in direct support of units as Regimental Administrative Officers or AGC Detachment Commanders. They hold Commander AGC(SPS) and SO2 AGC(SPS) posts in district/Divisional and Brigade HQs and fill posts at the Adjutant General's Information Centre (AGIC) and general staff appointments throughout the Army headquarters locations.

AGC(SPS) soldiers are employed as military clerks in direct support of units within the AGC Field Detachments, in fixed centre pay offices, in headquarters to provide staff support and in miscellaneous posts such as embassy clerks, as management accountants or in AGIC as programmer analysts.

The majority of AGC(SPS) soldiers, currently about 70 per cent are serving with field force units, with the remaining 30 per cent in base and training units or HQs, such as the MoD

Members of AGC(SPS) are first trained as soldiers and then specialise as Military Clerks. AGC(SPS). Officers complete the same military training as their counterparts in other Arms and Services, starting at the Royal Military Academy, Sandhurst. They are required to attend all promotion courses and to pass the standard career exams prior to promotion to the rank of Major.

The Role of the ETS Branch
The AGC(ETS) Branch has the responsibility for improving the efficiency, effectiveness and morale of the Army by providing support to operations and the developmental education, training, support and resettlement services that the Army requires to carry out its task. ETS personnel provide assistance at almost all levels of command but their most visible task is the manning of Army Education Centres wherever the Army is stationed. At these centres officers and soldiers receive the educational support necessary for them to achieve both civilian and military qualifications.

The Role of the ALS Branch
The AGC(ALS) Branch advises on all aspects of service and civilian law that may affect every level of the Army from General to Private soldiers. Members of the branch are usually qualified as solicitors or barristers. In addition to the AGC personnel attached to major units throughout the Army the Corps is directly responsible for the following:

SMALLER CORPS

THE INTELLIGENCE CORPS (Int Corps) – The Int Corps deals with operational intelligence, counter intelligence and security (Personnel strength during early 2014 probably about 1,300).

THE ROYAL ARMY VETERINARY CORPS (RAVC) – The RAVC looks after the many animals that the Army has on strength. Veterinary tasks in today's army are mainly directed towards guard or search dogs and horses for ceremonial duties (Personnel strength during early 2014 probably about 250).

THE ARMY PHYSICAL TRAINING CORPS (APTC) – Consists mainly of SNCOs who are responsible for unit fitness. The majority of major units have a representative from this corps on their strength. (Personnel strength during early 2014 probably about 300).

SMALL ARMS SCHOOL CORPS (SASC) – A small corps with the responsibility of training instructors in all aspects of weapon handling (Personnel strength during early 2014 probably about 120).

THE GENERAL SERVICE CORPS (GSC) – A holding unit for specialists. Personnel from this corps are generally members of the reserve army.

The Royal Gibraltar Regiment
Gibraltar also has its own single battalion of the Royal Gibraltar Regiment comprising one regular and two volunteer companies.

ARMY RESERVES

There have been reserve land forces in Britain since medieval times. Over time, the titles and structures of these reserve forces have changed, but until World War II these reserves essentially comprised four separate elements: Volunteers, Militia, and Yeomanry provided the part-time, voluntary territorial forces; while retired Regular Army personnel made up the Army Regular Reserve on a compulsory basis; subject to diminishing obligations with age. Today the Army Reserves comprise similar components – both Volunteers and Regulars, with the difference that the erstwhile Volunteers, Militia, and Yeomanry are now incorporated into a single volunteer force as the Territorial Army (TA).

The Territorial Army is the reserve element at the highest state of readiness. In mid 2013 the TA overall strength was 24,690 (19,230 trained and 5,460 untrained).

The Territorial Army consists mainly of people who have joined directly from the civilian community. These personnel form the main part of the active, ready reserve for the British Army, train regularly, and are paid at the same rates as the regular forces on a pro-rata basis.

Territorial Army Order of Battle, as identified in late 2013

Arm or Corps	Number of regiments or battalions
Infantry	14 (14)
Armour	4 (3)
Royal Artillery	7 (6)
Royal Engineers	5 (3)
Special Air Service	2 (2)
Royal Signals	5 (4)
Equipment Support	2 (6)
Logistics	16 (12)
Intelligence Corps	2 (4)
Aviation	1 (1)
Medical	15 (16) (1)
Total	73 (71)

(1) Total includes Medical Regiments and Field Hospitals.
Post 2015 figures are in brackets. Details of the late 2013 reorganisation of the Reserves will be included in the next edition of The British Army Guide.

Territorial Army units are widely dispersed across the country – much more so than the Regular Forces, and in many areas they are the visible face of the Armed Forces. They help to keep society informed about the Armed Forces, and of the importance of defence to the nation, and have an active role supporting the Cadet organisations. They provide a means by which the community as a whole can contribute to the security of the United Kingdom.

According to some sources the annual budget for the TA is in the area of £500 – £600 million but an accurate figure has yet to be disclosed. A now rather dated MoD Report published in 2009 suggested that the average annual cost of a TA Volunteer was in the region of £10,678. When related to the TA trained personnel strength of just over 19,000, this would result in an annual expenditure of around £200 million on personnel alone. During 2013 the Secretary of State for Defence confirmed and MoD allocation of £1.8 billion over 10 years for additional training, infrastructure and equipment for the reserves.

ARMY 2020 (RESERVE FORCES)

Plans for Army 2020 include raising the Reserve Forces current trained strength of just over 19,000 to a trained strength of 30,000 by 2020. This may include a change in name for the TA.

In the future greater use will be made of Reserves and they will be used routinely on enduring stabilisation operations or UN commitments. Reserve contributions will range from individual contributions, specialist teams and in some cases the deployment of complete units.

THE REGULAR ARMY RESERVE

Types of Reservist
We estimate the strength of the Regular Army Reserve during mid 2014 as follows:

Component	Category	Total (our estimates)
Regular Reserve (Retired)	Regular Army Reserve	50,000
Long Term Reserve	Individuals liable to recall	100,000

Regular Reserve (Retired)
The Regular Reserve is comprised of personnel who have a mobilisation obligation by virtue of their former service in the regular army. For the most part, these reservists constitute a standby rather than ready reserve, and are rarely mobilised except in times of national emergency or incipient war. Some 420 retired regular reservists were called-up for Iraq operations in 2003.

The Regular Reserve consists of Individual Reservists (IR), some of whom may have varying obligations in respect of training and mobilisation, depending on factors such as length of regular service, age and sex.

Many ex-regulars join the Volunteer Reserve Forces (TA) after leaving regular service – giving them a dual Reserve status.

Long Term Reserve
In general terms, consists of individuals who have left the service and have a statutory liability for service until their 45th birthday (for those who enlisted before 1997 and the age of 55 for those who enlisted after 1997.

ARMY CADETS

Consists of two separate organisations, The Combined Cadet Forces and the Army Cadet Force:

The Role of the CCF
The Combined Cadet Force (CCF) is a tri-Service military cadet organisation based in schools and colleges throughout the UK. Although it is administered and funded by the Services it is a part of the national youth movement.

The CCF receives assistance and support for its training programme from the Regular and Reserve Forces, but the bulk of adult support is provided by members of school staffs who are responsible to head teachers for the conduct of cadet activities. CCF officers wear uniform but they are not part of the Armed Forces and carry no liability for service or compulsory training.

There are some 240 CCF contingents with 45,000 cadets, of whom about 30,000 are Army Cadets. The role of the CCF is to help boys and girls to develop powers of leadership through training which promotes qualities of responsibility, self-reliance, resourcefulness, endurance, perseverance and a sense of service to the community. Military training is also designed to demonstrate why defence forces are needed, how they function and to stimulate an interest in a career as an officer in the Services.

The tri-service CCF is believed to receive about £11 million in funding each year.

The Role of the ACF
The role of the Army Cadet Force (ACF) is to inspire young people to achieve success with a spirit of service to the Queen, country and their local community, and to develop the qualities of good citizenship, responsibility and leadership.

Some reports suggest that Army cadets make up between 25 – 30 per cent of regular army recruits. There are about 1,674 ACF detachments based in communities around the UK with a strength of around 45,000 cadets. The ACF is run by over 8,000 adults drawn from the local community, who manage a broad programme of military and adventurous training activities designed to develop character and leadership. The Army Cadets are administered by the MoD. The total budget provided to the Army Cadets is believed to have been in the region of about £40 million annually.

ARMOURED VEHICLES

Challenger 2

(about 318 available – approximately 227 in service) Crew 4; Length Gun Forward 11.55 m; Height 2.5 m; Width 4.2 m with appliqué armour; Ground Clearance 0.51 m; Combat Weight 62.5 tonnes- MLC 76; Main Armament 1 x 120 mm L30 CHARM Gun; Ammunition Carried max 50 rounds stowed – APFSDS, HESH and Smoke; Secondary Armament Co-axial 7.62 mm Chain Gun; Loaders pintle mounted 7.62 mm GPMG; Ammunition Carried 4000 rounds 7.62 mm; Engine CV12 12 cylinder – Auxiliary Power Unit 4 – stroke

Challenger 2. (MoD Crown Copyright 2013)

diesel; Gearbox TN54 epicyclic – 6 forward gears and 2 reverse; Road Speed 59 kph; Cross-Country Speed 40 kph; Fuel Capacity 1,592 litres usable internal plus 2 x 175 litre external fuel drums.

Challenger 2 was manufactured by Vickers Defence Systems and production was undertaken at their factories in Newcastle-Upon-Tyne and Leeds. At 1999 prices Challenger 2 was believed to cost £4 million per vehicle. The first Challenger 2 were delivered in 1994.

Although the hull and automotive parts of the Challenger 2 are based upon that of its predecessor Challenger 1, Challenger 2 incorporates over 150 improvements that have achieved substantially increased reliability and ease of maintenance. The Challenger 2 turret is, however, of a totally new design. The vehicle has a crew of four – commander, gunner, loader/signaller and driver and is equipped with a 120 mm rifled Royal Ordnance L30 gun firing all current tank ammunition natures.

The design of the turret incorporates several of the significant features that Vickers had developed for its Mk 7 MBT (a Vickers turret on a Leopard 2 chassis). The central feature is an entirely new fire control system based on the Ballistic Control System developed by Computing Devices Company (Canada) for the US Army's M1A1 MBT. This second generation computer incorporates dual 32-bit processors with a MIL STD1553B databus and has sufficient growth potential to accept Battlefield Information Control System (BICS) functions and navigation aids (a GPS satnav system). The armour is an uprated version of Challenger 1's Chobham armour.

Following the 2010 SDSR it is likely that the majority of the UK' Challenger 2's will be stationed in the UK following the return of British Forces from Germany. Current plans appear to be for 3 x Regiments in the UK (each with 56 x Challenger 2) as part of a vehicle fleet of around 227 vehicles, some for training and some of which will be stationed at an overseas training area (possibly Suffield in Canada).

In 2014 the MoD will be publishing plans to extend Challenger 2 service life to 2035.

Fv 107 Scimitar

(Approx 320 available) Armament 1 x 30 mm Rarden L21 Gun; 1 x 7.62 mm Machine Gun; 2 x 4 barrel smoke dischargers; Engine BTA 5.9 Cummins diesel; Fuel Capacity 423 litres; Max Road Speed 80 kph; Combat Weight 8,000 kg; Length 4.9 m; Height 2.096 m; Width 2.2 m; Ground Clearance 0.35 m; Road Range 644 km; Crew 3; Ammunition Capacity 30 mm – 160 rounds; 7.62 mm – 3,000 rounds; Main Armament Elevation – 10 degrees to + 35 degrees.

CVR(T) Scimitar is the mainstay reconnaissance vehicle with which all Formation Reconnaissance regiments are equipped as well as all Close Reconnaissance troops and some platoons of Armoured Battlegroups. The Scimitar is an ideal reconnaissance vehicle, mobile and fast with good communications and excellent viewing equipment. The vehicle's small size and low ground pressure make it extremely useful where the terrain is hostile and movement difficult.

Scimitar in the desert. (Public Domain)

Scimitar is due to be replaced by the Scout Specialist Vehicle. Pre-production vehicle prototypes were delivered in 2013 and we expect an in-service date after 2015.

Panther Command and Liaison Vehicle (Panther CLV)

(Approximately 400 available); Crew 3; Weight 6.5 tons; Height 1.9 m; Width 2.05 m; Payload capacity 1,200 kg; Range 500 km; Speed 130 km/h (80 mph); Armament 1 x 7.62 mm GPMG with Remote Weapon Station.

The UK MoD announced in July 2003 that the BAE Systems Land Systems (formerly Alvis) Multi-role Light Vehicle (MLV) had been selected as the British Army's Future Command and Liaison Vehicle (FCLV). The first procurement contract was signed in November 2003 for an initial 401 vehicles, with an option for up to 400 more. The vehicle has been named the Panther Command and Liaison Vehicle (CLV).

Panther CLV is based on a design by Iveco Defence Vehicles Division of Italy and the vehicles were manufactured during the period 2006 to 2010. Acquisition cost for some 400 vehicles is £193 million spread over five years. The first batch of 50 vehicles was delivered in late 2007.

The vehicle is air transportable, underslung beneath a Chinook helicopter or carried inside C130, C17 and A400M aircraft and is capable of operations in all weathers, day and night using thermal imaging equipment. The vehicles are protected against a range of threats and are fitted with a 7.62 mm weapon system (capable of upgrade to 12.7 mm) which allows the user to operate the machine guns with a camera and joystick from inside the vehicle.

Panther is already in service and is replacing a range of vehicles that are reaching the end of their operational lives, for example some types of Land Rover, Saxon, some FV432 and a number of CVR(T) vehicles. Panther is also entering service with the Royal Air Force Regiment.

Panther CLV. (Copyright BAe Systems 2013)

Jackal 1/2 (4 x 4 Patrol Vehicle)

(Approximately 400 in service – early 2014); Length 5.39 m; Width 2.0 m; Height 1.97 m; Weight 6,650 kg.

During June 2007 the UK MoD announced the purchase of 130 new weapons-mounted patrol vehicles under an Urgent Operational Requirement for troops in Iraq and Afghanistan. The Jackal MWMIK (Mobility Weapon-Mounted Installation Kit) delivered a new level of power to the WMIK fleet, with more firepower and a better range and mobility. Ideal for deep

Jackal in Afghanistan. (MoD Crown Copyright 2013)

battlespace reconnaissance the vehicle has a top speed of around 80 mph. Further announcements since 2007 suggest that the over Jackal fleet is now in the region of 400 vehicles.

The vehicle can be fitted with a range of firepower including a .50 calibre machine gun or an automatic grenade launcher and a general purpose machine gun, as well as carrying a crew of four soldiers with their personal weapons. In the UK, Light Cavalry Regiments are equipped with Jackal.

First deployed on operations in 2008 Jackal was designed by Supacat Ltd and manufactured by Devonport Management Ltd (DML) at their facility in Plymouth.

Coyote

The Coyote is a larger version of the jackal (with six wheels) and mainly used to provide combat support and logistics. Coyote is an element in the Tactical Support Vehicle programme, the other vehicles being Husky and Wolfhound.

MCV – 80 Fv 510 (Warrior)

(740 available – probably about 365in service) Weight loaded 24,500 kg; length 6.34 m; Height to turret top 2.78 m; Width 3.0 m; Ground Clearance 0.5 m; Max Road Speed 75 kph; Road Range 500 km; Engine Rolls Royce CV8 diesel; Horsepower 550 hp; Crew 2 (carries 8 infantry soldiers); Armament L21 30 mm Rarden Cannon; Coaxial EX-34 7.62 mm Hughes Helicopter Chain Gun; Smoke Dischargers Royal Ordnance Visual and Infra Red Screening Smoke (VIRSS).

Warrior. (Copyright BAe Systems 2013)

Warrior is an Armoured Infantry Fighting Vehicle (AIFV) in service with armoured infantry battalions. The original purchase of Warrior was for 789 units (365 remaining in service with the infantry) and the vehicle is in service with 6 x armoured infantry battalions in 3 (UK) Division.

Warrior armed with the 30 mm Rarden cannon gives the crew a good chance of destroying enemy APCs at ranges of up to 1,500 m and the vehicle carries a crew of three and seven dismounted infantry.

The vehicle is CBRN proof, and a full range of night vision equipment is included as standard. Warrior variants include an Artillery Observation Vehicle and a Repair and Recovery version.

Warrior has seen successful operational service in the Gulf (1991), with British troops serving in the Balkans and more recently in Iraq in 2003. The vehicle has proven protection against mines, and there is dramatic BBC TV footage of a Warrior running over a Serbian anti-tank mine during the conflict in the Balkans with little or no serious damage to the vehicle or crew.

The hull and mechanical components of Warrior are exceptional and few other vehicles in the world can match it for reliability and performance. The Warrior armament fire control system and electronics require upgrading if the vehicle is to remain in service to 2025 as intended.

The future Warrior Capability Sustainment Programme (WCSP) will upgrade the current Warrior Infantry Fighting Vehicle to meet current and future operational requirements. This upgrade should maintain the capability of Warrior with enhanced lethality out to 2040 and beyond.

WCSP may include a new power pack, vehtronics enhancement, a digital fire control system (FCS) and a modern medium calibre cannon system.

Numbers in overall UK service are believed to include 365 x Warrior Basic; 37 x Warrior RA; 96 x Warrior Recovery and Repair. The Kuwait MoD has 230 Warrior vehicles some of which are Recce vehicles armed with a 90 mm Cockerill gun.

Mastiff 2 Force Protection Vehicle (FPV)

(300 available) Height 2.64 m; Width 2,53 m; Length 7.08 m; Top speed 90 kph; All up weight 23,500 kg; Payload 6,350 kg.

Mastiff 2 which replaced the earlier Mastiff 1 (Ridgeback) is a heavily armoured, wheeled, troop carrying vehicle suitable for road patrols and convoys and is the newest delivery in a range of protected patrol vehicles being used for operations. Manufactured by the US Company

Mastiff. (MoD Crown Copyright 2013)

Force Protection Inc (where it is named Cougar) Mastiff 2 is a 6 x 6 wheel-drive patrol vehicle which carries six people, plus two crew. It has a maximum speed of 90 kph and can be armed with a machine gun, 50 mm cannon or 40 mm automatic grenade launcher.

The UK MoD purchased some 108 vehicles in an original order worth approximately US$70.1 million (£35 million) and these vehicles were deployed in Iraq during December 2006. During October 2007 the MoD announced the purchase of another 140 Mastiff in a contract worth around £100 million.

Mastiff is in service with the 3 x Heavy Protected Mobility Battalions of 3(UK) Division

AFV 432 and Bulldog

Approximately 740 in service of which about 460 are base line vehicles (models include infantry and load carriers, command vehicles, and ambulances). Crew 2 (Commander and Driver); Weight loaded 15,280kg; Length 5.25 m; Width 2.8 m; Height 2.28 m; Ground Pressure 0.78 kg km squared; Armament 1 x 7.62 Machine Gun; 2 x 3 barrel smoke dischargers; Engine Rolls Royce K60 No 4 Mark 1-4; Engine Power 240 bhp; Fuel Capacity 454 litres; Max Road Speed 52 kph; Road Range 580 km; Vertical Obstacle 0.9 m; Trench Crossing 2.05 m; Gradient 60 degrees; Carries up to 10 men; Armour 12.7 mm max.

In service since the early 1960s the basic 432 armoured personnel carrier is NBC proof and when necessary can be converted for swimming when it has a water speed of 6 kph (if required). Properly maintained it is a rugged and reliable vehicle with a good cross-country performance.

In July 2006 the UK Mod announced the upgrading of about 900 c AFV 430 series vehicles to Bulldog specifications with about 150 being further upgraded for operations in Iraq.

Bulldog. (MoD Crown Copyright 2013)

For counter-insurgency operations the up-armoured FV432/Bulldog provides a similar level of protection to Warrior and the vehicle is able to carry out many of the same tasks.

In early 2014 the longer term future for AFV 432/Bulldog is uncertain.

Foxhound

(200 available) Height; 2.35 m; Length 5.2 m; Width 2.1 m; Weight 7,500 kg; Top speed 110 kph.

Foxhound is a light protected patrol vehicle that was procured under a £180 million contract for 200 vehicles signed in November 2010. Manufactured by Force Protection Europe whose HQ is in Leamington Spa Foxhound will replace many of the Snatch Land Rovers that have proved vulnerable on recent operations. Light and agile, Foxhound allows for options in operational scenarios that are not available when only heavier armoured is available.

Foxhound. (MoD Crown Copyright 2013)

The vehicle has a 'V' shaped hull to protect against blast and its engine can be removed and replaced in around 30 minutes. Crew and passengers sit inside a protective pod, which can be quickly adapted to transform the patrol vehicle into an ambulance or supply truck. It is claimed that Foxhound can drive away from an ambush on only three wheels.

First vehicles were in-service during 2011 with initial operational use in the Spring of 2012. In the longer term there would appear to be a requirement for another 200 vehicles.

In 1 (UK) Division there are 4 x Protected Mobility Infantry Battalions equipped with Foxhound vehicles.

AS 90

(116 in service) Crew 5; Length 9.07 m; Width 3.3 m; Height 3.0 m overall; Ground Clearance 0.41 m; Turret Ring Diameter 2.7 m; Armour 17 mm; Calibre 155 mm; Range (39 cal) 24.7 kms (52 cal) 30 kms;

Recoil Length 780 mm; Rate of Fire 3 rounds in 10 secs (burst) 6 rounds per minute (intense) 2 rounds per minute (sustained); Secondary Armament 7.62 mm MG; Traverse 6,400 mills; Elevation -89/+1.244 mills; Ammunition Carried 48 x 155 mm projectiles and charges (31 turret & 17 hull); Engine Cumminis VTA903T turbo-charged V8 diesel 660 hp; Max Speed 53 kph; Gradient 60%; Vertical Obstacle 0.75 m; Trench Crossing 2.8 m; Fording Depth 1.5 m; Road Range 420 kms.

AS 90 in Iraq. (US Government – Public Domain)

AS 90 was manufactured by Vickers Shipbuilding and Engineering (VSEL) at Barrow in Furness. 179 Guns were delivered under a fixed price contract for £300 million. These 179 guns completely equipped six field regiments replacing the older 120 mm Abbot and 155 mm M109 in British service. At the beginning of 2014 there remains three Regiments of 1 Artillery Brigade equipped with the system.

AS 90 is equipped with a 39 calibre gun fires the NATO L15 unassisted projectile out to a range of 24.7 kms (Base Bleed ERA range is 30 kms). The gun has been fitted with an autonomous navigation and gunlaying system (AGLS), enabling it to work independently of external sighting references. Central to the system is an inertial dynamic reference unit (DRU) taken from the US Army's MAPS (Modular Azimuth Positioning System). The bulk of the turret electronics are housed in the Turret Control Computer (TCC) which controls the main turret functions, including gunlaying, magazine control, loading systems control, power distribution and testing.

Artillery has always been a cost effective way of destroying or neutralising targets in the forward edge of the battlespace. When the cost of a battery of guns, (approx £20 million) is compared with the cost of a close air support aircraft, (£40 million plus) and the cost of training each pilot, (£4 million +) the way ahead for governments with less and less to spend on defence is clear.

227 mm GMLRS
(36 launchers in service) Crew 3; Weight loaded 24,756 kg; Weight Unloaded 19,573 kg; Length 7.167 m; Width 2.97 m; Height (stowed) 2.57 m; Height (max elevation) 5.92 m; Ground Clearance 0.43 m; Max Road Speed 64 kph; Road Range 480 km; Fuel Capacity 617 litres; Fording 1.02 m; Vertical Obstacle 0.76 m; Engine Cummings VTA-903 turbo-charged 8 cylinder diesel developing 500 bhp at 2,300 rpm; Rocket Diameter 227 mm;

The MLRS launch vehicle is based on the US M2 Bradley (M270) chassis and the system is self loaded with 2 x rocket pod containers, each containing 6 x rockets. The whole loading sequence is power assisted and loading takes between 20 and 40 minutes. There is no manual procedure. Currently (2009) the MLRS vehicle is used operationally to fire the GMRLS rocket.

GMLRS firing during acceptance trials. (MoD Crown Copyright 2013)

GMLRS rockets contain Global Positioning System (GPS) elements and the latest advanced computer technology giving them accuracy out to a range of up to 70 kms. Armed with a 200 lb (90 kg) high explosive warhead which carries a payload of 404 Dual Purpose Improved Conventional Munition (DPICM) submunitions, the improved missile can engage more targets with a lower risk of collateral damage and with a smaller logistical burden.

The GMLRS rocket has been developed by a five-nation collaboration of the UK, France Germany, Italy and the US. The overall programme was worth over £250 million and the UK took delivery of several thousand rockets. The approximate (2010) cost per GMLRS Rocket was £68,000.

Following a series of successful trials the Guided Multiple Rocket Launch System (GMLRS) was declared fit for deployment with UK troops in Afghanistan in mid 2007.

The US Army is currently operating 830 MLRS, the French have 58, the West Germans 154 and the Italians 21.

105 mm Light Gun

(Approximately 125 in service) Crew 6; Weight 1,858 kg; Length 8.8 m; Width 1.78 m; Height 21.3 m; Ammunition HE, HEAT, WP, Smoke, Illuminating, Target Marking; Maximum Range (HE) 17.2 kms; Anti Tank Range 800 m; Muzzle Velocity 709m/s; Shell Weight HE 15.1 kg; Rate of Fire 6 rounds per minute.

The 105 mm Light Gun has been in service with the Royal Artillery for 25 years, and has recently received a major upgrade. The enhancement is an Auto Pointing System (APS) which performs the same function as the DRU on the AS 90. The APS is based on an inertial navigation system which enables it to be unhooked and into action in 30 seconds. The APS replaces the traditional dial sight and takes into account trunion tilt without the requirement to level any spirit level bubbles as before.

105 mm Light Gun. (Copyright BAe Systems 2013)

The gun was first delivered to the British Army in 1975 when it replaced the 105 mm Pack Howitzer. A robust, reliable system, the Light Gun proved its worth in the Falklands, where guns were sometimes firing up to 400 rounds per day. Since then the gun has seen operational service in Kuwait, Bosnia, Iraq and Afghanistan.

The Light Gun is in service with four Artillery Regiments as a go-anywhere, airportable weapon which can be carried around the battlefield underslung on a Puma or Chinook.

During March 2005 the UK MoD placed a contract for an advanced and more effective light artillery shell. This contract for 105 mm Improved Ammunition that was awarded to BAE Systems led to an initial buy of 50,000 High Explosive rounds, and was worth around £17 million.

The new High Explosive munitions are more effective against a range of targets and incorporate Insensitive Munitions (IM) technology, making them even safer to transport and handle.

The Light Gun has been extremely successful in the international market with sales to Australia (59), Botswana (6), Brunei (6), Ireland (12), Kenya (40), Malawi (12), Malaysia (20), Morocco (36), New Zealand (34), Oman (39), Switzerland (6), UAE (50), United States (548) and Zimbabwe (12).

Starstreak HVM

60 Fire Units available on Stormer and 145 on Light Mobile Launcher; Missile Length 1.39 m; Missile Diameter 0.27m; Missile Speed Mach 3+; Maximum Range 5.5 kms; Missile ceiling 1,000 m; Flight time to max range is 8 secs.

Short Missile Systems of Belfast were the prime contractors for the HVM (High Velocity Missile) which continues along the development path of both Blowpipe and Javelin. The system can be shoulder launched by mounting on the LML (lightweight

Starstreak SAM mounted on Stormer. (Copyright Thales UK Ltd 2013)

multiple launcher) or vehicle borne on the Alvis Stormer APC. The Stormer APC has an eight round launcher and 12 reload missiles can be carried inside the vehicle.

HVM has been optimised to counter threats from fast pop-up type strikes by attack helicopters and low flying aircraft. The missile employs a system of three dart type projectiles which can make multiple hits on the target. Each of these darts has an explosive warhead. It is believed that the HVM has an SSK (single shot to kill) probability of over 95%.

Using the HVM Thermal Sighting System (TSS) the system has the capability to operate at night, through cloud or in poor visibility. Some 84 x TSS are believed to be in service.

12 Regiment RA stationed at Thorney Island in West Sussex are equipped with HVM and there is 1 x TA Artillery Regiment similarly equipped. On mobilisation and HVM Regiment is believed to be configured as follows:

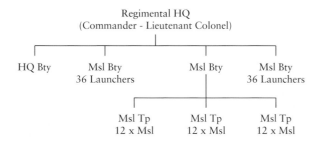

Note: An HVM detachment of four is carried in a Stormer armoured vehicle and in each vehicle there are four personnel. Inside the vehicle there are twelve ready to use missiles with a further eight stored inside as reloads.

Rapier (FSC)

(Possibly 32 in service) Guidance Semi Automatic to Line of Sight (SACLOS); Missile Diameter 13.3 cm; Missile Length 2.35 m; Rocket Solid Fuelled; Warhead High Explosive; Launch Weight 42 kg; Speed Mach 2+; Ceiling 3,000 m; Maximum Range 6,800 m; Fire Unit Height 2.13 m; Fire Unit Weight 1,227 kg; Radar Height (in action) 3.37 m; Radar Weight 1,186 kg; Radar Range 16 kms; Optical Tracker Height 1.54 m; Optical Tracker Weight 119 kg; Generator Weight 243 kg; Generator Height 0.91 m.

The Rapier system provides area 24 hour through cloud, Low Level Air Defence (LLAD) over the battlefield.

Rapier Field standard C (FSC) incorporates a range of technological improvements over its predecessor including an advanced three dimensional radar tracker acquisition system designed by Plessey. The towed system launcher mounts eight missiles (able to fire two simultaneously) which are manufactured in two warhead

Rapier firing. (Copyright MBDA 2013)

versions. One of these is a proximity explosive round and the other a kinetic energy round. The total cost of the Rapier (FSC) programme was £1,886 million.

The UK's future Rapier air defence capability will be 16 Regiment Royal Artillery (Thorney Island) The possible configuration of a Rapier Regiment on mobilisation will be four batteries each of two troops with three fire units per troop. In July 2004 the MoD announced the disbandment of the RAF Regiment Rapier squadrons.

Rapier in all of its versions has now been sold to the armed forces of at least 14 nations. We believe that sales have amounted to over 25,000 missiles, 600 launchers and about 350 radars.

Apache (AH Mk1)

(67 available – probably 48 in front line service)) Gross Mission Weight 7,746 kgs (17,077 lb); Cruise Speed at 500 m 272 kph; Maximum Range (Internal Fuel with 20 minute reserve) 462 kms; General Service Ceiling 3,505 metres (11,500 ft); Crew 2; Carries – 16 x Hellfire II missiles (range 6,000 metres approx); 76 x 2.75" CRV-7 rockets; 1,200 30mm cannon rounds; 4 x Air-to-Air Missiles; Engines 2 x Rolls Royce RTM-332.

Apache. (Copyright AgustaWestland 2013)

The UK MoD ordered 67 Apache based on the US Army AH-64D manufactured by Boeing in 1995. Boeing built the first eight aircraft, and partially assembled the other 59. The UK Westland helicopter company undertook final assembly, flight testing and programme support at their Yeovil factory. Full operating capability for Army Air Corps Apache Attack Regiments was achieved in mid 2007 and in UK service the aircraft is known as the AH Mk1.

We believe that there are 48 operational aircraft in two regiments (each of 24 aircraft). The remaining aircraft are used for trials, training and a war maintenance reserve (WMR).

The Apache can operate in all weathers, day or night, and can detect, classify and prioritise up to 256 potential targets at a time. Apart from the 'Longbow' mast-mounted fire control radar, the aircraft is equipped with a 127 x magnification TV system, 36 x magnification thermal imaging, and 18 x magnification direct view optics. The missile system incorporates Semi-Active Laser and Radio Frequency versions of the Hellfire missile, whose range is at least 6 kms. Apart from the Rolls-Royce engines, specific British Army requirements include a secure communications suite and a Helicopter Integrated Defensive Aids System (HIDAS). Programme cost was some £3 billion.

The night vision system of 67 Apache AH Mk1 attack helicopters is being upgraded. The M-TADS/PNVS, which is designated Arrowhead, is replacing the existing forward-looking infra-red (FLIR) and daylight television image intensifier with new sensors to provide improved target identification over longer ranges, better pilot performance and reduced life-cycle costs.

During May 2013 the MoD signed a £15 million contract to replenish the stock of Hellfire missiles used by Apache helicopters. Successful use of the missile in both Afghanistan and Libya (from the deck of HMS Ocean) had reduced UK stocks of the missiles and a replenishment was required. Current estimates suggest that the cost of each missile is in the region of £50,000.

A proposed Apache life extension programme should extend the life of the aircraft well beyond 2025.

Wildcat (AW159)

(38 being delivered) Crew 2 pilots and a door gunner; 6 x passengers at light scales; Length 15.2 m; Height 3.7 m; Main rotor diameter 12.8 m; Max take off weight 6,000 kg; Engine 2 x LHTEC CTS800-4N turboshaft, 1,015 kW (1,361 hp); Max speed 290 km/h (180 mph); Range: 770 km (480 miles).

The MoD has ordered 62 x Wildcat helicopters, 28 in the naval version (to replace Lynx Mk 8) and 34 in the army version (to replace Lynx AH Mark 7/9).

AW159 Wildcat. (Copyright Agusta Westland)

The prime contractor for the Wildcat contract is AgustaWestland who have subcontracted elements of the project to other companies. The most recent estimate of the cost of the project is £1.644 billion.

Essentially a Battlefield Reconnaissance Helicopter (BRH) the Wildcat is development of the older Lynx. Composed of around 95 per cent new components the Wildcat is the first AgustaWestland helicopter to be designed inside an entirely digital environment. The aircraft also has greater durability and stealth qualities. Both army and navy versions are based on a common airframe.

During late 2011 a further four helicopters were ordered and these four plus four from the army total of 34 were reconfigured as Wildcat Light Assault Helicopters.

Wildcat will be flown by 1 Regiment Army Air Corps operating from Yeovilton. The in-service date for the army variant is 2014.

In the longer term arming the Wildcat Lightweight Multirole Missile is one of the options being considered to meet the Future Anti Surface Guided Weapon (Light) (FASGW(L)) requirement.

Javelin LF ATGW (Light Forces Anti-tank Guided Weapon)

Launch Unit: Weight 6.4 kg; Sight magnification x 4; Missile: Range 2,500 m; Weight 11.8 kg; Length 1.08 m; Seeker – Imaging infra-red; Guidance – Lock on before launch, automatic self-guidance; Missile – Two stage solid propellant with a tandem shaped charge; Weight of Launch unit and missile 22 kg.

Javelin equips Light Forces, Mechanised and Armoured Infantry, and Formation Reconnaissance units. The UK version of the US Javelin ATGW system, is a more sophisticated guided weapon with a range of some 2,500 m A production contract was signed in early 2003 worth over £300 million and industry sources suggested that up to 5,000 missiles and 300 firing posts were ordered. The system replaced Milan ATGW and in UK service, Javelin has a number of modifications which include an enhanced Command Launch Unit (CLU) with a wider field of view, and the ability to recognise targets at longer ranges.

Javelin firing. (Copyright Eros Hoagland)

Although Javelin has been developed mainly to engage armoured fighting vehicles, the system can also be used to neutralise bunkers, buildings, and low-flying helicopters. Javelin's top-attack tandem warhead is claimed to defeat all known armour systems.

The US Army and Marine Corps have been using Javelin for some years and the system is either in service, or has been selected by Australia, Ireland, Jordan, Lithuania, New Zealand, and Taiwan. Over 7,000 Javelin launchers have been manufactured since 1995 and the average cost of each missile would be approximately £49,000.

Javelin is planned to be in UK service until 2025.

5.56 mm Individual Weapon (IW) (SA 80 and SA 80A2)
Effective Range 400m; Muzzle Velocity 940 m/s; Rate of Fire from 610-775 rpm; Weight 4.98 kg (with 30 round magazine); Length Overall 785 mm; Barrel Length 518 mm; Trigger Pull 3.12-4.5 kg.

SA 00A2. (MoD Crown Copyright 2013)

Designed to fire the standard NATO 5.56 mm x 45 mm round, the SA 80 was fitted with an x4 telescopic (SUSAT) sight as standard. The total buy for SA 80 was for 332,092 weapons. Issues of the weapon are believed to have been made as follows:

Royal Navy	7,864
Royal Marines	8,350
Royal Air Force	42,221
MoD Police	1,878
Army	271,779

At 1991/92 prices the total cost of the SA80 contract was in the order of £384.16 million. By late 1994 some 10,000 SA 80 Night Sights and 3rd Generation Image Intensifier Tubes for use with SA80 had been delivered.

The SA 80 had a mixed press and following some severe criticism of the weapons mechanical reliability the improved SA 80A2 was introduced into service during late 2001.

SA 80A2 (180,000 in service)
Some 13 changes were made to the weapon's breech block, gas regulation, firing-pin, cartridge extractor, recoil springs, cylinder and gas plug, hammer, magazine and barrel. Since modification the weapon has been extensively trialled.

Mean time before failure (MTBF) figures from the firing trials for stoppages, following rounds fired are as follow:

	SA 80A2	LSW
UK (temperate)	31,500	16,000
Brunei (hot/wet)	31,500	9,600
Kuwait (hot/dry)	7,875	8,728
Alaska (cold/dry)	31,500	43,200

The first SA 80A2 entered operational service during early 2002 and these weapons were in service across the army by late 2004. The cost of the programme was £92 million and some 200,000 weapons were modified by the time the programme ended in May 2006.

5.56mm Light Machine Gun (Minimi)
(4,500 in service) Effective range 800 m; Calibre 5.56 mm; Weight 7.1 kg; Length 914 mm; Feed 100-round disintegrating belt; Cyclic rate of fire 700 to 1000 rounds per minute.

FN Herstal's Minimi belt fed 5.56mm Light Machine Gun (LMG), has entered service on a scale of one per four-man fire team. The Minimi has been used operationally by British troops in Afghanistan and Iraq and the UK MoD has bought 2,472 weapons. The contract that boosted the firepower within infantry sections was believed to have been completed in late 2007.

The Minimi is in service with the Australian, Canadian and New Zealand Armies as well as the US Armed Forces.

7.62 mm General Purpose Machine Gun (GPMG)
(8,450 in service) available) Range 800 (Light Role) 1,800 m (Sustained Fire Role); Muzzle Velocity 538 m/s; Length 1.23 m; Weight loaded 13.85 kg (gun + 50 rounds); Belt Fed; Rate of Fire up to 750 rpm; Rate of Fire Light Role 100 rpm; Rate of Fire Sustained Fire Role 200 rpm.

An infantry machine gun which has been in service since the early 1960s, the GPMG can be used in the light role fired from a bipod or can be fitted to a tripod for use in the sustained fire role. The gun is also found pintle-mounted on many armoured vehicles and will be mounted on Wildcat helicopters. Used on a tripod the gun is effective out to 1,800 m although it is difficult to spot strike at this range because the tracer rounds in the ammunition belt burns out at 1,100 m.

Machine Gun platoons in air assault battalions remain equipped with the GPMG in the sustained fire role. GPMG performance has recently been enhanced by the issue of a Maxi Kite night image intensification sight giving excellent visibility out to 600 m.

60 mm Light Mortar

(215 in service) Max Range 3,800 m; Barrel weight 5.3 kg; Bipod weight 12 kg; Base plate weight 4.8 kg.

Procured under an Urgent Operational Requirement (UOR) in 2007 the M6-895 60 mm Mortar provides the infantry with a light mortar capability out to almost 4 kms in both the direct and indirect fire roles. Capable of firing up to 12 rounds per minute the M6-895 has replaced the 51 mm Mortar in operational service.

60 mm Mortar fired in support of UK troops in Afghanistan. (MoD Crown Copyright 2013)

Figures suggest that in the 12 months to November 2009 more than 3,500 60 mm mortar rounds were fired on operations and training. The cost of a 60 mm mortar round varies from between £185 – £640 dependent upon the type of round that is fired. In the main high explosive (HE) and illuminating rounds are used.

CHAPTER 4 – THE ROYAL AIR FORCE

PERSONNEL SUMMARY (MID 2013)

Royal Air Force		*Trained and Untrained Strength (mid 2013)*
Officers		8,230
	Males	6,890
	Females	1,340
Other Ranks		28,790
	Males	25,000
	Females	3,790
	Total	35,350

	Personnel in training (mid 2013)
Officers	130
Other Ranks	1,170

RAF AIRCRAFT IN SERVICE (EARLY 2014)

Aircraft type	*Fleet number*
Typhoon	108 (total of 160 on order)
Tornado GR4/4A	88
Hawk (all types)	84
Tristar	5 (being withdrawn by early 2014)
Voyager	8 (total of 14 on order replacing VC10 & Tristar)
Sentry	4
Sentinel	3
Shadow R1	5
Hercules C1/3/4/5	24 (8 x C1/C3 being withdrawn)
C-17	8
BAe 146	2
BAe 125	5
Sea King HAR 3/3A	16
Reaper	5
Tucano	30 (Training)
Tutor	119 (Training)
Chinook (JFH)	38 (14 x Mk 6 on order)
Merlin (JFH)	25
Puma (JFH)	24 (Mk 2 entering service)

22 x A400M Atlas will replace Hercules C1/C3 later in the decade

RAF Chinook, Merlin and Puma helicopters are assigned to the Joint Force Helicopter (JFH)

RAF Merlin helicopters will transfer to the Royal Navy's Commando Helicopter Force beginning in 2014

In late 2013 the RAF is believed to have about 500 qualified fast jet pilots and about 45 trained Reaper Remotely Piloted Aircraft (RPA) pilots.

ROYAL AIR FORCE FRONTLINE SQUADRONS (AS OF LATE 2013)

Strike/Attack/ Fast Jet Squadrons	11
Unmanned Air Vehicle (UAV) Squadrons	2
Airborne Early Warning Squadrons	2
ISTAR	3
Transport Squadrons	5
Air to Air Refuelling Squadrons	3
Heavy Lift Helicopter Squadrons	3
Medium Lift Helicopter Squadrons	4
Search and Rescue Squadrons	2
Reserve Squadrons (OEU and Training)	11
RAF Regiment Field Squadrons	8

ISTAR – Intelligence, Surveillance, Target Acquisition, and Reconnaissance: OEU   Operational Evaluation Units)

RAF SQUADRON LISTING (AS OF MID 2013)

Aircraft numbers are our estimates

1 (F) Sqn	12 x Typhoon FGR4	RAF Lossiemouth (Leuchars until 2014)
II (AC) Sqn	12 x Tornado GR4A	RAF Marham (Recce)
3 Sqn	12 x Typhoon FGR4	RAF Coningsby
4 (R) Sqn	12 x Hawk T2	RAF Valley (4 FTS)
5 (AC) Sqn	5 x Sentinel R1 (ASTOR)	RAF Waddington
6 Sqn	12 x Typhoon FGR4	RAF Lossiemouth (Leuchars until 2014)
7 Sqn	11 x Chinook HC4/11C4A/HC5	RAF Odiham (JHC)
8 Sqn	3 x E3D Sentry AEW1	RAF Waddington
9 (B) Sqn	12 x Tornado GR4/4A	RAF Marham
10 Sqn	A330 Voyager	RAF Brize Norton (From May 2014) (3)
11 Sqn	12 x Typhoon FGR4	RAF Coningsby
12 (B) Sqn	12 x Tornado GR4	RAF Lossiemouth
13 Sqn	MR-9 Reaper	RAF Waddington
14 Sqn	Shadow R1	RAF Waddington
15 (R) Sqn	12 x Tornado GR4/4A	RAF Lossiemouth (OCU)
16 (R) Sqn	Tutor T1	RAF Cranwell (1 EFTS)
17 (R) Sqn	12 x Typhoon FGR4	RAF Coningsby (OCU)
18 Sqn	10 x Chinook HC4/HC4A/HC5	RAF Odiham (JHC)
22 Sqn	8 x Sea King HAR3/3A	RAF Valley (Sqn HQ) (1)
23 Sqn	3 x E3D Sentry AEW1	RAF Waddington
24 Sqn	6 x Hercules C4/C5	RAF Brize Norton
27 Sqn	9 x Chinook HC4/HC4A/HC5	RAF Odiham (JHC)
28 Sqn	12 x Merlin HC 3/3A	RAF Benson (JHC)
29 (R) Sqn	12 x Typhoon FGR4	RAF Coningsby
30 Sqn	6 x Hercules C4/C5	RAF Brize Norton
31 Sqn	12 x Tornado GR4/4A	RAF Marham
32 (The Royal) Sqn	6 x BAe 125 CC3; 3 x Augusta A109; 2 x BAe 146 CC2/3	RAF Northolt
33 Sqn	12 x Puma HC2	RAF Benson (JHC)
39 Sqn	MR-9 Reaper	RAF Waddington
41 Sqn	12 x Tornado GR4/4A	RAF Coningsby (FJWOEU)

43 Sqn	16 x Tornado F3	RAF Leuchars
45 (R) Sqn	8 x Beech King Air	RAF Cranwell
47 Sqn	6 x Hercules C4/C5	RAF Brize Norton
51 Sqn	3 x RC-135W (from 2014)	RAF Waddington
56 (R) Sqn	ISTAR	RAF Waddington (OCU)
57 (R) Sqn	Tutor T1	RAF Cranwell (3 FTS)
60 (R) Sqn	Griffin HT1, Bell 412	RAF Shawbury
70 Sqn	6 x Hercules C4/C5	RAF Brize Norton
72 (R) Sqn	Tucano T1	RAF Linton-on-Ouse
78 Sqn	12 x Merlin HC 3/3A	RAF Benson (JHC)
84 Sqn	4 x Griffin HAR2	RAF Akrotiri (JHC)
99 Sqn	8 x C-17	RAF Brize Norton
100 Sqn	16 x Hawk T1/T1A	RAF Leeming
101 Sqn	A330 Voyager	RAF Brize Norton (From May 2014) (3)
202 Sqn	8 x Sea King HAR3/3A	RAF Valley (Sqn HQ) (2)
203 (R) Sqn	Sea King HAR3/3A	RAF Valley (OCU)
208 (R) Sqn	12 x Hawk T2	RAF Valley (4 FTS)
216 Sqn	A330 Voyager	RAF Brize Norton (From May 2014)
230 Sqn	12 x Puma HC2	RAF Benson (JHC)
617 Sqn	12 x Tornado GR4/4A	RAF Lossiemouth

(1) 22 Sqn – Although headquartered at RAF Valley, the Squadron maintains three detachments at Chivenor (A Flight), Wattisham (B Flight) and Valley (C Flight).

(2) 202 Sqn – Although headquartered at RAF Valley, the Squadron maintains detachments at Boulmer (A Flight), Lossiemouth (D Flight), Valley (C Flight) and Leconfield (E' Flight).

(3) 14 x A330 Voyager on order.

Other Flying Units

Display Team	12 x Hawk T1A	RAF Scampton (Red Arrows – RAFAT)
DHFS	20 x Squirrel HT1	RAF Shawbury (provided by contractor)
	60 x Griffin HT1,	
Battle of Britian	Spitfire, Hurricane, Lancaster,	RAF Coningsby
Memorial Flight	Dakota	
1310 Flight	Chinook HC4/HC4A/HC5	Kandahar, Afghanistan
1312 Flight	Voyager, Hercules	Falkland Islands
1419 Flight	Various helicopters	Camp Bastion, Afghanistan
1435 Flight	Typhoon FGR	Falkland Islands
1564 Flight	Sea King HAR3/3A	Falkland Islands
Op Herrick	Tornado GR4/4A	Kandahar, Afghanistan (on detachment)

RAF Lossiemouth Squadrons (as of mid 2013)
Aircraft numbers are our estimates

1 (F) Sqn	12 x Typhoon FGR4	RAF Lossiemouth (Leuchars until 2014)
6 Sqn	12 x Typhoon FGR4	RAF Lossiemouth (Leuchars until 2014)
12 (B) Sqn	12 x Tornado GR4	RAF Lossiemouth
15 (R) Sqn	12 x Tornado GR4/4A	RAF Lossiemouth
617 Sqn	12 x Tornado GR4/4A	RAF Lossiemouth

There will eventually be 3 x Typhoon Squadrons at RAF Lossiemouth.

RAF Marham Squadrons (as of mid 2013)

Aircraft numbers are our estimates

II (AC) Sqn	12 x Tornado GR4A	RAF Marham (Recce)
9 (B) Sqn	12 x Tornado GR4/4A	RAF Marham
31 Sqn	12 x Tornado GR4/4A	RAF Marham

By 2016 RAF Marham will become the main operating base for the Lightening II (JSF)

RAF Coningsby Squadrons (as of mid 2013)

Aircraft numbers are our estimates

3 Sqn	12 x Typhoon FGR4	RAF Coningsby
11 Sqn	12 x Typhoon FGR4	RAF Coningsby
17 (R) Sqn	12 x Typhoon FGR4	RAF Coningsby
29 (R)	12 x Typhoon FGR4	RAF Coningsby
41 Sqn	12 x Tornado GR4/4A	RAF Coningsby (FJWOEU)

RAF Waddington Squadrons (as of mid 2013)

Aircraft numbers are our estimates

5 (AC) Sqn	5 x Sentinel R1 (ASTOR)	RAF Waddington
8 Sqn	3 x E3D Sentry AEW1	RAF Waddington
13 Sqn	MR-9 Reaper	RAF Waddington
14 Sqn	Shadow R1	RAF Waddington
23 Sqn	3 x E3D Sentry AEW1	RAF Waddington
39 Sqn	MR-9 Reaper	RAF Waddington
51 Sqn	3 x RC-135W (from 2014)	RAF Waddington
56 (R) Sqn	ISTAR OCU	RAF Waddington

RAF Brize Norton Squadrons (as of mid 2013)

Aircraft numbers are our estimates

24 Sqn	6 x Hercules C4/C5	RAF Brize Norton
30 Sqn	6 x Hercules C4/C5	RAF Brize Norton
47 Sqn	6 x Hercules C4/C5	RAF Brize Norton
70 Sqn	6 x Hercules C4/C5	RAF Brize Norton
99 Sqn	8 x C-17	RAF Brize Norton
10 Sqn	A330 Voyager	RAF Brize Norton (From May 2014)
101 Sqn	A330 Voyager	RAF Brize Norton (From May 2014)
216 Sqn	A330 Voyager	RAF Brize Norton (From May 2014)

RAF Odiham Squadrons (as of mid 2013)

Aircraft numbers are our estimates

7 Sqn	11 x Chinook HC4/HC4A/HC5	RAF Odiham (JHC)
18 Sqn	10 x Chinook HC4/HC4A/HC5	RAF Odiham (JHC)
27 Sqn	9 x Chinook HC4/HC4A/HC5	RAF Odiham (JHC)

RAF Benson Squadrons (as of mid 2013)

Aircraft numbers are our estimates

28 Sqn	12 x Merlin HC 3/3A	RAF Benson (JHC)
33 Sqn	12 x Puma HC2	RAF Benson (JHC)
78 Sqn	12 x Merlin HC 3/3A	RAF Benson (JHC)
230 Sqn	12 x Puma HC2	RAF Benson (JHC)

JHC (Joint Helicopter Command).
24 x upgraded Puma HC 2 being delivered

RAF Valley Squadrons (as of mid 2013)
Aircraft numbers are our estimates

4 (R) Sqn	16 x Hawk T2	RAF Valley (4 FTS)
22 Sqn	8 x Sea King HAR3/3A	RAF Valley (Sqn HQ)
202 Sqn	8 x Sea King HAR3/3A	RAF Valley (Sqn HQ)
208 (R) Sqn	12 x Hawk T2	RAF Valley (4 FTS)
203 (R) Sqn	Sea King HAR3/3A	RAF Valley (OCU)

RAF Flying Training Squadrons (as of mid 2013)
Aircraft numbers are our estimates

4 (R) Sqn	16 x Hawk T2	RAF Valley (4 FTS)
16 (R) Sqn	Tutor T1	RAF Cranwell (1 EFTS)
45 (R) Sqn	8 x Beech King Air	RAF Cranwell (3 FTS)
57 (R) Sqn	Tutor T1	RAF Cranwell (3 FTS)
60 (R) Sqn	Griffin HT1, Bell 412	RAF Shawbury (DHFS)
72 (R) Sqn	Tucano T1	RAF Linton-on-Ouse (1 FTS)
208 (R) Sqn	12 x Hawk T2	RAF Valley (4 FTS)
Central Flying School (CFS)	Various	RAF Cranwell

BRITISH COMMERCIAL AVIATION

In an emergency, the UK Government has the power to enlist the assistance of the United Kingdom's civil airline and aircraft charter fleets. In total, there are over 50 registered airlines and aircraft charter companies (Type A and B) operating about 1,000 fixed-wing passenger and transport aircraft and over 600 helicopters. The largest of the British-registered airlines is British Airways operating about 255 aircraft, carrying on average about 35 million passengers per year. Other major British airlines include Jet 186, Virgin Atlantic with 40 aircraft, Britair with 40 aircraft and the discount airline Easyjet with 167 aircraft. Bristow Helicopters is the largest helicopter charter operator with a fleet of almost 500 helicopters. The UK Civil Aviation Authority (CAA) license about 50,000 active professional and private pilots.

HIGHER MANAGEMENT OF THE ROYAL AIR FORCE

The Ministry of Defence (MoD) is a Department of State, headed by the Secretary of State for Defence (SofS) who implements national defence policy and plans the expenditure of the defence budget. The MoD is the highest level of headquarters for the Armed Forces, both administrative and operational. All major issues of policy are referred to the SofS or to one of his Ministerial colleagues:

Minister of State for the Armed Forces
Minister of State for Defence Personnel, Welfare and Veterans
Parliamentary Under Secretary of State for Defence Equipment, Support and Technology
Parliamentary Under Secretary of State for International Security Strategy
Under Secretary of State and the House of Lords Spokesman for Defence

Under the direction of the Defence Council (described in Chapter 1) management of Armed Forces is the responsibility of the Service Boards, in the case of the Royal Air Force the Air Force Board is the senior management directorate.

AIR FORCE BOARD

The routine management of the Royal Air Force is the responsibility of the Air Force Board, the composition of which is as follows:

The Secretary of State for Defence
Minister of State for the Armed Forces
Minister of State for Defence Personnel, Welfare and Veterans
Parliamentary Under Secretary of State for Defence Equipment, Support and Technology
Parliamentary Under Secretary of State for International Security Strategy
Under Secretary of State and House of Lords Spokesman for Defence
Permanent Under Secretary
Chief of the Air Staff
Deputy Commander Operations
Deputy Commander Capability & Personnel
Chief of Materiel (Air)
Assistant Chief of the Air Staff
Specialist officers as required

Air Force Board Standing Committee (AFBSC)

Attended by senior RAF commanders, the AFBSC dictates the policy required for the Royal Air Force to function efficiently and meet the aims required by the Defence Council and government. The Chief of the Air Staff is the chairman of the Air Force Board Standing Committee.

Decisions made by the Defence Council or the Air Force Board are implemented by the air staff at various headquarters world-wide. The Chief of the Air Staff is the officer ultimately responsible for the Royal Air Force's contribution to the national defence effort. He maintains control through the AOC (Air Officer Commanding), and the staff branches of the various Royal Air Force Headquarters.

CHIEF OF THE AIR STAFF

Air Chief Marshal Sir Andrew Pulford KCB CBE

Air Chief Marshal Sir Andrew Pulford was appointed Chief of the Air Staff in July 2013.

Air Chief Marshal Pulford was commissioned into the Royal Air Force as a pilot in 1977 and after flying training, joined No 72 Squadron, flying Wessex helicopters. During his flying career he accumulated over 5,000 hours on both Wessex and Chinook helicopters, serving primarily in Germany with No 18 Squadron but including exchange tours with the Royal Navy's Commando Helicopter Force and the Royal Australian Air Force. He has commanded in every officer rank and has seen operational service in Northern Ireland , the Falkland Islands, Lebanon , the Balkans and the Gulf.

Sir Andrew's staff appointments have included command of the Support Helicopter Tactics and Trials Flight, a short spell in Headquarters Northern Ireland as the Royal Air Force and Army Air Corps Operational Requirements desk officer, a tour in the British Army's doctrine organisation and two years as Personal Staff Officer to the Chief of Air Staff. He attended No 85 Advanced Staff Course at the Royal Air Force Staff College Bracknell in 1993 and graduated from the Higher Command and Staff Course in 2001.

Air Chief Marshal Pulford was Officer Commanding Royal Air Force Odiham for two years from December 2001, which included a period of unprecedented

Air Chief Marshal Sir Andrew Pulford KCB CBE.
(MoD Crown Copyright 2013)

operational activity for his command, and included large scale deployments to Afghanistan and Iraq. He moved to the Directorate of Air Resources and Plans in December 2003 and in August 2004 was appointed to the position of Director, on promotion to Air Commodore. He was promoted to Air Vice-Marshal in February 2007 when he commenced an 18 month tour as Air Officer Commanding No 2 Group. He assumed the post of Assistant Chief of the Defence Staff (Operations) in the Ministry of Defence in October 2008, after which he became the Deputy Commander Capability and Air Member for Personnel and Capability in August 2010.

He was appointed as Knight Commander of the Most Honourable Order of the Bath in the 2013 New Year Honours List.

RAF Command Organisation
The Chief of the Air Staff commands the RAF via the subsidiary headquarters at HQ Air Command.

HQ AIR COMMAND

HQ Air Command is located at RAF High Wycombe in Buckinghamshire. The Command was formed in April 2007 following the merger of RAF Strike Command and RAF Personnel and Training Command. HQ Air Command works with the MoD and the Joint Forces Command to provide the correct mix of airpower to various operational areas.

Headquarters Air Command

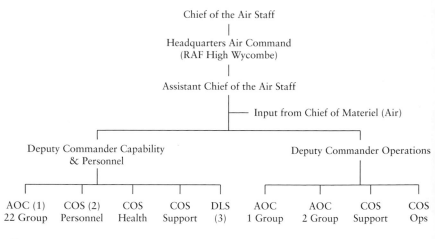

Notes:

(1) AOC – Air Officer Commanding; (2) COS – Chief of Staff; (3) DLS – Director Legal Services.

Personnel strength at HQ Air Command is believed to be in the region of 1,800 (1,200 service and 600 civilian).

Groups are normally commanded by Air Vice Marshals.

NO 1 GROUP

From its Headquarters at High Wycombe No 1 Group is responsible for all, front line combat aircraft. No 1 Group squadrons and units are involved in the whole range of military operations ranging from UK Homeland Defence to operations in Afghanistan and elsewhere.

Iraq. No 1 Group has around 10,000 personnel under command who operate from eight major flying stations. The group has 14 squadrons and one support unit under command.

No 1 Group – Squadrons and Stations
Aircraft numbers are our estimates

RAF Lossiemouth

1 (F) Sqn	12 x Typhoon FGR4	RAF Lossiemouth (Leuchars until 2014)
6 Sqn	12 x Typhoon FGR4	RAF Lossiemouth (Leuchars until 2014)
12 (B) Sqn	12 x Tornado GR4	RAF Lossiemouth
15 (R) Sqn	12 x Tornado GR4/4A	RAF Lossiemouth
617 Sqn	12 x Tornado GR4/4A	RAF Lossiemouth

There will eventually be 3 x Typhoon Squadrons at RAF Lossiemouth.

RAF Marham

II (AC) Sqn	12 x Tornado GR4A	RAF Marham (Recce)
9 (B) Sqn	12 x Tornado GR4/4A	RAF Marham
31 Sqn	12 x Tornado GR4/4A	RAF Marham

By 2016 RAF Marham will become the main operating base for the Lightning II (JSF)

RAF Coningsby

3 Sqn	12 x Typhoon FGR4	RAF Coningsby
11 Sqn	12 x Typhoon FGR4	RAF Coningsby
17 (R) Sqn	12 x Typhoon FGR4	RAF Coningsby
29 (R)	12 x Typhoon FGR4	RAF Coningsby
41 Sqn	12 x Tornado GR4/4A	TAF Coningsby (FJWOEU)

RAF Leeming

100 Sqn	16 x Hawk T1/T1A	RAF Leeming

NO 2 GROUP

The role of 2 Group is to provide the operational 'reach' and the associated support to UK operations world-wide from its Headquarters at High Wycombe.

No 2 Group provides the RAF with Air Transport, Air-to-Air Refuelling (AT/AAR), and ISTAR (Intelligence Surveillance, Targeting and Reconnaissance). The Group operates from 5 major flying stations with 26 squadrons. Aircraft and ground stations operate a large array of defensive and offensive systems.

No 2 Group is also responsible for Expeditionary Air Groups, Force Protection (FP) with units under command including the RAF Regiment, RAF Police and the CBRN protection capability at RAF Honington.

No 2 Group – Squadrons and Stations
Aircraft numbers are our estimates

RAF Brize Norton

24 Sqn	6 x Hercules C4/C5	RAF Brize Norton
30 Sqn	6 x Hercules C4/C5	RAF Brize Norton
47 Sqn	6 x Hercules C4/C5	RAF Brize Norton
70 Sqn	6 x Hercules C4/C5	RAF Brize Norton
99 Sqn	8 x C-17	RAF Brize Norton
10 Sqn	A330 Voyager	RAF Brize Norton (From May 2014)

| 101 Sqn | A330 Voyager | RAF Brize Norton (From May 2014) |
| 216 Sqn | A330 Voyager | RAF Brize Norton (From May 2014) |

RAF Odiham

7 Sqn	11 x Chinook HC4/HC4A/HC5	RAF Odiham (JHC)
18 Sqn	10 x Chinook HC4/HC4A/HC5	RAF Odiham (JHC)
27 Sqn	9 x Chinook HC4/HC4A/HC5	RAF Odiham (JHC)

RAF Benson

28 Sqn	12 x Merlin HC 3/3A	RAF Benson (JHC)
33 Sqn	12 x Puma HC2	RAF Benson (JHC)
78 Sqn	12 x Merlin HC 3/3A	RAF Benson (JHC)
230 Sqn	12 x Puma HC2	RAF Benson (JHC)

JHC (Joint Helicopter Command).
24 x upgraded Puma HC 2 being delivered

RAF Waddington

5 (AC) Sqn	5 x Sentinel R1 (ASTOR)	RAF Waddington
8 Sqn	3 x E3D Sentry AEW1	RAF Waddington
13 Sqn	MR-9 Reaper	RAF Waddington
14 Sqn	Shadow R1	RAF Waddington
23 Sqn	3 x E3D Sentry AEW1	RAF Waddington
39 Sqn	MR-9 Reaper	RAF Waddington
51 Sqn	3 x RC-135W (from 2014)	RAF Waddington
56 (R) Sqn	ISTAR OCU	RAF Waddington

RAF Valley (Search and Rescue)

22 Sqn	8 x Sea King HAR3/3A	RAF Valley (Sqn HQ) (1)
202 Sqn	8 x Sea King HAR3/3A	RAF Valley (Sqn HQ) (2)
203 (R) Sqn	Sea King HAR3/3A	RAF Valley (OCU)

(1) 22 Sqn – Although headquartered at RAF Valley, the Squadron maintains three detachments at Chivenor (A Flight), Wattisham (B Flight) and Valley (C Flight).

(2) 202 Sqn – Although headquartered at RAF Valley, the Squadron maintains detachments at Boulmer (A Flight), Lossiemouth (D Flight), Valley (C Flight) and Leconfield (E' Flight).

NO 22 (TRAINING) GROUP

No 22 (Training Group) from its Headquarters at High Wycombe recruits RAF personnel, provides initial and through career training for RAF personnel and provides other specialist training to members of the Army and Royal Navy.

The Group operates over 300 training aircraft and has a staff of about 7,000 personnel who work out of eight major UK sites.

No 22 Group provides training and support as follows:

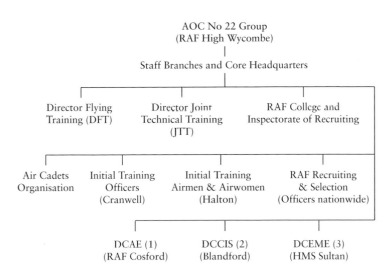

AOC No 22 Group
(RAF High Wycombe)

Staff Branches and Core Headquarters

Director Flying Training (DFT) | Director Joint Technical Training (JTT) | RAF College and Inspectorate of Recruiting

Air Cadets Organisation | Initial Training Officers (Cranwell) | Initial Training Airmen & Airwomen (Halton) | RAF Recruiting & Selection (Officers nationwide)

DCAE (1) (RAF Cosford) | DCCIS (2) (Blandford) | DCEME (3) (HMS Sultan)

Notes:

The following are Joint Service Colleges: (1) DCAE – Defence College of Aeronautical Engineering with HQ at RAF Cosford and operating from other tri-service sites. (2) DCCIS – Defence College of Communications and Information Systems with HQ at the Blandford (Royal School of Signals) and operating from other tri-service sites. (3) DCEME – Defence College of Electro and Mechanical Engineering Communications and Information Systems with HQ at HMS Sultan and operating from other tri-service sites.

No 22 Group Flying Training Squadrons
Aircraft numbers are our estimates

4 (R) Sqn	16 x Hawk T2	RAF Valley (4 FTS)
16 (R) Sqn	Tutor T1	RAF Cranwell (1 EFTS)
45 (R) Sqn	8 x Beech King Air	RAF Cranwell (3 FTS)
57 (R) Sqn	Tutor T1	RAF Cranwell (3 FTS)
60 (R) Sqn	Griffin HT1, Bell 412	RAF Shawbury (DHFS)
72 (R) Sqn	Tucano T1	RAF Linton-on-Ouse (1 FTS)
208 (R) Sqn	12 x Hawk T2	RAF Valley (4 FTS)
Central Flying School (CFS)	Various	RAF Cranwell
RAFAT	12 x Hawk T1A	RAF Scampton (The Red Arrows)

RAF Valley hosts the Search and Rescue Training Unit (SARTU).

FLYING TRAINING OVERVIEW

Flying training is carried out at the following locations:

RAF Cranwell
Elementary Flying Training HQ
Central Flying School HQ
No 3 Flying Training School
Joint Elementary Flying Training School
Fast Jet Navigation Training

RAF Linton on Ouse
No 1 Flying Training School
Basic Fast Jet Training

RAF Valley
No 4 Flying Training School
Advanced Fast Jet Training
Search and Rescue Training Unit

RAF Scampton
Royal Air Force Aerobatic Team (RAFAT)

RAF Shawbury
Central Flying School Helicopter Squadron
Defence Helicopter Flying School (Joint Service)

Elementary Flying Training Flow Chart (Direct Entrant)

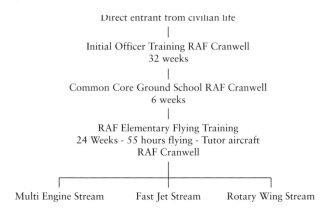

Direct entrant from civilian life
|
Initial Officer Training RAF Cranwell
32 weeks
|
Common Core Ground School RAF Cranwell
6 weeks
|
RAF Elementary Flying Training
24 Weeks - 55 hours flying - Tutor aircraft
RAF Cranwell
|

Multi Engine Stream   Fast Jet Stream   Rotary Wing Stream

The most recent figures for the average flying hours per month per fast jet pilot on an operational Typhoon Squadron is 17.5 hours. The standard flying hour cost for a Typhoon is £3,875, including the cost of fuel.

Recent UK MoD figures suggest that putting a pilot through the flying training programme (up to the OCU) costs £3.2 million per pilot for fast jet aircraft, about £600,000 per pilot for multi-engine aircraft and about £800,000 per pilot for helicopters. These are all inclusive cost estimates that include all expenses relating to aircraft, instructors, simulators, airfield support etc.

Fast jet pilots are considered combat ready following Operational Conversion Unit (OCU) training and a period of post OCU training on an allocated squadron. Some figures suggest that the cost of training a Typhoon pilot at the OCU is in the region of £9 million, putting the total cost of Typhoon pilot training at around £12 million.

During FY 2007–2008 the RAF trained pilot requirement was 126. Following recent SDSR reductions we believe that the trained pilot requirement will now be at around 90 per year.

All RAF and Royal Navy Reaper (RPAS) pilots are qualified in flying either fast jets, helicopters and multi-engine types.

JOINT HELICOPTER COMMAND (JHC)

The UK armed forces' Joint Helicopter Command (JHC) became operational on 1 April 2000. During late 2013 the JHC had about 190 aircraft from the Royal Navy, Army Air Corps and Royal Air Force under command.

Royal Air Force helicopters deployed with the JHC include Chinook HC4/HC4A/HC5; Puma HC2; Merlin HC3; Sea King HAR3.

More detail relating to the JHC is given in Chapter 5.

UK AIR SURVEILLANCE AND CONTROL SYSTEM (ASACS)

One of Air Command's major responsibilities is the UK Air Surveillance and Control System (ASACS). Air Command is tasked with providing early warning of air attack against the UK air defence region; to provide fighter and missile defences and the associated ground control system; fighter co-ordination with Royal Naval ships operating in adjacent waters and to maintain the integrity of UK air space in war.

ASACS comprises a number of individual static and mobile units that provide the minute-to-minute information on air activity required to defend the UK and NATO partners. Manned by officers of Fighter Control under the Operations Support Branch with the support of airmen Aerospace Systems Operators, ASACS is a computer-based system which gathers and disseminates information on all aircraft flying in and around the UK Air Defence Region. The information within is used by the Air Defence Commander when deciding whether to investigate or perhaps even destroy an aircraft flying in an area without permission. Information comes from the RAF's ground-based radars and from the air defence systems of neighbouring NATO partners. ASACS can also receive information via digital data-links from other ground, air or sea based units.

NATO Control and Reporting Centres (CRC) provide state-of-the-art air defence radar cover across the NATO region. Each CRC has geographical areas of responsibility and within their own areas, the CRCs receive and process information provided round-the-clock by military and civilian radars. In addition to this radar data, the CRCs also exchange information using digital data-links with neighbouring NATO partners, AEW aircraft and ships.

The UK CRCs are supported by a number of Reporting Posts/Remote Radar Heads across the UK that are the locations of the major RAF Air Defence radars. These radars feed information into the overall UK ASACS (and the NATO NADGE/Aegis) architecture. In addition to the radars, units have varying capabilities for the exchange of data-link information and radars operate around the clock.

ASACS Command and Reporting Units

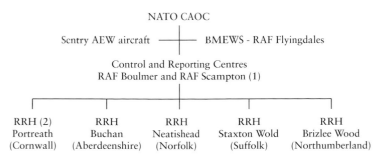

NATO CAOC

Sentry AEW aircraft ———— BMEWS - RAF Flyingdales

Control and Reporting Centres
RAF Boulmer and RAF Scampton (1)

RRH (2)	RRH	RRH	RRH	RRH
Portreath	Buchan	Neatishead	Staxton Wold	Brizlee Wood
(Cornwall)	(Aberdeenshire)	(Norfolk)	(Suffolk)	(Northumberland)

Note:

(1) The CRC at RAF Scampton is an integral part of No1 Air Control Centre

(2) RRH – Remote Radar Head

During 2008 the MoD confirmed the retention of RAF Boulmer as the ASACS Headquarters with No.1 Air Control Centre (1 ACC) at RAF Scampton.

In the Falkland Islands there are Reporting Posts at Mount Kent, Mount Alice and Byron Heights.

Air Defence Aircraft

The second ASACS function is the control of air defence aircraft. Fighter Controllers provide the tactical control required for air defence aircraft to police the UK's airspace in peace and war, and they are also involved in the peacetime training of the RAF air defence assets. Fighter Controllers also provide support to ground attack forces when undertaking training with their air defence counterparts.

Quick Reaction Alert (QRA) aircraft are held at immediate readiness for 24 hours a day and investigate all unidentified intrusions into UK airspace. RAF Coningsby provides the Typhoon aircraft for the QRA (South) and the QRA (North) is provided for by Typhoon aircraft from RAF Lossiemouth.

NATO Combined Air Operations Centre

To identify unknown aircraft in the NATO Air Policing Area, the NATO Combined Air Operations Centre at Finderup in Denmark issues direction to United Kingdom Control and Reporting Centres for the launch of RAF (QRA) aircraft. There are about 20 RAF/UK personnel stationed at CAOC Finderup.

The CAOC at Finderup is responsible for the overall coordination of the Air Defence, Ground Attack and Maritime Air elements of the NATO Region together with the response of the air forces and navies of our NATO partners. Within the NATO CAOCs (seven in total across the NATO area), control and reporting centres are linked with other elements of the NATO Air Defence Ground Environment (NADGE) and with the Ballistic Missile Early Warning Systems (BMEWS) station at RAF Fylingdales in North Yorkshire. The latter is networked with the US operated BMEWS at Thule (Greenland) and Clear (Alaska). By extending high-level radar cover some 3,000 miles across Eastern Europe, Fylingdales provides advance warning of intermediate range ballistic missiles launched against the UK and Western Europe and of inter-continental ballistic missiles against the North American continent. Fylingdales also tracks satellites and space debris.

No 1 Air Control Centre (1 ACC)

1 ACC at RAF Scampton provides the RAF with a mobile command and control capability able to deploy within the UK or anywhere in the world at short notice. The unit has recently been transformed into a fully capable Tactical Air Command and Control System (TACCS) following delivery of state-of-the-art communications and data-link equipment to supplement the two new mobile radars recently delivered into its inventory.

Sentry AEW

The Sentry AEW1 makes a large contribution to ASACS using digital datalinks. The Sentry can deploy rapidly in response to crisis or conflict to provide Air Defence Commander with information on potential aggressors. The roles within the Mission Crew of the Sentry mirror those within the UK ASACS CRCs, the posts being filled again with Fighter Controllers and Aerospace Systems Operators.

RAF COMMUNICATIONS

Overview

RAF signals communications fall into three categories. First, there is a large complex of HF transmitter and receiver facilities in the UK, including communications centres with automatic message routing equipment. Operations include those on behalf of Air Command, the Military Air Traffic Organisation, NATO, and the Meteorological Office.

Second, the RAF Signals Staff operate message relay centres, both automatic and manual and also manages the RAF's General Purpose Telephone network. RAF command operating procedures are monitored on all networks to ensure high standards are achieved and maintained. To reduce risk of compromise, all RAF communications facilities designed to carry classified information are checked for communications electrical security by command staff. For the use of the all the armed forces, the MoD has procured a fixed telecommunications network called Boxer under a Private Finance Initiative (PFI) contract, which will save the increasing expense of renting lines from the private sector.

Third, the main operation of the Skynet Satellite Communications System, which offers overseas formations telegraphed, data and speech communications, is controlled from Oakhanger (Paradigm / Astrium Services). Skynet 5D entered service in 2013 and provides the next generation of flexible and survivable satellite communications services for defence purposes.

Robust military satellite communications services are essential to support inter and intra-theatre information exchange requirements and ensure that deployed and mobile forces are not constrained by the need to remain within the range of terrestrial communications.

Commander Signals has a large engineering design staff of engineers, technicians and draughtsmen. Manufacturing resources include a general mechanical engineering and calibration capacity, plus a facility for the systems design, development and installation of certain airborne signals role equipment.

The majority of the RAF Signals (communications) units are located at RAF Leeming and RAF Digby.

RAF Leeming
90 Signals Unit (90 SU)
With almost 900 personnel, 90 SU concentrates on support to Expeditionary Operations and has two major sub units:

Force Generation Wing (FGW)
FGW provides the majority of the support required to deploy and sustain 90 SU on its expeditionary missions. FGW has sub units (mainly squadron size that provide engineering support, information services, operational evaluation and conversion and a squadron dedicated to the provision of planning and sustaining missions.

Tactical Communications Wing (TCW)
The Tactical Communications Wing (TCW) is the Force Element at Readiness within 90 Signals Unit providing communications support world-wide. There are four sub-units (Field Communications Squadrons) providing a complete range of communications services to deployed RAF formations.

RAF Digby
Joint Service Signals Organisation (JSSO)
A Joint Service organisation, the JSSO provides specialist communications support to deployed units and researches future communications systems that might be of interest to the UK.

Joint Services Signals Unit (Digby) (JSSU (D))
One of several JSSUs operating under the command of the JSSO. JSSU(D) provides support in the UK and overseas for specialist communications systems.

591 Signals Unit (591 SU)
Concentrates on computer security.

Aerial Erector School
Responsible for training Aerial Erectors at basic and advanced levels plus all aspects of fibre optics.

RAF Mount Pleasant in the Falkland Islands has No 7, 303 and 751 Signals Units under command.

Joint Tactical Information Distribution/Display System (JTIDS)
JTIDS is a secure tactical datalink network to enable the UK armed forces to participate in Allied operations. JTIDS is now in service throughout the UK armed Forces. The RAF is believed to operate JTIDS terminals on Typhoon, Tornado GR4, E-3D Sentry, Sentinel R1, VC10, TriStar, Hercules C130 and Sea King Mk7. In the future it is likely to be fitted to Lightening II, Voyager, Atlas and RC-135W Rivet Joint.

Falcon
From late 2013 the RAF's Transportable Telecommunications System/Deployable Local Area Network will be replaced by Falcon. This new system will operate at all levels of command in conjunction with systems such as Bowman, Cormorant, Skynet 5 and with allies' communication and information systems.

LOGISTIC SUPPORT

In 2000 the three distinct separate service logistic functions were fused into one and the Defence Logistic Organisation was formed. In a further amalgamation, from 1 April 2007 the Defence Logistic Organisation (DLO) and the Defence Procurement Agency (DPA) were merged to form Defence Equipment and Support (DE&S).

DE&S is the engine that delivers 'Through Life' equipment and logistic support to the Royal Air Force, attempting to ensure that the whole factory to front line process is seamless and properly integrated.

More detail regarding the DE&S is provided in Chapter 5.

The RAF's logistics hub moved from RAF Wyton and was established at RAF Wittering in April 2006. The following logistic and support units are located at RAF Wittering:

RAF Expeditionary and Logistic Units
No 83 Expeditionary Air Group
No 83 Expeditionary Air Group supports the Joint Forces Command and associated operations with a number of deployable Expeditionary Air Wings (EAW) that assist in enabling the force package required:

901 EAW supports coalition operations in the Middle East with a number of specialist flights that have responsibilities for activities such as air movements, air transport and passenger handling.

902 EAW provides ongoing operational support for Operations in Afghanistan.

903 EAW is the RAF headquarters element at Camp Bastion, Afghanistan. Until recently Camp Bastion has been one of the RAF's busiest airfields with around a 1000 aircraft movements a week.

904 EAW is the RAF headquarters element based at Kandahar Airfield in Afghanistan.

905 EAW supports RAF Mount Pleasant in the Falkland Islands.

906 EAW with about 50 personnel is based at Al Minhad in the United Arab Emirates and provides support to air transport links between the UK and operations in Afghanistan.

No 42 (Expeditionary Support) Wing
The headquarters of 42 (ES) Wing commands the following specialist squadrons based at RAF Wittering:

71 (Inspection and Repair) Squadron.
5001 (Airfield Construction) Squadron
5131 (Bomb Disposal) Squadron
93 (Expeditionary Armaments) Squadron (RAF Marham)

No 85 (Expeditionary Logistics (EL)) Wing
The headquarters of 85 (EL) Wing commands the following specialist squadrons based at RAF Wittering:

1 (Expeditionary Logistics) Squadron.
2 (Mechanical Transport) (MT) Squadron
3 (Mobile Catering) Squadron Sqn

RAF STATION ORGANISATION

An indication of the manner in which an RAF Station might be organised is as follows:

This example is an RAF Station with 4 x Tornado GR4 flying squadrons – each with 12 x aircraft. The 48 aircraft will have cost at least £1.4 billion (at 1980s prices) in total purchase costs, and the combined running costs for the operation of these squadrons will be in the region of some £120 million pounds per annum.

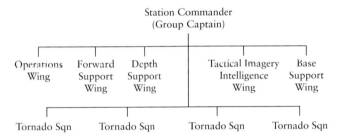

Flying Squadron Organisation

Note:
Generally 1 x Tornado GR4 will be held in reserve (IUR).
Note. (1) These departmental leaders have responsibility for weapons, airframes, propulsion, electronics, flight guidance and control systems, communications, automatic navigation and attack controls and report to the squadron commander.

Operations Wing is responsible for the management of the airfield and its supporting services. Wing sub-units include:

♦ Air Traffic Control Squadron (including Fire Services and the Bird Control Unit)
♦ Standards and Evaluation Squadron (STANEVAL responsible for the standardization of flying units, the Tornado Simulator and Electronic Warfare).
♦ Meteorological Services (a civilian agency).
♦ Operations Support Squadron (responsible for the Combat Operations Centre.
♦ C4i Support Squadron, encompassing IS Flight, and Communications Flight, Station Intelligence Flight (responsible for the Station Intelligence services).
♦ Security Squadron; responsible for RAF Police, the Dog Section, Criminal
♦ Station RAF Regiment Flight.

Forward Support Wing (FSW) might consist of the following:

♦ Forward Engineering Squadron (FES).
♦ Forward Logistics Squadron (FLS) .
♦ Engineering Operations Squadron (EOS).

Depth Support Wing could include:

♦ Tornado Components Squadron (TCS)
♦ Tornado Propulsion Squadron (TPS)
♦ Tornado Engineering Squadron (TES)
♦ Tornado Structures Squadron
♦ Tornado Lean Team.

Tactical Imagery Intelligence Wing (TIW) covers:

♦ Intelligence
♦ Surveillance
♦ Target – Acquisition
♦ Reconnaissance

Base Support Wing usually consists of:

♦ Personnel Administration
♦ Property Management
♦ Financial Services and Resources
♦ Force Development
♦ Community Support and Media Communications Officer
♦ Catering Squadron
♦ Facilities Management Squadron
♦ Medical and Dental Centres
♦ Chaplaincy Services.

OVERSEAS BASES

Air Command has responsibility for all RAF bases overseas.

RAF Akrotiri, Cyprus

The RAF use the airfield at Akrotiri as a staging post for transport aircraft, and as a temporary operating base for aircraft carrying out Armament Practice Camps. Akrotiri is the permanent base of 84 Squadron who perform Search and Rescue duties as well as a support role for the UN peacekeeping forces on the island. In addition, a detachment of the RAF Regiment is stationed at Akrotiri to assist with airfield defence.

RAF Ascension Island

Situated in the middle of the Atlantic Ocean, and over 700 miles from its nearest neighbour, Wideawake Airfield on Ascension Island was used extensively as a staging base during the Falklands War. This is still the major role for the Station, which it performs for both the RAF and the USAF.

RAF Gibraltar

Although aircraft are no longer stationed at RAF Gibraltar a complete range of RAF aircraft transit through.

Mount Pleasant, Falkland Islands

Mount Pleasant was opened in 1984 to establish a fighter and transport presence in the Islands following the Falklands War. Currently based at Mount Pleasant are No 1435 Flight with 4 x Typhoon FGR4 , No 1312 Flight with 1 x VC10 tanker (Voyager) and 1 x Hercules, as well as a detachment with Chinook and 2 x Sea King HAR3. Ground units include Signals Units and a Rapier surface to air missile detachment.

Mobile Air Movement Squadron (MAMS)

During operations and exercises, aircraft often visit overseas airfields where no regular RAF ground handling organisation exists. For this purpose, Air Command has a Mobile Air Movement Squadron (MAMS) at RAF Brize Norton that provides teams who are expert in all aspects of loading and unloading aircraft.

TORNADO GR-4

In late 2013 the latest strike variant of the Tornado – the GR4 is in service with:

Aircraft numbers are our estimates

12 (Bomber) Sqn	12 x Tornado GR4	RAF Lossiemouth
15 (R) Sqn	12 x Tornado GR4/4A	RAF Lossiemouth
617 Sqn	12 x Tornado GR4/4A	RAF Lossiemouth
II (AC) Sqn	12 x Tornado GR4A	RAF Marham (Recce)
9 (B) Sqn	12 x Tornado GR4/4A	RAF Marham
31 Sqn	12 x Tornado GR4/4A	RAF Marham
41 Sqn	12 x Tornado GR4/4A	RAF Coningsby (FJWOEU)

Crew 2; Wingspan (open) 13.9m; Wingspan (swept) 8.6m; Height 5.9m; Length 16.7m; Max Weapon Load 18,000lb/8,180kg; Max Take Off Weight 27,900kg; Max Speed Mach 2.2 (1,452 mph/2,333kph); Max Ferry Range approx 3,900km; Required Runway Length approx 900m. Engines 2 x Turbo-Union RB 199-34R Mk103 Turbofans; Armament 1 x 27mm Mauser Cannon, 3 x weapon points under fuselage, 4 x weapon points under wings; AIM-9L Sidewinder AAM; ALARM; JP233; BL755 CBU; Paveway II, III, EPR (IV); Brimstone; Storm Shadow CASOM.

The Tornado Multi-Role Combat aircraft (MRCA) has been the RAF's principal strike weapon system over the past three decades. Designed during the Cold War to penetrate Soviet air defence at low level, the Tornado is nuclear-capable but since the withdrawal from service of the WE177 nuclear bomb in 1998, the Tornado strike capability has been restricted to conventional weapons. The Tornado was jointly developed by the UK, West Germany and Italy under a collaborative agreement and manufactured by a consortium of companies formed under the name of Panavia. The first prototype flew in 1974 and the first RAF Squadron equipped with the GR-1 became operational in 1982.

Tornado GR4 from IX(B) Squadron RAD during training for overseas deployment. (MoD Crown Copyright 2013)

During the 1990 Gulf War, Tornado GR1s were amongst the first aircraft in action from 17 January 1991. During the war, the Tornado GR1 force flew 1,500 operational sorties divided almost equally between offensive counter air targets such as airfields and air defence sites, and interdiction targets such as bridges. The RAF deployed 48 x GR1 in the area during hostilities. A total of six GR1s was lost in action, five of which were involved in low-or medium- level attacks with 1,000 pound bombs and one that was flying a low-level JP233 mission. The final three weeks of the air war saw the Tornado GR1 force concentrating almost exclusively on day and night precision attacks dropping LGBs from medium altitude.

142 x Tornado GR-1s were upgraded to GR4 standard under the Tornado Mid-Life Update (MLU) programme costing some £943m. Deliveries began in 1998 and were completed by the end of 2003. Compared to the GR1, the GR4 has a Forward-Looking Infra-Red (FLIR), a wide angle Head-Up Display (HUD), improved cockpit displays, Night-Vision Goggle (NVG) compatibility, new avionics and weapons systems, updated computer software, and Global Positioning System (GPS). The upgrade also re-armed the Tornado with the Storm Shadow stand-off missile, Brimstone advanced anti-armour weapon, and the Paveway EPW LGB. New sensors include the RAPTOR and Vicon reconnaissance pods and an improved Thermal Imaging Airborne Laser Designator (TIALD) targeting pod. A separate programme covered an integrated Defensive Aids Suite consisting of the radar warning receiver, Sky Shadow radar jamming pod and BOZ-107 chaff and flare dispenser. The standard Tornado GR4 can also fulfil tactical reconnaissance tasks when equipped with an external camera pod. The GR4A is used as a combat reconnaissance aircraft – also upgraded under the GR1 series MLU.

During the Iraq War of 2003 (Operation Telic), GR4s from all five active Tornado squadrons were deployed. One Tornado was lost to friendly fire. The Storm Shadow air-launched cruise missile was fired operationally for the first time from a Tornado GR4 during conflict.

During the 2011 Libyan campaign (Operation Ellamy) 16 x Tornado GR4s attacked targets using both Brimstone (230 employed) and Storm Shadow missiles. The average cost of a Tornado mission from RAF Marham to a target in Libya was approximately £37,000.

Expect a Tornado GR4 squadron to have 15 established crews.

The assumed out of service date for the RAF Tornado GR4 aircraft is 2019 (subject to confirmation in the 2015 SDSR).

TYPHOON FGR4

In service with:

Aircraft numbers are our estimates

3 Sqn	12 x Typhoon FGR4	RAF Coningsby
11 Sqn	12 x Typhoon FGR4	RAF Coningsby
17 (R) Sqn	12 x Typhoon FGR4	RAF Coningsby
29 (R)	12 x Typhoon FGR4	RAF Coningsby
1 (F) Sqn	12 x Typhoon FGR4	RAF Lossiemouth (Leuchars until 2014)
6 Sqn	12 x Typhoon FGR4	RAF Lossiemouth (Leuchars until 2014)

There will eventually be 3 x Typhoon Squadrons at RAF Lossiemouth.

Crew 1; Length 15.96m; Height 5.23m; Wingspan 10.95m; Max Speed 1,321mph/2,125kph; Empty Weight 22,000lb/9,999kg; Max Take-Off Weight 46,305lb/21,000kg; Engine 2 x Eurojet EJ200 turbofans; Ferry Range 5,382 km (3,310 miles) with 4 x drop tanks; Armament 1 x 27mm (first RAF batch only); Air Interdiction. 2 x Storm Shadow, 2 x ALARM, 4 x AMRAAM, 2 x ASRAAM, 2 x1,500 litre fuel tank, 1 x 1,000 litre fuel tank; Close Air Support. 18 x Brimstone, 4 x AMRAAM, 2 x ASRAAM, 1 x 1,000 litre fuel tank. SEAD. 6 x ALARM, 4 x AMRAAM, 2 x ASRAAM, 1 x 1,000 litre fuel tank; Maritime Attack. 4 x Penguin, 4 x AMRAAM, 2 x ASRAAM, 2 x 1,500 litre fuel tank, 1 x 1,000 litre fuel tank; also Sidewinder AAM; Meteor BVRAAM; Paveway II,III, EPR (IV) LGB; JDAM or other PGB.

The first production aircraft flew in 2003, and delivery of the first aircraft started during early 2004. The Typhoon replaced the Tornado F3 and the Jaguar in RAF Service. It is planned that the Typhoon front-line will comprise seven squadrons, of which four will be primarily air defence, two swing-role, and one offensive support, covering a full range of Combat Air Operations.

The Typhoon (formerly EFA – European Fighter Aircraft) is a single seat, STOL capable aircraft optimised for air superiority/air defence and ground attack roles. Germany, Italy and Spain are UK partners in the most costly European collaboration programme to date. The air forces of the four countries have ordered a total of 571 Eurofighters (UK 160, Germany 143, Italy 96, and Spain 73). The UK is to receive its aircraft in 3 x Tranches. Tranche 1 – 53 aircraft (mainly air defence aircraft with some multi-role towards the end of the tranche). Tranche 2 – 67 aircraft (mainly air defence aircraft with an enhanced air-to-surface capability scheduled to be integrated on Tranche 2 aircraft from 2012). Tranche 3 – 40 aircraft. Export orders have been received from Austria 15, Oman 12 and Saudi Arabia 72.

Typhoon is a fifth-generation combat aircraft with fully digital, integrated aircraft, avionics and weapon systems. The aircraft is designed to perform at least five air missions: air superiority, air interdiction, Suppression of Enemy Air Defence (SEAD), Close Air Support (CAS) and Maritime Attack.

No 9 Squadron RAF Typhoon over Malaysia in 2013. (Copyright 2013 BAe Systems)

The aircraft is configured to carry 6 x medium-range and 2 x short-range air-to-air missiles. Typhoon has 13 x store stations and an internal gun fitted on the starboard side. A range of air-to-ground weapons can be carried, including the new Storm Shadow CASOM, Brimstone anti-armour weapon, and the future Precision Guided Bomb (PGB). No modifications are necessary to carry 'smart' weapons and three stations can carry external fuel pods. The Captor radar is a collaboration European design. Other sensors include the Infra-Red Search and Track (IRST) system. The Defensive Aids Sub-System (DASS) equipment is carried in 2 x wing pods that are an integral part of the wing. The datalink is provided by the Multiple Image Data System (MIDS). If required, the aircraft will be able to operate from a 500 metre strip.

The latest estimated cost of the RAF Typhoon programme was some £17.6 billion (demonstration and manufacture) – making it the most expensive weapon system yet produced for the UK Armed Forces. A rough unit cost estimate is £110 million (demonstration and manufacture divided by 160 aircraft). These figures do not include estimates of the through life support costs. The cost of flying a Typhoon for one hour is believed to be in the region of £3,875.

In 2011 the RAF deployed 10 x Typhoon aircraft to its base in Italy for operations in Libya and achieved 4,500 flying hours without an engine change. The aircraft operated in its air-to-air role and for the first time attacked ground targets using laser-guided Paveway bombs. Some sources suggest that 561 Typhoon missions were flown over a six month period (average 93 missions per month) and that 209 air-to-ground weapons were released.

In 2006 a senior United States Air Force general who, fresh from an exhilarating first flight in Typhoon and, naturally, quite excited, was heard to say, "This is the best fast jet in the world". Typhoon is due to be replaced in the late 2030s and the MoD is expected to decide what mix of manned and unmanned aircraft will replace its Typhoons sometime between 2015 and 2020.

F-35B LIGHTNING II (JOINT STRIKE FIGHTER – JSF)

Crew 1; Max speed Mach 1.8; Length 15.6 m; Span 10.67 m; Weight empty 14,700 kg; Max take off weight 27,200 kg; Combat radius (internal fuel) 860 km; Range 1,670 km; Max altitude 50,000 feet; Armament – Paveway IV, AMRAAM, ASRAAM, Brimstone, Storm Shadow.

Lightning II (formerly the Joint Strike Fighter) was selected to meet the UK's Joint Combat Aircraft requirement for a survivable, stealthy, multi-role, all-weather, day and night, fighter/attack air system, able to operate from land and sea. Using secure links the aircraft will operate as an ISTAR (Intelligence, surveillance, target, acquisition and reconnaissance) platform.

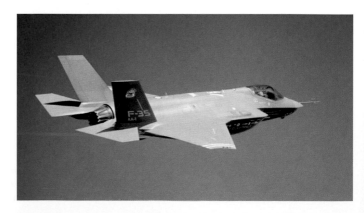

F-35. *(Copyright 2013 BAe Systems)*

Once in service we would expect the Lightning II to be capable of undertaking air interdiction operations, making low or medium level attacks using precision-guided, freefall or retarded bombs. Close air support missions against targets in the forward edge of the battle area and fleet air defence patrols in the area of vessels that require protection from enemy air attack.

Although the US Company Lockheed Martin is the prime contractor, the UK is a Level 1 partner with the US Government and a number of British companies, including BAE Systems and Rolls-Royce are participating. These UK companies have had extensive involvement in building and developing the aircraft. Under current plans about 15 per cent of the aircraft will be manufactured in the UK securing about 25,000 jobs.

The UK's first three Lightning II aircraft are currently participating in the US test and evaluation programme at Elgin Airforce Base in the US. Frontline aircraft are expected to be delivered from 2015 onwards with an initial operating capability from land in 2018, followed by first of class flights from HMS Queen Elizabeth later that year. In March 2013 the MoD confirmed that RAF Marham would be the main operating base for Lightning II.

Decisions on the overall order for joint strike fighters will not be made until the strategic defence and security review in 2015. However most analysts believe that there will be an initial UK order for about 50 aircraft. Current cost estimates vary but there seems to be a reasonable consensus around a unit cost of between £100 -£125 million per aircraft. Current expectations are that the aircraft will remain in service until at least 2040.

PREDATOR MR-9 REAPER

In service with:

13 Sqn	MR-9 Reaper	RAF Waddington (5)
39 Sqn	MR-9 Reaper	RAF Waddington (5)

Operated by one pilot and one sensor operator; Length 11m; Wingspan 20m; Weight 1,676kg(empty); 4,760kg (max); Operational Altitude 25,000ft; Endurance 16–28hrs; Range 3,682 miles; Payload 4,200lb; Max Speed 400kph/250mph; Cruise Speed 160kph/100mph; Engines 670 kW Honeywell TP331-10 turboprop; Armament 6 x hardpoints under the wings, can carry a payload mix of 1,500lb (680kg) on each of its two inboard weapons stations, 500–600lb (230–270kg) on the two middle stations and 150–200lb (68–91kg) on the outboard stations. Up to 14 x AGM-114 Hellfire air to ground missiles can be carried or four Hellfire missiles and two 500lb (230kg) GBU-12 Paveway II laser-guided bombs. The ability to carry the JDAM in the future is also possible, as well is the AIM 9X, Air to Air missile.

38 Squadron RAF Reaper in Afghanistan. (MoD Crown Copyright 2013)

Reaper is a Remotely Piloted Air System (RPAS) with a primary ISTAR (mission to act as an (intelligence, surveillance, target, acquisition and reconnaissance) platform. During Operation Herrick in Afghanistan Reaper has been used to provide close air support on opportunity targets to troops operating in the forward part of the battlespace. We believe that Reaper (RPAS) currently in RAF service employ two types of munitions; the Hellfire AGM 114 guided missile and the GBU 12 laser guided bomb.

During April 2013 the RAF began operating Reaper RPAS from RAF Waddington in addition to those operated from Creech Air Force Base in Nevada by 39 Squadron. 'Operational since October 2012 at RAF Waddington, 13 Squadron has about 100 personnel including pilots, engineers and systems operators. Personnel from 39 Squadron will return to the UK (RAF Waddington) in 2013.

The UK MoD states that "Reaper is not an autonomous system and all weapons employment depends upon commands from the flight crew. The weapons may be released under the command of a pilot who uses Rules of Engagement that are no different to those used for manned UK combat aircraft. The targets are always positively identified as legitimate military objectives, and attacks are prosecuted in strict accordance with the Law of Armed Conflict and UK Rules of Engagement. Every effort is made to ensure the risk of collateral damage, including civilian casualties, is minimised." By the end of January 2013 approximately 365 weapons were launched by UK Reapers.

US sources suggest that the 'flyaway cost' of an MQ-9 Reaper is in the region of US$16.9 million (£11.2 million).

TARANIS

The RAF has also taken the first steps towards developing its own Unmanned Combat Aircraft Systems (UCAS), Project "Taranis" was announced in 2008 and a demonstrator flying in 2013 in Australia being used to evaluate how UCAVs will contribute to the RAF's future mix of aircraft.

The demonstrator is believed to be the size of a BAe Hawk, weigh about 8 tons and will be configured for reconnaissance and attack missions. Some analysts believe that a system developed from Project Taranis could be operational by 2020.

Other than BAE Systems the project includes a teaming arrangement between Rolls-Royce, the Systems division of GE Aviation (formerly Smiths Aerospace) and QinetiQ who work alongside UK military personnel and scientists to develop and fly the system.

Taranis. (Copyright 2013 BAe Systems)

E-3D SENTRY AEW1

In service with:

8 Squadron	3 x Sentry AEW1	Waddington
23 Squadron	3 x Sentry AEW1	Waddington

Some reports in 2013 suggest that only four aircraft are in operational service.

Crew 5 x Flight Crew and 12/13 x Mission Crew; Length 46.61m; Wingspan 44.42m; Height 12.73m; All Up Operational Weight 147,400kg; Max Speed 853kph (530 mph); Patrol Endurance 6 hrs (can be enhanced by AAR); Ferry Range 3,200km; Engines 4 x CFM-56-2A-3; Armament provision for self-defence air-to-air missiles.

Deliveries of the Sentry AEW1, commenced in March 1991 and delivery of all seven airframes was complete in early 1992. These seven aircraft are of the same type as the 18 delivered to the multi national NATO early warning force between 1982/1985. Powered by four CFM 56-2A-3 engines, the Sentry is designed to cruise at 29,000 feet whilst detecting air and surface contacts with its AN/APY-2 surveillance radar. Information is then transmitted back to interceptor aircraft and, ground air-and-ship-based units using a wide variety of digital datalinks. All are equipped with the Joint Tactical Information Distribution System (JTIDS) and a 665,360 word memory secure communication system. Between 1998 and 2000, RAF Sentry aircraft were upgraded under the Radar System Improvement Programme (RSIP) costing some £120 million. New Global Positioning System navigation equipment was also installed.

AEW Sentry has a long flight endurance of up to 18 hours and the six UK aircraft form about 25 per cent of the total NATO AEW Force. During the past decade Sentry AEW1 aircraft were deployed in support of Operation Telic during the 2003 Iraq War and for Operation Oracle in support of ISAF in Afghanistan from 2002. During 2011 Sentry was deployed over Libya in support of Operation Ellamy.

Sentry is due to leave service in 2025.

RAF Sentinel R1.
(Copyright Alan Radecki Akradecki)

SENTINEL R1 (ASTOR)

In service with:

5 Sqn	5 x Sentinel R1 (ASTOR)	RAF Waddington

Crew 2 with 3 mission systems operators; Length 30.3m; Height 7.57m; Wingspan 28.6m; Empty Weight 22,817kg; Max Take-Off Weight 43,094kg; Range 6,500nm/12,000km; Endurance 14 plus hours; Operating altitude 15,000m; Engines 2 x RR BR710; Systems ASARS-2 radar derivative; narrowband datalink subsystem (NDLS), wideband data link based on Common Data Link (CDL); Defensive Aids Subsystem (DASS) developed for the Nimrod MRA4, including missile warning system, radar warning receiver, towed radar decoy and chaff and flare dispensers.

The Airborne Stand-off Radar (ASTOR) is a new British capability for operations over and around the battlefield forming the the UK equivalent to the US E-8 Joint Surveillance Target Attack Radar System (JSTARS). ASTOR is to provide a long range all weather theatre surveillance and target acquisition system capable of detecting moving, fixed and static targets designed to meet a joint Army and RAF requirement. The production contract was signed in December 1999 for the supply of 5 x air-platforms, 8 x ground stations, and contractor logistic support. The principal elements of ASTOR are the Bombardier Global Express aircraft and the Raytheon ASARS-2 side looking airborne radar used on the U-2. The radar operates at high altitude and in all weathers to provide high resolution. ASARS-2 has been reported to provide images of the battlefield at ranges of 160 km, at altitudes up to 47,000 feet. High speed data links transfer the data from aircraft to ground stations in near real time. The system has directional and broadcast data links which are interoperable with existing US U-2Rs, JSTARS and command and control networks.

Number 5 (Army Cooperation) Squadron was reformed on 1st April 2004 at RAF Waddington and operates the 5 x modified Bombardier Global Express long-range aircraft and 8 x ground stations. In RAF service, the aircraft type will be known as the Sentinel R Mk 1, with the R acknowledging its Reconnaissance role.

The first Sentinel R1 arrived at RAF Waddington in 2007 and in February 2009 the aircraft made its operational debut in Afghanistan. The projected procurement cost is just over £1bn.

The 2011 UK SDSR announced the intention of the MoD "withdraw the Sentinel airborne ground surveillance aircraft once it is no longer required to support operations in Afghanistan." However, in February 2013 it was announced that it might be possible to retain Sentinel after 2015 and that a decision would be made as part of the next SDSR

In 2013 Sentinel were deployed in support of French operations in Mali.

HAWK T1/T1A/T2

In service with:

4 (R) Sqn	16 x Hawk T2	RAF Valley (4 FTS)
100 Sqn	16 x Hawk T1/T1A	RAF Leeming
208 (R) Sqn	12 x Hawk T2	RAF Valley (4 FTS)
Display Team	12 x Hawk T1A	RAF Scampton (Red Arrows – RAFAT)

The Hawk first flew in 1974, and entered RAF service two years later both as an advanced flying trainer and a weapons training aircraft. Hawks are used to teach operational tactics such as air-to-air and air-to-ground firing, air combat and low-level operating procedures to pilots destined for the "fast-jet" squadrons. As a weapons trainer, the Hawk is armed with an Aden cannon carried beneath the fuselage, and rocket pods or practice bombs can be fitted to under-wing pylons. To fulfil its mobilisation role as a fighter aircraft, the Hawk carries a 30 mm Aden cannon and two Sidewinder air-to-air missiles, and is designated T1A (89 previous delivered to the RAF). The Hawk is a strong and rugged aircraft designed to cut training and maintenance costs.

The Hawk has been widely exported as a trainer and single-pilot fighter ground attack aircraft – in numerical terms, by far the most successful British export programme since the Hawker Hunter. By late 2012 about 1,000 Hawks had been exported or ordered world-wide.

The RAF has two types of the Hawk in service the T1/T1A and the T2.

The T1/T1A remains in service with 100 Squadron and the Red Arrows with the current out of service date for the T1/T1A as 2020.

T1/T1A Characteristics: Crew 2; Span 9.39m; Length 11.96m; Height 3.99m; Weight Empty 3,647kg; Max Take Off Weight 8,569kg; Max Speed 622 mph/1,000 kph at sea level; Mission Radius 556 km (345 miles); Engine 1 x Rolls Royce/Turbomeca Adour Mk 151 turbofan; Armament. (Hawk T1) 1 x 30mm Aden cannon pack and up to 5,600lb (2,540kg) of under-wing stores for rockets, bombs and missiles, (Hawk T1A) – in addition has inboard pylons for Sidewinder AIM-9 AAM.

Note: Reports regarding the operational status of the Aden cannon are contradictory.

HAWK T2

Crew 2; Length 12.43m; Height 3.98m; Span 9.94m; Max Speed 1,028kph/638mph; Service Ceiling 13,565m; Range 2,520km; Engine Rolls-Royce Adour 951 turbofan.

In July 2003 the Hawk T2 was selected as the new Advanced Jet Trainer (AJT) for the RAF and Royal Navy fast-jet aircrew training. Aircrew trained on the Hawk T2 move onto operational service with Tornado, Typhoon and the Lightning II (from 2015). Hawk T2 will be able to provide pilots in training with the all-digital, fly-by-wire experience necessary for pilots flying the latest generation of fast jets.

There appear to be 28 Hawk T2 available for service with 24 in the Forward Fleet at RAF Valley. It is believed that 22 aircraft were delivered in 2009 and six in 2010. The in-service date of the aircraft was November 2009 and it is likely to be in service for at least 20 years.

Based on past evidence, for every 1,000 applicants to the RAF for pilot training, about 115 complete initial pilot training and of those, about 40 are selected for fast-jet training.

TUCANO

In service with:

| 72 (R) Sqn | 30 x Tucano T1 | RAF Linton-on-Ouse (1 FTS) |

Crew 2; Length 9.86m; Height 3.40m; Span 11.28m; Max Speed 507kph/315mph; Service Ceiling 8,750m; Range 1,916kms; Engine 1,100shp Garrett TPE-331 turboprop.

Originally designed by the Brazilian aerospace company Embraer, the Tucano was selected in 1985 to replace the Jet Provost as the RAF basic trainer. The development and production contract was awarded to Shorts of Belfast under licence. The first squadron aircraft was delivered in June 1988. Student training on the aircraft started at RAF Church Fenton in December 1989. The RAF version of the Tucano, designated the Tucano T1, has been modified in many ways from the basic Embraer 312. A Garrett TPE 331 engine is fitted in place of the original PT6 and represents a 50% power increase. Fatigue life has been extended from 8,000 to 12,000 hours by fitting strengthened wings and landing gear, a ventral air brake has been added, plus a new canopy which is bird strike resistant up to 270 knots. The original RAF purchase was for 126 x Tucano. Two training sorties can be completed before the aircraft requires refuelling.

RAF Tucano T1. (Photo Adrian Pingstone)

C-130 HERCULES

In service with:

24 Squadron	6 x Hercules C-130J	Brize Norton
30 Squadron	6 x Hercules C-130J	Brize Norton
47 Squadron	6 x Hercules C-130J	Brize Norton
70 Squadron	6 x Hercules C-130J	Brize Norton

The squadron totals are given as a guide to what we believe are the average aircraft figures per squadron at any one time.

C-130J Hercules

Crew: 2 Pilots and 1 Loadmaster; Engines: Four Allison AE 2100D3 turboprops; Max speed; 355kts Range: 3,700 nautical miles; Max altitude: 32,000ft; Length: 34.34m; Span: 40.38m; Payload 19,958 kg; Range 5,250 kms; Take off distance 950 m at 70,300 kg gross weight.

The C-130 Hercules has been the workhorse of the RAF transport fleet since 1967 when the first aircraft entered service. Over the years it has proved to be a versatile and rugged aircraft, primarily intended for tactical operations including troop carrying, parachuting, supply dropping and aeromedical duties. The Hercules can operate from short unprepared airstrips, but also possesses the endurance to mount long range strategic lifts if required. The aircraft was a derivative of the C-130E used by the United States Air Force, but fitted with British Avionic equipment, a roller-conveyor system for heavy air-drops and with more powerful engines. The crew of five (K version) included, pilot, co-pilot, navigator, air engineer and air loadmaster.

The K Series aircraft finally retired from RAF service in late 2013.

HERCULES C-130J C4/C5

The RAF has replaced its Hercules K C1/C3 aircraft with second-generation C-130Js on a one-for-one basis. Twenty-five Hercules C4 and C5 aircraft were ordered in December 94, and the first entered service in 2000. Deliveries were completed by 2003 at a total cost of just over £1bn. The C4 is the same size as the older Hercules C3 which features a fuselage lengthened by 4.57 m (15ft 0 in) than the original C1. The Hercules C5 is the new equivalent of the shorter model. With a flight deck crew of two plus one loadmaster, the C-130J can carry up to 128 infantry, 92 paratroops, 8 pallets or 95 medical stretchers.

The C4/C5s has Allison turboprop engines, R391 6-bladed composite propellers and a Full Authority Digital Engine Control (FADEC). This propulsion system increases take-off thrust by 29 per cent and is 15 per cent more efficient. Consequently, there is no longer a requirement for the external tanks to be fitted. An entirely revised 'glass' flight deck with head-up displays (HUD) and 4 multi-function displays (MFD) replaced many of the dials of the original aircraft. These displays are compatible with night-vision goggles (NVG). MoD figures suggest that there are 24 C-130J in service.

Latest reports suggest that the C-130J will be retired in 2022.

C-17 GLOBEMASTER

In service with:

| 99 Squadron | 6 x C-17A | Brize Norton |

Crew of 2 pilots and 1 loadmaster. Capacity Maximum of 154 troops. Normal load of 102 fully-equipped troops, up to 172,200lb (78,108kg) on up to 18 standard freight pallets or 48 litters in the medevac role; Wingspan 50.29m; Length overall 53.04m; Height overall 16.8m; Loadable width 5.5m; Cruising speed 648kph (403 mph); Range (max payload) 4,444km (2,400 miles); Engines 4 x Pratt and Whitney F117 turbofans.

The C-17 meets an RAF requirement for an interim strategic airlift capability pending the introduction into service of the A400M Atlas. The decision to lease four C-17 aircraft for some £771m from Boeing was taken in 2001, and the aircraft entered service in 2001. The lease was for a period of seven years, with the option to buy or extend at the end of that period. The option to buy the leased aircraft was exercised in August 2006 together with signature of the contract to procure a fifth new C-17 aircraft which was delivered in April 2008. A sixth C-17 was ordered as a result of a £130 million contract signed in December 2007 and was delivered in July 2008. Two more were ordered in 2010 and 2012.

The C-17 fleet is capable of the deployment of 1,400 tonnes of freight over 3,200 miles in a seven day period. The aircraft is able to carry one Challenger 2 MBT, or a range of smaller armoured vehicles, or up to three WAH-64 Apache aircraft at one time. Over 150 troops can be carried. In-flight refuelling increases the aircraft range.

By 2013 the unit cost of a C-17 was believed to have risen to around £200 million.

No 99 Sqn has some 180 flight crew and ground staff.

RAF C-17. (MoD Crown Copyright 2013)

A400M ATLAS (PREVIOUSLY FUTURE LARGE AIRCRAFT – FLA)

Crew 2 pilots and 1 loadmaster; Length 45.1 m; Wingspan 42.4 m; Height 14.7 m; Payload 37,000 kg; Cruising speed 780 km/h (485 mph); Range 3,298 km (2,049 miles) at maximum payload; Ferry range 8,710 km (5,412 miles); Take off distance 980 m; Passengers 116 fully equipped troops or 66 stretchers accompanied by 25 medical personnel.

In 2000 the MoD committed to 25 x Airbus A400M (later reduced to 22) to meet the Future Transport Aircraft (FTA) requirement for an air lift capability to replace the remaining Hercules C-130K and C-130J fleet.

The A400 is a collaborative programme involving eight European nations (Germany, France, Turkey, Spain, Portugal, Belgium, Luxembourg and United Kingdom), procuring a total of 174 aircraft. The expected UK project cost is some £3.2 billion for 22 aircraft and the first aircraft will be delivered to the RAF in 2014 with an in-service date of March 2015. Full Operating Capability (FOC) should be possible in 2018 when 12 aircraft should be in service.

The A400M will provide tactical and strategic mobility to all three Services. Atlas's capabilities will enable the aircraft to operate from well established airfields and semi-prepared rough landing areas in extreme climates and all weather by day and night; to carry a variety of vehicles and other equipment, freight, and troops over extended ranges; to be capable of air dropping paratroops and equipment; and to be capable of being unloaded with the minimum of ground handling equipment. Atlas will also meet a requirement for an airlift capability to move large single items such as attack helicopters and some Royal Engineers' equipment. In short, Atlas is capable of transporting 32 tonnes of cargo over a range of 4,500 km.

Airbus Military SL of Madrid, a subsidiary of Airbus Industrie, is responsible for management of the whole of the A400M programme. Companies involved in the programme are: BAE Systems (UK), EADS (Germany, France and Spain), Flabel (Belgium) and Tusas Aerospace Industries (Turkey).

It now looks likely that the RAF will probably retain its C-17s, and will operate a mixed transport fleet comprising the C-130J, A-400 Atlas and C-17 until at least the end of the decade.

Orders for other nations include Germany 53; France 50; Spain 27; Belgium 7; Turkey 10; Luxembourg 1 and Malaysia 4.

A400M. (Photo – MillborneOne – Creative Commons)

AIR-TO-AIR REFUELLING (AAR) AIRCRAFT

Until recently the RAF's AAR fleet mainly comprises 15 x VC10 K3 and K4 aircraft flown by No 101 Squadron based at RAF Brize Norton. These were supported by 8 x Tristar K1/KC1/C2/C2A (216 Sqn, Brize Norton) aircraft used for both transport and AAR. The RAF AAR capability is the most specialised in NATO, and has been extensively deployed in recent allied coalition operations in Afghanistan, and Iraq. From 2014 onwards RAF AAR operations will be undertaken by A330 Voyager aircraft.

VOYAGER (FUTURE STRATEGIC TANKER AIRCRAFT-FSTA)

Crew 3; Max speed 648 kph (405 mph); Engines 2; Thrust 72,000 lbs each engine; Length 193 ft.

On 27 March 2008 the UK Ministry of Defence signed a deal to lease 14 aircraft under a PFI agreement from the EADS-led consortium AirTanker Ltd. This PFI contract is based on the firm assumption that the FSTA aircraft are both operated from, and maintained at RAF Brize Norton. The AirTanker consortium comprises Cobham, EADS, Rolls-Royce, Thales and VT Group. The Airbus Military division of EADS were responsible for designing, developing and converting the tankers based on the Airbus A300-200 aircraft, and for delivering the completed aircraft to AirTanker.

FSTA (now Voyager) will replace the in-service Tri Star and VC10 aircraft.

There are two versions: Voyager KC2 fitted with two Cobham 905E under-wing refuelling pods and Voyager KC3 fitted with a Cobham 805E Fuselage Refuelling Unit in addition to the under-wing pods. Voyager is powered by two Rolls-Royce Trent 772B-60 engines.

Voyager will probably remain in service until about 2040, and the aircraft will refuel combat aircraft such as the Tornado, Typhoon and the F35B which will enter service during the next decade.

In its air-to-air refuelling role Voyager has the ability to offload 60 tonnes of fuel 1,000 miles from base, and remain on station for 2 hours. On a typical deployment over about 3,000 miles, a single A330 would be able to refuel four Tornados and still carry 11,000lb (5000kg) of freight and/or 290 passengers.

The in-service date for Voyager is May 2014 when 9 of the 14 aircraft on order will be available for AAR operations.

The PFI payment terms means that the MoD will only pays for the service delivered depending on number of aircraft booked per day, and hours flown.

Voyager at Farnborough in 2010. (MoD Crown Copyright 2013)

CHINOOK HC4/HC4A/HC5

In service with:

7 Squadron	11 x Chinook HC4/HC4A/HC5	Odiham
18 Squadron	10 x Chinook HC4/HC4A/HC5	Odiham
27 Squadron	9 x Chinook HC4/HC4A/HC5	Odiham

All the above aircraft are under the control of the Joint Helicopter Command (JHC). Squadron numbers will increase as more aircraft become available.

Crew 3/4; Fuselage Length 15.54m; Width 3.78m; Height 5.68m; Weight (empty) 10,814kg; Internal Payload 8,164kg; Rotor Diameter 18.29m; Cruising Speed 158mph/270 kph; Service Ceiling 4,270m; Mission Radius (with internal and external load of 20,000kgs including fuel and crew) 55kms; Rear Loading Ramp Height 1.98m; Rear Loading Ramp Width 2.31m; Engines 2 x Avco Lycoming T55-712 turboshafts.

The Chinook is a tandem-rotored, twin-engined medium-lift helicopter and the first aircraft of this type entered service with the RAF in 1982. It has a crew of four (pilot, navigator and 2 x crewmen) and is capable of carrying 54 fully equipped troops or a variety of heavy loads up to approximately 10 tons. The triple hook system allows greater flexibility in load carrying and enables some loads to be carried faster and with greater stability. In the ferry configuration with internally mounted fuel tanks, the Chinook's range is over 1,600 km (1,000 miles). In the medical evacuation role the aircraft can carry 24 stretchers.

RAF Chinook aircraft were upgraded to the HC2 standard between 1993 and 1996 for some £145m. The HC2 upgrade modified the RAF Chinooks to the US CH-47D standard. New equipment included infra-red jammers, missile approach warning indicators, chaff and flare dispensers, a long-range fuel system, and machine gun mountings. In 1995, the UK MoD purchased a further 14 x Chinooks (6 x HC2 and 8 x HC2a – now Mk3) for £240 million.

During 2003 the Chinook Night Enhancement Package (NEP) was installed in the HC2 fleet. The NEP was based upon experience gained during operations in Afghanistan and allows Chinook aircraft to operate at night and in very low-light conditions, often at the limit of their capabilities.

A £62 million contract with Boeing to convert eight Chinook Mk3 helicopters to a support helicopter role was announced by the Ministry of Defence in December 2007. The first helicopters were operational in Afghanistan in 2010.

RAF Chinook. (Photo Adrian Pingstone)

The RAF currently has a fleet of 46 Chinook delivered between 1981 and 2001 of which we believe 30 are available to the Forward Fleet at any one time. There appear to be plans to procure another 14 Mk 6 aircraft to bring the Chinook inventory up to a total of 60. The purchase cost for 14 x Mk 6 aircraft is £841 million and the first of these aircraft will enter service in May 2014. All 14 aircraft should be fully operational by early 2017.

The most recent upgrade and currently underway is Project Julius. This enhancement introduces an integrated digital 'glass' cockpit, moving map tablet and new crewman's workstation across the whole of the fleet of Chinook helicopters. Pilots will now be able to determine what flight and tactical information is displayed to them at any given time, improving the ergonomics of the cockpit. Under Project Julius HC2/HC2A's are being upgraded to the HC4/HC4A standard, and the HC3's to the HC5 standard. Following the upgrade these aircraft will be better positioned for the switch between Special Forces and Support Helicopter tasks.

PUMA HC2

In service with:

33 Squadron	12 x Puma HC2	Benson
230 Squadron	12 x Puma HC2	Benson

All the above aircraft are under the control of the Joint Helicopter Command (JHC).

Crew 2 or 3; Capacity up to 20 troops or 7,055lb underslung; Fuselage Length 14.06m rotors turning 18.15m; Width 3.50m; Height 4.38m; Weight (empty) 3,615kg; Maximum Take Off Weight 7,400kg; Max Speed 163mph/261 kph; Service Ceiling 4,800m; Range 550kms; 2 x Turbomeca Turmo 111C4 turbines.

Following the retirement of the last Wessex in 2003, the Puma is now the oldest helicopter in RAF service. The "package deal" between the UK and France on helicopter collaboration dates back to February 1967. The programme covered the development of three helicopter types – the Puma, Gazelle and Lynx. Production of the aircraft was shared between the two countries, the UK making about 20% by value of the airframe, slightly less for the engine, as well as assembling the aircraft procured for the RAF. Deliveries of the RAF Pumas started in 1971.

Capable of many operational roles, Puma can carry 16 fully equipped troops or 20 at light scales. In the casualty evacuation role (CASEVAC), six stretchers and six sitting cases can be carried. Underslung loads of up to 3,200 kg can be transported over short distances and an infantry battalion can be moved using about 34 Puma lifts.

RAF Pumas MoD. (Crown Copyright 2013)

The first of 24 upgraded Puma Mk2 aircraft entered service in 2012 with the entire fleet upgraded in early 2014. The entire upgrade package cost about £300 million including one-off costs associated with developing modifications, trials activity, provision of initial support and conversion training for aircrew and maintainers. The actual cost of modifying each helicopter was in the region of £10 million.

Pumas upgraded to HC2 standard should be able to remain in service until about 2025.

MERLIN HC3

In service with:

28 Squadron	12 x Merlin HC3/3A	Benson
78 Squadron	12 x Merlin HC3/3A	Benson

All the above aircraft are under the control of the Joint Helicopter Command (JHC).

Note: RAF Merlin aircraft will be transferred to the Royal Navy Commando Helicopter Force during 2014.

Crew 4; Capacity up to 24 combat-equipped troops, or 16 stretchers and a medical team, or 4 tonnes of cargo (2.5 tonnes as an underslung load). Length 22.81m; Rotor Diameter 18.59m; Max Speed 309k/ph (192mph); Engine 3 x Rolls Royce/Turbomeca RTM 322 turboshafts.

The RAF ordered 22 x EH101 (Merlin) support helicopters for £755m in March 1995. Merlin is a direct replacement for the Westland Wessex, and it operates alongside the Puma and Chinook in the medium-lift role. Its ability to carry troops, artillery pieces, light vehicles and bulk loads, means that the aircraft is ideal for use with the UK Army's 16 Air Assault Brigade. Deliveries took place between 2000–2002.

The aircraft can carry a load of 24–28 troops with support weapons. The maximum payload is 4,000 kg and Merlin has a maximum range of 1,000km, which can be extended by external tanks or by air-to-air refuelling. The Merlin Mk 3 has sophisticated defensive aids, and the aircraft is designed to operate in extreme conditions with corrosion-proofing for maritime operations. All weather, day/night precision delivery is possible because of GPS navigation, a forward-looking infra-red sensor and night vision goggle compatibility. In the longer term, the aircraft could be fitted with a nose turret mounting a .50 calibre machine gun.

Merlin. (Copyright Augusta Westland 2013)

During March 2007 the UK MoD announced the acquisition of 6 x additional Merlin Mk 3a from Denmark. These aircraft were ordered to support operations in Afghanistan.

After four years of continuous front line support.RAF Merlin aircraft returned from Afghanistan in June 2013.The Merlins had flown for more than 18,000 hours in the dust and heat of Helmand, moving more than 7,900 tonnes of equipment and transporting over 130,000 personnel during the period. In Afghanistan Merlin had been used mainly as a troop transporter.

In 2013 a Merlin Life Sustainment Programme is in its Assessment Phase. This upgrade assessment is looking at options to enhance the Merlin Mk3/3A aircraft's ability to support amphibious operations.

Following an upgrade we would expect Merlin Mk 3/3A aircraft to remain in service until 2030.

SEA KING HAR3/3A

In service with:

22 Squadron	Headquarters	RAF Valley
A Flight	3 x Sea King HAR3/3A	RMB Chivenor
B Flight	3 x Sea King HAR3/3A	Wattisham
C Flight	2 x Sea King HAR3/3A	Valley
202 Squadron	Headquarters	Valley
A Flight	3 x Sea King HAR3/3A	Boulmer
D Flight	3 x Sea King HAR 3/3A	Lossiemouth
E Flight	2 x Sea King HAR 3/3A	Leconfield

Note: Both 22 and 202 Squadrons have 8 x Sea King HAR3/3A. Numbers of aircraft (our estimates) have been allocated to flights for rounding purposes.

Crew 4; Length 17.01m; Height 4.72m;Rotor Diameter 18.9m; Weight (empty) 6,201kg; Cruising Speed 129mph/208 kph; Range 1,230kms; Engine 2 x Rolls Royce Gnome H1400-1 turboshafts.

The Westland Sea King HAR3 Search and Rescue helicopter entered RAF service in 1978. The aircraft is fitted with advanced all-weather search and navigation equipment, as well as autopilot and onboard computer to assist positioning and hovering at night or in bad weather. In addition to four crew members, the HAR3 can carry up to six stretchers, or 18 x survivors. Under normal conditions, expect the HAR3 to have an operational radius of approximately 448 km (280 miles).

An early 1990s MoD report concluded that a total of 25 Sea Kings was required to ensure that SAR duties were carried out effectively and the Sea King HAR3A replaced the Wessex HC2 in the SAR role

Sea King HAR 3.
(Photo Alistar Taylor)

during 1996. An announcement was made in 1992 of an order for six more HAR3, to bring the total up to the required 25. Of these 25 aircraft, 16 are allocated for SAR duties in the UK, two in the Falkland Islands, three for conversion training and the remaining three form an engineering and operational pool.

RAF Sea King HAR3/3A are due to be phased out of service in 2017.

During March 2013 a £1.6 billion, 10 year contract was signed to provide a search and rescue helicopter service for the whole of the UK with Bristow Helicopters Ltd. Operations will commence progressively from 2015 and the service will be fully operational across the United Kingdom by summer of 2017 when the RAF (and Royal Navy) will withdraw from SAR operations. Sea King HAR3/3A will then be retired.

Bristow Helicopters will operate a mixed fleet of 22 helicopters from 10 locations around the UK. Sikorsky S92 aircraft will be based at the Maritime and Coastguard Agency (MCA) locations at Stornoway and Sumburgh, and at new locations at Newquay, Caernarfon and Humberside airports. AW 189 aircraft will be based at Lee on Solent, Prestwick, St Athan, Inverness and Manston. These bases will ensure maximum operational coverage across the UK.

The UK Government states that "Helicopters will be able to reach a larger area of the UK search and rescue region within one hour of take off than is currently possible, and based on historic incident patterns we estimate that there will be an overall 20% improvement in flying times, with the average flight time reducing from 23 minutes to 19. Presently, approximately 70 per cent of high and very high risk areas are reachable within 30 minutes. Under the new contract, approximately 85 per cent of the same areas are reachable within this time frame".

RAF WEAPONS

Air to Air Missiles

Sidewinder AIM-9L

Diameter 0.13m; Span 0.63m; Length 2.85m; Total Weight 85.3kg; Warhead Weight 9.5kg; Propulsion Solid fuel rocket; Speed Mach 2.5; Range 10–18km; Guidance Solid-state, infrared homing system.

The Sidewinder missile, which is carried by all the RAF combat aircraft including (as required) the Hawk, is an infra-red weapon which homes onto the heat emitted by a hostile aircraft's engines. Sidewinder is a within visual range missile that the pilot can direct to the target manually and has an excellent dogfight capability. Sidewinder can operate independently of the aircraft's radar, and provides the air defence aircraft with an alternative method of attacking targets at shorter ranges.

Sidewinder AIM-9.
(Photo US Air Force)

ASRAAM

Length 2.9m; Diameter 0.17m; Weight 88kg; Cruising speed Mach 3.5+; Range over 10 miles; Guidance Imaging IR 128 x 128 element focal plane array.

ASRAAM is a fast, highly agile, fire and forget IR missile for short range air-to-air combat, able to counter intermittent target obscurity in cloud and severe Infra Red countermeasures. It is carried on the Typhoon and is replacing Sidewinder AIM-9L, although Sidewinder will remain in service in parallel for a period. The programme cost some £857 million and there were considerable technical problems and delays before service entry in 2002.

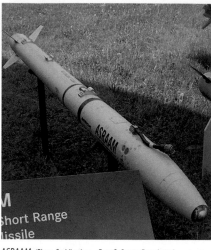

ASRAAM. *(Photo Stahlkocher – Free Software Foundation)*

AMRAAM

Length 3.66m; Diameter 0.18m; Span 0.48m; Weight 161.4kg/336lbs; Cruising speed Mach 4; Range approx 30 miles; Guidance System Active radar terminal/inertial midcourse.

AMRAAM (Advanced medium-range air-to-air missile) is a US air fighting weapon that matches the fire-and-forget capability of the ASRAAM, but with greater range. There is increased immunity over electronic countermeasures and a low-smoke, high-impulse rocket motor to reduce the probability of an enemy sighting the missile. This system is in use by the Typhoon. AMRAAM has been in service since 1995, and the initial purchase was believed to be some 210 missiles worth some £50m.

AMRAAM being fitted. *(Photo US Air Force)*

In 2004 Raytheon Missile Systems was awarded an £80 million contract by the UK MoD for the AIM-120 C5 variant. Having entered service in 2007 the new missile, includes a greater immunity to countermeasures, longer range and a more powerful warhead. The C model has replaced the earlier B model.

Meteor (BVRAAM)

Range Over 100 km (60 miles); Speed over Mach 4; Weight 185 kg; Length 3.65 m; Diameter 0.17 m; Warhead HE blast fragmentation – proximity impact.

The Beyond Visual Range Air-to-Air Missile (BVRAAM) (also known as Meteor) should provide Typhoon with the capability to combat projected air-to-air threats and sustain air superiority throughout the life of the aircraft. The weapon is required to operate in all weather conditions and will complement the Typhoon Advanced Short Range Air-to-Air Missile (ASRAAM). Until Meteor enters service, Typhoon will be armed with the Advanced Medium Range Air-to-Air Missile (AMRAAM). Meteor is a collaborative programme with 5 partner nations; Germany, Spain and Italy (for Typhoon), Sweden (for JAS 39 Gripen) and France (for Rafale).

Intergration of the Meteor to the Typhoon continues and the RAF expects an initial operating capability in 2015 with an in-service date of 2016/2017. The overall cost is projected at £1.4 billion (demonstration and manufacturing phase).

AIR-LAUNCHED AIR-TO-GROUND CRUISEMISSILE

Storm Shadow

Length 5.1m; Diameter 0.48m; Span 2.84m; Weight 1,300kg; Range Estimate 350km (210 miles); Propulsion TRI 60-30 Turbofan; Guidance Navigation using TERrain PROfile Matching) system as well as GPS, Terminal guidance using imaging infra-red sensor, Autonomous target recognition algorithms, BROACH warhead.

Storm Shadow (also known as Conventionally-Armed Stand-Off Missile or CASOM) is a long-range, air-launched, stand-off attack missile that will allow the RAF to attack high-priority targets deep inside enemy territory without exposing the launch aircraft to high-intensity enemy air defences. The missile is the BAe version (with some UK enhancements) of the French Matra APACHE/SCALP missile and entered service in late 2002. It is fitted to Tornado GR4 and the Typhoon (integration ongoing). The RAF is believed to have purchased an initial batch of 500 missiles. The programme cost is some £980m.

Some 27 Storm Shadow missiles were launched from Tornado aircraft with tremendous success during the 2003 Iraq War (Operation Telic). Although the exact figure for Storm Shadow launched during Operation Ellamy (Libya 2011) is not known, MoD sources state UK forces employed a combined total of around 80 Storm Shadow and Tomahawk land attack missiles.

Storm Shadow in Flight. (Copyright MBDA 2013)

AIR-TO-GROUND ANTI-RADIATION MISSILE ALARM

Length 4.3m. Diameter 0.22m. Span 0.72m. Weight 265kg. Propellant 1 x Royal Ordnance Nuthatch solid fuel two-stage rocket. Guidance Passive Radar Homing/Strap-down INS; Range 93km.

ALARM stands for Air-Launched Anti-Radiation Missile and this type was introduced into RAF Service in the early 1990s. The missile is launched at low level near the suspected site of an enemy radar and, after launch, rapidly climbs

ALARM on Tornado GR4. (Creative Commons)

to about 12,000 m. At this height, a small parachute opens and the missile descends earthwards while the on-board radar searches the broadband for emissions from enemy radar. Once a target has been identified, the motor is re-ignited and the missile makes a supersonic dive onto the target. The total RAF buy in the first manufacturing run was believed to be some 750 missiles. Since its original entry into service, radars have become increasingly more sophisticated in their ability to avoid detection and attack by anti-radiation weapons such as ALARM. As a result, the missile has been upgraded and its capability improved.

ALARM was used extensively during the 2003 Iraq War (Operation Telic) and the 2011 Libyan campaign Operation Ellamy. The missile is expected to remain in service until at least 2020.

AREA WEAPONS

Brimstone – Air-to-Ground Anti-Armour Missiles

Length 1.81m; Diameter 0.18m; Weight 49kg; Propulsion cast double-base propellant rocket motor; Guidance inertial guidance + seeker determination to target acquisition, then seeker control; Cruising speed boost to supersonic; Range 12 km (8 miles).

The Advanced Air-launched Anti-Armour Weapon (AAAW), known as Brimstone, is an area weapon to attack enemy armoured forces as early and as far forward as possible. It replaces the BL755 cluster bomb in the anti-armour role,

and is carried by Tornado GR4/4a and Eurofighter Typhoon. These fixed-wing aircraft will compliment the capability provided by the Apache AH64-D, which is armed with the Hellfire anti-armour weapon.

Brimstone operates automatically after launch, which helps reduce the hazard to the attacking aircraft from enemy fire. Development and

ALARM on Tornado GR4. (Creative Commons)

procurement of Brimstone has cost the RAF some £822m since 1996. The weapon entered RAF service in mid 2005.

In 2007 an Urgent Operational Requirement (UOR) for a precision guide missile for use in Afghanistan resulted in an upgrade to the Brimstone guidance system. This upgraded version is known as the Dual Mode Seeker Brimstone. It is believed that 300 of the older Brimstones missiles were upgraded to Dual Mode Seeker Brimstone standard and some sources state that about 500 have been delivered.

During Operation Ellamy (Libya 2011) UK forces launched a total of 230 Dual Mode Seeker Brimstone.

Each missile costs approximately £100,000 (excluding development and support costs).

PRECISION GUIDED MUNITIONS

Paveway II

Length 3.7m; Weight 520kg; Laser Guidance.

Paveway II is the standard 1,000 lb (454 kg) general purpose bomb for used against moderately well-protected targets. Paveway II can be fitted with a laser guidance kit, and the bomb can be used in the freefall or retarded mode. Used on the Tornado GR4 and Eurofighter Typhoon.

Paveway III

Length 4.4m; Weight 1,130kg; Laser Guidance.

Paveway III is a 2,000 lb (908 kg) laser guided bomb (LGB) for use against well-protected targets. The bomb is guided to its target by a TIALD (Thermal Imaging and Laser Designation) pod that is carried on the aircraft or by a ground based observer using a target designator. The weapon can be carried on the Tornado GR4, Harrier, and Typhoon. Unlike the Paveway II, this weapon uses proportional guidance – the control canards on the front of the bomb move only the exact amount necessary to guide the weapon. This conserves energy, improves accuracy capability and increases the range of the weapon, thus allowing delivery aircraft to engage their targets with greater stand-off. When the weapon is released, it flies a pre-programmed autopilot profile into the target area, using the energy given to it by the releasing aircraft. These autopilot profiles are designated to provide the best attack conditions for different types of target and also to use to maximum effectiveness the increased stand-off capability of the weapon.

ENHANCED PAVEWAY

Length (EPWII) 3.7m; (EPWIII) 4.4m); Weight (EPW2) 545kg (EPW3) 1,130kg); GPS guidance.

Shortcomings in target acquisition during the 1999 Kosovo conflict resulted in a requirement for the RAF to obtain a weapon to satisfy all-weather 24-hour tasking. The Enhanced Paveway (EPW) family of weapons meets this requirement, and the EPWII entered service in 2001 and the larger EPWIII entered service in late 2002. Both EPWII and EPWIII are based on their laser-guided bomb variants, the Paveway II and Paveway III respectively, and utilise the same warheads and fin sections. However, the EPW weapons have a modified guidance section and wiring to accommodate a Global Positioning System Aided Inertial Navigation System (GAINS). EPW (also known as Paveway IV) is carried by the Tornado GR4.

In Iraq, during Operation Telic in early 2003 the RAF used 360 x Enhanced Paveway PGMs, and 255 Paveway II/III LGBs. Enhanced Paveway was described by the RAF officers as "the weapon of choice". In November 2007 the Typhoon dropped its first in-service bomb, the Paveway II and was declared operational in the ground attack role.

Paveway IV

In late 2003 the UK MoD selected the Paveway IV PGM in preference to the Boeing Joint Direct Attack Munition (JDAM). Paveway IV has the ability to engage targets in all types of weather with laser guidance for high terminal accuracy.

The Paveway IV kit, is equipped with a GPS/INS (Global Positioning System/Inertial Navigation System) and a SAL (Semi-Active Laser) terminal seeker. The total value of the contract is believed to be in the region of £100 million. Paveway IV is a joint development by the UK-based Raytheon Systems Ltd (RSL) and Raytheon Missile Systems (RMS) in the US.

Paveway IV kits, fitted to 227 kg (500 lb) bombs, entered service in 2008.

During Operation Ellamy (Libya 2011) the UK's precision guided bombing capability was provided by 240 x Enhanced Paveway II and 900 x Paveway IV.

Freefall bombs

Conventional 1,000 lb (454 kg) bombs are still in service, as are Mark 1 and Mark 2 bombs weighing 570 lb (260 kg). By adding the Hunting 118 retarding tail, the weight of the latter is increased to 670 lb (304 kg).

CVR-7 Rocket

This is an air-to-air and air-to-surface rocket system. Each rocket pod, weighing 240 kg, carries 19 rockets. The HE warhead is designed for use against light armour, vehicles, small vessels and helicopters.

BALLISTIC MISSILE DEFENCE

In 2002, the unilateral withdrawal of the United States from the 1972 Anti-Ballistic Missile Treaty with the then Soviet Union opened the way for the deployment of limited national and theatre ballistic missile defence (BMD) systems. In early 2003, the UK government agreed to a US government request to upgrade BMEWS system at RAF Fylingdales for BMD applications. That upgrade is now complete.

In an early 2006 statement the Secretary of State for Defence said that "The UK Government have not yet decided whether or not to pursue missile defence for the United Kingdom, but continues to examine, with our NATO allies, the developing threat from ballistic missiles and the appropriate responses. We have agreed to the upgrading of the radar at RAF Fylingdales as part of the United States missile defence system, and we also have a programme of joint technical and research projects with the US exploring the relevant technologies."

In a more recent announcement the MoD stated that RAF Fylingdales and another station at RAF Menwith Hill simply feed essential tracking information into the US system and that both sites remain under UK command. There are no plans to site interceptor missiles in the UK.

RAF REGIMENT

The need to raise a dedicated specialist force to protect air installations became apparent during WWII when unprotected aircraft on the ground were vulnerable to enemy air and ground attack. Consequently, the RAF Regiment was raised on 1 February 1942 by a Royal Warrant of King George VI. At the end of WWII, there were over 85,000 personnel serving in the RAF Regiment manning 240 operational squadrons. As of 2013, the strength of the RAF Regiment is some around 2,100 airmen with approximately 300 officers and 500 part-time reservists. The Regiment is generally formed into Squadrons of 100 to 150 personnel. Currently the RAF Regiment exists to provide defence for RAF installations, and to train all the RAF's combatant personnel to enable them to contribute to the defence of their units. RAF Regiment units are under the operational command of No 2 Group.

The annual cost of the core RAF Regiment force (2013) is around £120 million.

As of late 2013 RAF Regiment Squadrons/units are as follows:

SQUADRONS & WINGS

No 1 Squadron	Honington	Field Squadron
No 2 Squadron	Honington	Field/Parachute Sqn
No 3 Squadron	Wittering	Field Squadron
No 15 Squadron	Honington	Field Squadron
No 34 Squadron	Leeming	Field Squadron
No 51 Squadron	Lossiemouth	Field Squadron
No 58 Squadron	Leuchars	Field Squadron
No 63 (QCS)	Uxbridge	Ceremonial/Field Sqn

Note: The future of 58 Squadron following the closure of RAF Leuchars in 2014 is undecided/

RAF Regiment Depot	Honington
RAF Force Protection HQ	Honington

NO 20 WING RAF REGIMENT

No 20 Wing at RAF Honington is responsible for the Defence CBRN Wing . This organisation provides the CBRN (Chemical, biological, radiological and nuclear) reconnaissance, monitoring, detection and decontamination support required by the three armed services, and where necessary the civilian authorities. 20 Wing has two squadrons:

No 26 Squadron	Honington
No 27 Squadron	Honington

Specialist RAF Regiment training for gunners is given at the RAF Regiment Depot at Honington. On completion of training at the RAF College Cranwell officers also undergo further specialist training at RAF Honington and, in some cases, the School of Infantry at Warminster in Wiltshire.

The RAF Regiment also mans the Queen's Colour Squadron (QCS) which undertakes all major ceremonial duties for the Royal Air Force. These duties involve mounting the Guard at Buckingham Palace on an occasional basis, and providing Guards of Honour for visiting Heads of State. The Queen's Colour Squadron also has a war role as a field squadron.

The regiment is not alone in defending any RAF station. Every airman based at a station has a ground defence role and is trained to defend his place of work against ground attack and attack by NBC weapons. Training for this is given by RAF Regiment instructors who provide courses at station level for all personnel on various aspects of ground defence.

RAF FORCE PROTECTION WINGS

The former Survive to Operate HQ were restructured in 2006 to become rapidly deployable RAF Force Protection Wings (FPWs). The units integrated elements of the RAF Regiment, RAF Police, Intelligence and Support to deliver a full range of capability from policing and security (including dogs) to close combat. RAF FPWs have been extremely active in Afghanistan.

There are RAF Force Protection Wings at:

No 1 Force Protection Wing – RAF Wittering
No 2 Force Protection Wing – RAF Leeming
No 3 Force Protection Wing – RAF Marham

No 5 Force Protection Wing – RAF Lossiemouth
No 6 Force Protection Wing – RAF Leuchars
No 7 Force Protection Wing – RAF Coningsby

Note: The future of No 6 Force Protection Wing following the closure of RAF Leuchars in 2014 is undecided.

RAF RESERVES

The reserve component of the Royal Air Force was as follows:

RAuxAF & RAFVR Reserves	1,360 (about 200 x officers and 1,160 other ranks)
Royal Air Force Reserve	6,600 (about 350 x officers and 6,250 other ranks)
University Air Squadrons	850 (approximate figure)

The number of retired officers and airmen who have completed pensionable service and are liable to recall is possibly in the region of 5,000 officers and 15,000 airmen/airwomen.

The Controller Reserve Forces (RAF) is located at HQ Air Command. He is responsible for all of the non-operational aspects of reserve forces policy and co-ordination, ranging from recruitment, through training, promotions and welfare to future planning. The following are the formed Reserve Units for which he is responsible.

The RAuxAF is the RAF volunteer element that provides trained personnel to reinforce the regular units. It consists of volunteers who give up their weekends and holiday for training. RAuxAF Units provide resilience and strength in depth to the RAF operations world wide, generally by providing individual reinforcements to regular units.

Under the Future Force 2020 programme the RAuxAF will grow to a trained strength of around 1,800 with the principal growth will be in the specialist areas of logistics, flight operations, medical, intelligence, media, RAF police and cyber operations.

ROYAL AUXILIARY AIR FORCE

Royal Auxiliary Air Force units include:

3 Sqn	RAF Henlow	Tactical Provost Wing
501 Sqn	RAF Brize Norton	Operations Support Squadron
503 Sqn	RAF Aldergrove	Operations Support Squadron
504 Sqn	RAF Wittering	Awaiting re-role
600 Sqn	RAF Northolt	HQ Augmentation Unit
602 Sqn	Glasgow	Operations Support Squadron
603 Sqn	Edinburgh	Force Protection
606 Sqn	RAF Benson	Helicopter Support Squadron
609 Sqn	RAF Leeming	Operations Support Squadron
611 Sqn	RAF Woodvale	Operations Support Squadron
612 Sqn	RAF Leuchars	Airmobile Surgical Squadron
622 Sqn	RAF Brize Norton	Aircrew Augmentation Unit
4624 Sqn	RAF Brize Norton	Operations Support Squadron
4626 Sqn	RAF Brize Norton	Aeromedical Evacuation Unit
7006 Sqn	RAF Waddington	Intelligence Sqn
7010 Sqn	RAF Waddington	Photographic Interpretation Sqn
7630 Sqn	RAF Waddington	Intelligence Sqn
7644 Sqn	RAF Halton	Media Operations Squadron
Mobile Met Unit	RAF Benson	Meteorological Services

Royal Auxiliary Air Force Regiment (RAuxAF Regt)

Airfield defence is further enhanced by squadrons of the RAuxAF Regt who are recruited locally and whose role is the ground defence of the airfield and its associated outlying installations.

A RAuxAF Regiment Squadron has an all-up strength of about 120 personnel and costs approximately £500,000 a year to keep in service. As a general rule, a squadron has a headquarters flight, two mobile flights mounted in Land Rovers and two flights for static guard duties. RAuxAF Regt squadrons are as follows:

2503 Sqn RAuxAF Regt	RAF Waddington	Field Squadron
2620 Sqn RAuxAF Regt	RAF Marham	Field Squadron
2622 Sqn RAuxAF Regt	RAF Lossiemouth	Field Squadron
2623 Sqn RauxAF Regt	RAF Honington	Force Protection
2624 Sqn RauxAF Regt	RAF Brize Norton	Force Protection

Royal Auxiliary Air Force Regiment squadrons are generally based alongside regular units in order to maximise training opportunities and give the auxiliary personnel access to equipment held by the regular unit.

CHAPTER 5 – JOINT FORCES COMMAND AND JOINT SERVICE ORGANISATIONS

JOINT FORCES COMMAND

Joint Forces Command (JFC) was established in April 2012 and reached full operating capability in April 2013. The creation of the Joint Forces Command was recommended by Lord Levene's 2011 Defence Reform Review.

The JFC was created to ensure the Joint Capabilities of all three of the UK's fighting services were fully optimised, with an additional JFC aim of creating a more direct link between front line experience and top-level planning. The headquarters of the Joint Forces Command, is at Northwood in Middlesex (just north of London) and consists of around 150 civilian and military staff.

Across the whole command, the JCF's day to day personnel total will probably number about 30,000 military and civilian personnel, a figure that includes forces deployed on operations under command of the Chief of Joint Operations (CJO). These personnel are at locations across the UK, overseas in the Permanent Joint Operating Bases (PJOBs), and on operations world-wide.

Included in the overall JFC budget are the costs of the UK forces in the Falkland Islands, Cyprus, the British Indian Ocean Territory and Gibraltar. Major operations such as the ongoing operational commitment in Afghanistan are funded separately by way of a supplementary budget, and in almost all cases, this requires government- level approval. Small operations and the cost of reconnaissance parties are funded from the standard JFC budget.

JFC responsibilities are now so wide-ranging and complex it is probably easier to comment on operational areas with which this Headquarters will not be involved. These include Defence of the UK Home Base; Integrity of UK Airspace and Seaspace; Strategic Nuclear Deterrent; Counter-terrorism in the UK; Northern Ireland and NATO General War (Article V) operations.

General Richard Barrons took command of the JFC in succession to Air Chief Marshal Sir Stuart Peach in mid-April 2013.

GENERAL SIR RICHARD BARRONS

General Barrons was commissioned into the Royal Regiment of Artillery in 1977, prior to reading for a degree in Philosophy, Politics and Economics at Queen's College, Oxford. He then served in a variety of regimental appointments based in the UK and Germany, which included periods of training in Belize, Canada, France, Hong Kong and Brunei, and two years at the MoD, London.

He completed a Masters degree in Defence Administration in 1990 before attending the Army Staff College, Camberley in 1991.

As Chief of Staff of HQ 11 Armoured Brigade in Minden, Germany, he was despatched at a week's notice in October 1993 to form the first HQ British Forces in Bosnia and Croatia. This was followed by a short tour in the Directorate of Military Operations as the Balkans desk officer, before assuming command of B Battery, 1st Regiment Royal Horse Artillery in 1994 for two years – including a period of Northern Ireland duty.

On promotion to Lieutenant Colonel in 1996 he served as a Military Advisor to the High Representative in Bosnia, also leading on liaison with HQ NATO and SHAPE. In 1997 he was appointed Military Assistant (MA) to the Chief of the General Staff. He assumed command of 3rd Regiment Royal Horse Artillery in Hohne, Germany in 1999, deploying the Regiment to Kosovo and Bosnia in 2001 and commanding the first KFOR deployments alongside Serbian forces.

He was promoted to Colonel in December 2001 and appointed Chief of Staff of 3rd (United Kingdom) Division, deploying to Afghanistan the next day as the Headquarters established the International Security Assistance Force in Kabul for the first half of 2002. Having attended the Higher Command and Staff Course in 2003, he deployed again with the Headquarters as the Chief of Staff of HQ Multinational Division (South East) in Basra until October 2003.

As a Brigadier, he commanded 39 Infantry Brigade, covering Belfast and South Armagh from December 2003 to December 2005 when he assumed the appointment of ACOS (Assistant Chief of Staff) Commitments at HQ Land Forces, responsible for intelligence, security and operations – especially force generation for Iraq and Afghanistan.

General Sir Richard Barrons KCB, CBE, ADC Gen. (Crown Copyright MoD 2013)

On promotion to Major General in 2008 he served as a Deputy Commanding General of Multinational Corps Iraq (Baghdad), leading on operations with the Iraqi Army.

He was appointed Chief of Staff of the Allied Rapid Reaction Corps in April 2009. In October 2009 he was posted at very short notice to HQ ISAF to establish a Force Reintegration mechanism.

General Barrons was appointed MBE in 1993, OBE in 1999, CBE in 2003, awarded QCVS in 2004 and 2006, and appointed as an Officer of the US Legion of Merit in 2009.

JFC STRUCTURE

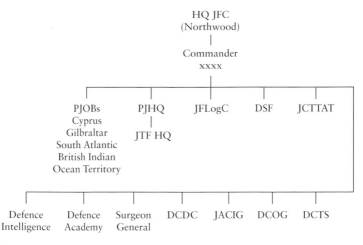

Abbreviations:
PJOBs – Permanent Joint Operating Bases; JFHQ – Joint Force Headquarters; JFLogC – Joint Force Logistics Component: JCTTAT – Joint Counter-Terrorist Training and Advisory Team; DSF – Director Special Forces; Def Ac – Defence Academy; DCDC – Development Concepts and Doctrine Centre; JACIG – Joint Arms Control Implementation Group; (DCTS); DCOG – Defence Cyber Operations Group; DCTS – Defence Centre of Training Support.

Notes:

(1) PJHQ and DSF are within JFC, however the commanders report directly to the Chief of the Defence Staff.

(2) PJHQ is commanded by the Chief of Joint Operations (CJO)

PJOB costs during FY 2012–2013 were as follows:

British Indian Ocean Territory	2 million
Falkland Islands	67 million
Gibraltar	53 million
Cyprus (Akrotiri & Dhekelia)	188 Million

Chief of Defence Intelligence and his staff advise the MoD on all aspects of defence intelligence.

Head of the Defence Academy Group directs the activities of the various Joint Service Staff Colleges and Academies.

The Surgeon General is the professional head of the Defence Medical Services and responsible for the healthcare and medical operational capability of the Armed Forces.

Defence Cyber Operations Group leads on Cyber Security, Cyber Policy and plans.

PERMANENT JOINT HEADQUARTERS (PJHQ)

Now an essential element of the JFC, Permanent Joint Headquarters (PJHQ) was established as a headquarters for joint military operations at Northwood in Middlesex in April 1996. This headquarters is the UK's national operational level command and contains elements of a rapidly deployable in-theatre Joint Task Force Headquarters (JTF HQ), that has the capability of commanding front line forces.

PJHQ is commanded by the Chief of Joint Operations (CJO) who is responsible for the planning and execution of joint, or potentially joint, national and UK-led multinational operations conducted outside the UK. CJO (a three star officer) reports direct to CDS for advice on a number of matters including the conduct and resourcing of military operations.

CJO commands UK forces assigned for a specific operation and is responsible at the operational level for the deployment, direction, sustainment and recovery of deployed forces. CJO acts as the Joint Force Commander and is usually based at Northwood. Forces in the operational area are commanded by a Joint Task Force (JTF) Commander or in cases where the UK is operating alongside allies, the UK National Contingent Commander.

Principal Additional Tasks of PJHQ Include:

♦ Monitoring designated areas of operational interest
♦ Preparing contingency plans
♦ Conducting Joint Force exercises
♦ Focus for Joint Rapid Reaction Force planning and exercising

Chain of Command for Joint Operations

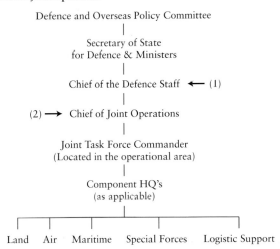

Notes:

(1) CDS has the option of advice from the three service commanders and the Commander JFC.

(2) Chief of Joint operations is provided with force packages (as required) by the three service commanders.

(3) CJO has a civilian Command Secretary who provides a wide range of policy, legal, presentational, financial and civilian human resources advice.

(4) The Defence and Overseas Policy Committee (DOPC) is responsible for the strategic direction of the UK Government's defence and overseas policy. The DOPC is chaired by the Prime Minister and members include the Secretary of State for Foreign and Commonwealth Affairs (Deputy Chair); Deputy Prime Minister and First Secretary of State; Chancellor of the Exchequer; Secretary of State for Defence; Secretary of State for the Home Department; Secretary of State for International Development; Secretary of State for Trade and Industry. If necessary, other ministers, the Heads of the Intelligence Agencies and the Chief of Defence Staff may be invited to attend.

PJHQ operates through the following staff branches:

J1 Personnel and Admin	J6 Communication and Information Systems
J2 Intelligence	J7 Doctrine and Joint Training
J3 Operations	J8 Finance
J4 Logistics & Medical	J9 Policy, legal and presentation
J5 Policy and Crisis Planning	

JOINT RAPID REACTION FORCE (JRRF)

The JRRF is essentially the fighting force that PJHQ has immediately available. The JRRF provides a force for rapid deployment operations using a core operational group of the Army's 16th Air Assault Brigade and the Royal Navy's 3rd Commando Brigade, supported by a wide range of air and maritime assets such as the Joint Helicopter Command and the Royal Navy's Response Task Group.

The JRRF uses what the MoD has described as a 'golfbag' approach with a wide range of units available for specific operations. For example, if the operational situation demands assets such as heavy armour, long range artillery and attack helicopters, these assets can easily be assigned to the force.

This approach means that the JRRF can be tailored for specific operations, ranging from support for a humanitarian crisis to missions including high intensity operations.

The 'reach' of the JRRF is enhanced by the Royal Navy's amphibious vessels HMS Albion and HMS Bulwark. Both of these vessels have the ability to carry 650 troops plus a range of armoured vehicles including main battle tanks. A flight deck allows for ship-to-shore helicopter operations.

Responsibility for providing units to the JRRF remains with the single service commanders who ensure that units assigned are at an extremely high state of readiness. Units assigned to the JRRF are trained to Joint standards and be committed to NATO, EU, UN or other coalition operations as required.

Under normal circumstances, it would be expected that the Army would ensure the following land forces were available to the JRRF: a brigade sized grouping held at High Readiness and two Strategic Reserves—the Spearhead Land Element (SLE) held at Extremely High Readiness and the Airborne Task Force (ABTF) held at Very High Readiness.

The force commander is the JTF Commander (Joint Task Force Commander) who is responsible to the Chief of Joint Operations (CJO) at PJHQ. JTF Commander is supported by the Joint Force Operations Staff at PJHQ who provide a fully resourced Joint Task Force Headquarters (JTFHQ) at 48 hours notice to move anywhere in the world.

JOINT FORCE LOGISTICS COMPONENT

The Joint Force Logistics Component (JFLogC) provides a joint logistic headquarters for operations with force logistics under the command of PJHQ. It delivers coordinated logistic support to the deployed Joint Force in accordance with the commander's priorities. The composition of the JFLogC will be determined by PJHQ during the mission planning stage. If necessary, 2 x logistic brigades can be assigned to JFLogC.

SPECIAL FORCES

Although the exact detail is highly classified, the UK Special Forces Group (UKSF) is under the command of the Director Special Forces (DSF). DSF's department is within the JFC but DSF reports directly to the Chief of the Defence Staff.

Units known to be part of the UK Special Forces Group include:

22nd Special Air Service Regiment (Army)	22 SAS
Special Boat Service (Royal Marines)	SBS
Special Forces Support Group	SFSG
Special Reconnaissance Regiment	SRR
18 (UKSF) Signal Regiment	18 SIG REGT
Reserve Components	

Special Forces Support Group

Based around a core group from the 1st Battalion The Parachute Regiment, the Special Forces Support Group (SFSG) is a unit within the UK Special Forces, that was established in April 2006. SFSG directly supports Special Forces operations worldwide and also provides an additional counter-terrorist capability. Personnel for the SGSG also come from the Royal Marines, and the Royal Air Force Regiment. Members of the Special Forces Support Group (SFSG) retain the cap badges of their parent units but also wear the SFSG insignia.

All SFSG personnel have passed either the Royal Marines Commando course, the Airborne Forces Selection course run by the Parachute Regiment or the RAF Pre-Parachute Selection course. Quaified personnel are then equipped and provided with additional training to fit their specific specialist role on joining the SFSG.

The UK MoD has described the main role of the SFSG as "Providing direct support to UK Special Forces intervention operations around the world. They will be prepared to operate in war-fighting, counter-insurgency and counter-terrorism operations at short notice. Their roles may include provision of supporting or diversionary attacks, cordons, fire support, force protection and supporting training tasks. Prior to the creation of the SFSG, these tasks have been carried out by other units on an ad hoc basis".

SFSG consists of four strike companies and a support company with specialist units such as as a CBRN detection troop and tactical air control parties. The group is believed to be equipped with Jackal vehicles.

Special Reconnaissance Regiment
The Special Reconnaissance Regiment (SRR) was formed in April 2005 to meet a growing worldwide demand a for special reconnaissance capability. The term 'special reconnaissance' covers a wide range of highly classified specialist skills and activities related to covert surveillance.

The SRR draws its personnel from existing units and can recruit new volunteers from serving members of the Armed Forces where necessary.

Other sub-units provide combat and combat service support.

18 (UKSF) SIGNAL REGIMENT

This regiment provides communications and electronic warfare support to the whole of the UK Special Forces Group. Squadrons under command include:

264 (SAS) Signals Squadron
SBS Signals Squadron
267 (SRR) Signals Squadron
268 (SFSG) Signals Squadron

Special Forces Reserve (SF-R)
The two reserve SAS Regiments (21 and 23 SAS) together with 63 SAS Signal Squadron and the SBS Reserve have evolved into the Reserve Component of the UKSF Group.

JOINT HELICOPTER COMMAND (JHC)

The majority of UK service helicopters are assigned to the Joint Helicopter Command, a formation under the command of Commander Land Forces. The primary role of the JHC is to deliver and sustain effective Battlefield Helicopter and Air Assault assets, operationally capable under all environmental conditions, in order to support the UK's defence missions and tasks. Major formations under JHC command are as follows:

- ◆ All Army Aviation Units
- ◆ RAF Support Helicopter Force
- ◆ Commando Helicopter Force
- ◆ 16 Air Assault Brigade
- ◆ Combat Support Units
- ◆ Combat Service Support Units
- ◆ Joint Helicopter Command and Standards Wing

Our estimate for the JHC service personnel total is approximately 13,000 from all three services. During operations elements of the JHC would probably be assigned to formations/units under the command of the Joint Forces Command (JFC).

Our figures suggest that the JHC appears to have about 195 aircraft available as follows.

Possible UK Helicopter types available during 2014

Royal Navy

Sea King Mk 4	22

Army Air Corps

Apache	49
Gazelle	12
Lynx/Wildcat	30
Defender/Islander	9

Royal Air Force

Chinook	29
Merlin Mk 3/3A	20
Puma Mk 2	24

Note: These figures suggest numbers of aircraft available for operations and not the total inventory which includes aircraft being used for training or being upgraded etc.

In a normal non-operational environment (with the exception of Lynx), each individual aircraft is resourced to fly approximately 400 hours per year. The Lynx fleet is generally resourced for 23,900 hours, which averages about 405 hours per aircraft.

Helicopters not under the command of the JHC include the Royal Navy's fleet helicopters (in support of ships at sea), and the Royal Air Force and Royal Navy's search and rescue aircraft.

DEFENCE MEDICAL SERVICES (DMS)

The Defence Medical Services include the whole of the medical, dental, nursing, health professional, paramedical, veterinary and support personnel (about 7,000 uniformed personnel) including civilian staff, employed by the three Armed Services. These elements are responsible for providing healthcare to service personnel serving in the UK and overseas and on operations. In addition and where appropriate the families of service personnel and entitled civilians (possibly about 260,000 people). DMS also provides some aspects of healthcare to other countries' personnel overseas, in both permanent military bases and in areas of conflict and war zones.

The range of services provided by the Defence Medical Services includes:

- ◆ Primary healthcare
- ◆ Dental care
- ◆ Hospital care
- ◆ Rehabilitation
- ◆ Occupational medicine
- ◆ Community mental healthcare
- ◆ Specialist medical care

Defence Medical Services also provide healthcare in a range of facilities, including medical and dental centres, regional rehabilitation units and in field hospitals.

The Deputy Chief of Defence Staff – Health (DCDS(H)) is accountable for the overall outputs of the Defence Medical Services.

The Surgeon General is the professional head of the Defence Medical Services and responsible for the healthcare and medical operational capability. His responsibilities include defining the standard and quality of healthcare needed in both operational and non-operational environments and assuring its delivery. He is also responsible for setting the strategy and the associated (non-clinical) policies for the Defence Medical Services.

These two senior officers oversee the work of three separate organisations:

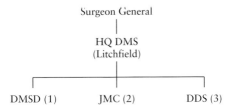

Surgeon General

HQ DMS
(Litchfield)

DMSD (1)   JMC (2)   DDS (3)

Notes:

(1) The Defence Medical Services Department (DMSD) is the headquarters for the Defence Medical Services providing strategic direction to ensure delivery of defence medical outputs. The DMSD operates through the following four directorates: Medical Operations; Medical Policy; Healthcare; Finance and Secretariat.

(2) Joint Medical Command (JMC) – This is a joint service agency providing secondary care personnel to meet requirements for operational deployments. It also supports the front line units by educating and training medical personnel through the Defence Medical and Training Agency (DEMTA). DMETA runs about 2,000 clinical courses (providing about 300,000 training days) to all three services. JMC has responsibility for the following:

♦ MDHUs (Ministry of Defence Hospital Units)
♦ RCDM (The Royal Centre for Defence Medicine)
♦ DMRC (The Defence Medical Rehabilitation Centre at Headley Court
♦ DMSTC (The Defence Medical Services Training Centre in Aldershot
♦ The Defence Medical Postgraduate Deanery

The JMC provides a single headquarters responsible for healthcare delivery.

(3) Defence Dental Services (DDS) – this is a joint service organisation employing both Armed Forces and civilian personnel that provides dental services in the UK at service establishments and to personnel on operations overseas. The DDS will come under the 'umbrella' of the JMC from mid 2009.

Single Service Medical Care
The three armed services are responsible for delivering primary healthcare to their respective services and for providing the required medical support on operations.

Royal Naval Medical Service (RNMS)
Army Medical Services (AMS)
Royal Air Forces Medical Services (RAF MS)

Mid 2012 personnel figures for these agencies were as follows:

	Regular personnel	Reserve personnel	Personnel total
Royal Navy	1590	60	1650
Army	5200	2840	8040
Royal Air Force	1930	190	2120
Tri-service Totals	8720	3090	11810

Defence Nursing Staff

On operations, nursing staff and medical officers from all three services deliver primary and emergency care at the front line and secondary and critical care in field hospitals. Aeromed evacuation of casualties is supported by defence nurses who deliver intensive care nursing during patient transfers both in theatre and on return to the UK working within the Critical Care Air Support Teams.

When not deployed on operations, defence nurses work within Ministry of Defence Hospital Units within NHS Trusts across the UK to maintain their clinical skills and care for the general public. In particular, Defence Nurses working at the Royal Centre for Defence Medicine in Birmingham and at the Defence Medical Rehabilitation Centre at Headley Court contribute directly to the health care provision of military personnel.

Hospital Care

In the UK hospital care is provided at Ministry of Defence Hospital Units (MDHU).

The Defence Medical Services Department (DMSD) has contracts with the NHS for provision of care in MDHUs, which are run as military units embedded within selected NHS hospitals. There are MDHUs at Derriford (Plymouth), Frimley Park (Aldershot), Northallerton (near Catterick), Peterborough and Portsmouth.

In addition, the Defence Medical Services runs a number of other units which include the Royal Centre for Defence Medicine (Birmingham), Defence Services Medical Rehabilitation Centre (Headley Court) and the Duchess of Kent's Psychiatric Unit (Catterick). There are also about 245 DMS medical and dental primary care facilities mostly located in the UK. Outside of the UK primary healthcare, and some secondary healthcare, is provided on board Royal Navy ships and in overseas bases and theatres of military operations.

The Military Ward at the new Queen Elizabeth Hospital in Birmingham started taking patients in 2010 and service personnel are cared for in single rooms or four-bedded bays that have additional features for the exclusive use of military patients. The ward has more staff than a normal NHS ward, a quiet room for relatives as well as a communal space for military patients to gather. A dedicated physiotherapy area has also been provided close to the ward for service patients.

On operations in Afghanistan and other overseas locations **Field Hospitals** provide medical support that includes primary surgery, an intensive care unit, medium and low dependency nursing care beds and diagnostic support, as well as emergency medical care. These Field Hospitals may be staffed by medical personnel from all three services.

Service personnel serving in Germany who require hospital care are treated in one of the five German Provider Hospitals. As the withdrawal from Germany gathers pace these services will be reduced.

Royal Centre for Defence Medicine (RCDM)

The RCDM in Birmingham provides a centre for military personnel requiring specialised care, and incorporates a facility for the treatment of service personnel who have been evacuated from an overseas deployment area after becoming ill or wounded/injured. RCDM also acts as a centre for the training of Defence Medical Service personnel.

In operation since 2001 the RCDM operates on a contract between the DMSD and the University Hospitals Birmingham (UHB) NHS Trust.

The RCDM is a Joint Service establishment with medical personnel from all three of the armed services wearing their respective Naval, Army, or Air Force uniforms.

Midlands Medical Accommodation Project

From 2010 Whittington Barracks in Lichfield became the home of military medicine The Midlands Medical Accommodation project (MMA) will ensure that the area becomes the central focus for military medical expertise and assets. About 2,000 military and civilian staff will eventually work at the barracks when the MMA project completes in late 2014.

The first phase – MMA Increment 1 – has already delivered a modern headquarters office building for the DMS at Whittington Barracks that incorporates both the Surgeon General's strategic Headquarters and those of the Joint Medical Command, both of which are fully operational.

The second phase – MMA Increment 2 – will see the DMS elements relocate from Keogh Barracks near Aldershot to a new modern training centre at Whittington Barracks. The new complex will include training facilities, a learning centre; lecture theatre, messes for Officers, Warrant Officers and Senior Non Commissioned Officers, living accommodation for permanent staff and a new Junior Ranks' dining and leisure facility.

Work began at the beginning of 2011, and relocation should be complete by early 2014.

MMA1 and 2 will see around £200M invested in the redevelopment of Whittington Barracks.

DEFENCE EQUIPMENT AND SUPPORT

In parallel with the establishment of PJHQ at Northwood it became important to combine the separate logistics functions of the three Armed Services. As a result, in 2000 the three distinct separate service logistic functions were fused into one and the Defence Logistic Organisation was formed.

From 1 April 2007 the Defence Procurement Agency (DPA) and the Defence Logistic Organisation (DLO) were merged to form Defence Equipment and Support (DE&S).

DE&S has been described as 'the engine' that delivers 'Through Life' equipment and logistic support, and making sure the whole factory to front line process is seamless and properly integrated.

The Headquarters of DE&S is at Abbey Wood (Bristol) a site that is the largest MoD facility in the UK with a site workforce of about 10,000. DE&S is a Top Level Budget Holder and employs about 29,000 personnel (about 77 per cent civilian).

DE&S Structure

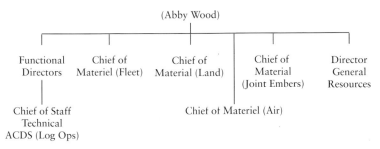

Over the next ten years, the UK Government plans to spend about £150 billion on new equipment and equipment support as follows:

Procurement of new equipment	£60 billion
Support for new equipment entering service	£18 billion
Support for existing in-service equipment (1)	£68 billion
Contingency against risk	4.8 billion

(1) Includes spending on routine spares and maintenance, ship refits, support arrangements for our communications and information infrastructure, and the running costs of the nuclear propulsion and nuclear weapons production facilities.

Expenditure by service sectors over the next ten years is shown under the following headings:

Ships	£17.4 billion
Submarines and Deterrent	£35.8 billion
Combat Air	£18.5 billion
Air Support	£13.9 billion
Helicopters	£12.1 billion
Information Systems and Services	£15.7 billion
ISTAR	£4.4 billion
Land Equipment	£12.3 billion
Weapons	£11.4 billion

In a normal year expect the MoD to spend about 40 per cent of its budget on equipment and equipment support.

Finances already allocated to equipment and equipment support over the period 2013 to 2017 are as follows:

Financial year	13/14	14/15	15/16	16/17
£ Billions	13.8	14.3	15.5	15.3

Some of the DE&S responsibilities to Joint Operations include:

Logistics planning, resource management, contractual support and policy
Global fleet management and land-based equipment
Support of the naval fleet and all naval systems
Communication and Information Systems
Transport and movements
Food and ration packs
Ammunition
Fuel, Oil and Lubricants
Postal Services
Clothing and tentage
Storage for all equipment and materiel

In 2013 the MoD announced that an assessment phase was in progress for a future DE&S business model based around a Government – Owned Contractor – Operated (GOCO) entity. If finally approved the GOCO would be implemented in stages.

DEFENCE INFRASTRUCTURE ORGANISATION (DIO)

Formed on 1 April 2011 and with a headquarters in Sutton Coldfield the DIO replaced the former Defence Estates organisation and brings together the majority of property and infrastructure functions from across the Ministry of Defence.

The DIO, a Top Level Budget Holder (TLB) has an annual expenditure of approximately £3.3 billion and assets worth over £20 billion. The overall area of the Defence Estate is estimated at being in the region of 2,400 sq kms.

The Defence Estate includes docks, airfields, barracks, training areas, schools and colleges, married quarters and roads owned and managed by the MoD.

There are five operating divisions:

◆ Major Projects – Responsible for the management of high value corporate projects.
◆ Land Management Services – Responsible for managing the entire estate portfolio.
◆ Defence Training Estate – responsible for all MoD Training Areas.
◆ Hard Facilities Management – Responsible for routine construction projects, mechanical and electrical support to the estate.
◆ Security Services Group – Responsible for the provision of security at all levels.
◆ Soft Facilities Management – Responsible for providing cleaning and catering type support across the MoD.

JOINT CHEMICAL, BIOLOGICAL, RADIOLOGICAL AND NUCLEAR DEFENCE

During July 2011 the MoD announced the specialist Chemical, Biological, Radiological and Nuclear (CBRN) capabilities of the 1st Royal Tank Regiment were to be transferred to the RAF Regiment's Defence CBRN Wing (20 Wing RAF Regiment) by December 2011.

No 20 Wing at RAF Honington is now responsible for the Defence CBRN Wing .This organisation provides the CBRN reconnaissance, monitoring, detection and decontamination support required by the three armed services, and where necessary the civilian authorities.

20 Wing has three squadrons:

No 26 Squadron RAF Regiment	RAF Honington
No 27 Squadron RAF Regiment	RAF Honington
No 2623 Squadron RAuxAF Regt	RAF Honington

20 Wing possesses extremely sophisticated detection, monitoring and decontamination capabilities, including systems related to the Sampling and Identification of Biological Chemical and Radiological Agents (SIBCRA) task. 20 Wing personnel also provide support to the civil authorities as part of the UK Nuclear Event Response Organisation (NERO). In one example an RAF Regiment monitoring team was deployed to an overseas British Embassy where there was a potential contamination threat.

Winterbourne Gunner (Wiltshire) is the location of the Defence Chemical Biological Radiological and Nuclear Centre (DCBRNC). The Centre designs and runs courses that qualify individuals of all three services for CBRN defence operational and training appointments.

Porton Down (Wiltshire) houses theDefence Science and Technology Laboratory (Dstl) and the Health Agency's Centre for Emergency Preparedness and Response. Both of these organisations have important inputs relating to the defence of the UK and its population against CBRN events.

Continuing TA Yeomany support to Defence CBRN activities remains unclear.

JOINT SERVICES SIGNAL ORGANISATION (JSSO)

With its headquarters at RAF Digby the JSSO is a joint service organisation providing specialist communications support to military operations in both the UK and overseas. At times this support can also be provided for allied nations during multi-national operations.

Commanded by either an Army Colonel or an RAF Group Captain on rotation the JSSO also researches new systems and techniques to provide enhanced support to units of all three armed forces.

SKYNET

Astrium Services operates the Skynet military satellite constellation on a concession basis and provides the three armed services with the ground terminals to provide all Beyond Line of Sight (BLOS) communications to the MoD.

Under a £4 billion Private Finance Initiative (PFI) Astrium is contracted to provide this service until 2022.

A number of Skynet satellites have been launched over the past decade and the fourth of the Skynet 5 series, Skyney 5D was launched from French Guiana (South America) in December 2012. . Skynet 5A and Skynet 5B entered service in April 2007 and January 2008 respectively. Skynet 5C was launched in June 2008. Skynet 5D will travel at speeds of around 6,200 miles per hour when in orbit.

The Land, Air and maritime environments utilise different equipment for their principal terminal capabilities. The Land and Air environments primarily use Reacher. The maritime environment uses the Satellite Communications Terminal (SCOT).

MINISTRY OF DEFENCE POLICE AND GUARDING AGENCY

This agency has two major elements, The Ministry of Defence Police and the Ministry of Defence Guarding Agency:

Ministry of Defence Police (MDP)
The MDP has its headquarters at Wethersfield, in Essex, and is deployed across the British Isles at over 80 MoD sites from Culdrose in Cornwall to the Clyde in Scotland. Organised into five divisional commands, with headquarters at York, Aldershot, Aldermaston, Foxhill and the Clyde Naval Base, the personnel total is approximately 3,400 (including about 150 in the Defence Police Criminal Investigation Department).

The majority of MDP tasks are security orientated and include the security of military bases, protecting against the sabotage of assets and the threat of terrorist incursion. At the same time the MDP has a role as a civilian police force creating a safe crime free environment. The MDP is supported by a number of specialist units that include the largest fraud squad in the UK, marine units that are equipped with a large number of amphibious craft, over 400 police dogs, a special escort group and a multi-capability operational support unit.

During early 2011 it was announced that the MDP had established a Defence Crime Board, to provide strategic direction to the defence-wide effort to reduce the harm done to the defence budget, safety, security and military operational capability by crime and fraud.

All MDP officers are trained in the use of firearms and at any one time about 70 per cent of MDP officers on duty will be armed.

Ministry of Defence Guard Service
The Ministry of Defence Guard Service (MGS) is the uniformed, unarmed element forming part of the larger Ministry of Defence Police and Guarding Agency. The Ministry of Defence Guard Service was formed into a corporate structure as part of the Ministry of Defence Police and Guarding Agency in April 2004. The MGS has a personnel total of around 2,800 personnel who are located at over 200 locations across the UK. There are six regional headquarters locations at Aldershot, Bath, Clyde Naval Base, London, Shrewsbury and York. Primary duties of the MGS include:

♦ Control of entry and exit
♦ Issue of entry passes
♦ Searching of vehicles and personnel
♦ Perimeter patrolling
♦ Key control

The Training Centre is at Wethersfield in Essex.

We would expect the annual cost of the MGS to be in the region of £100 million.

MILITARY CORRECTIVE TRAINING CENTRE (MCTC)

The MCTC takes servicemen and women who have been sentenced to periods of detention from 14 days to two years. The vast majority are serving periods of detention to which they have been sentenced by court martial or after summary hearing by their commanding officers. Most detainees have offended against Armed Forces law rather than criminal law, and few are committed for offences that would have resulted in custody had they been in civilian life.

All detainees are held in accordance with rules determining committal to custody within the Armed Forces Act 2006.

Staff at the MCTC are drawn mainly from the Military Provost Staff Corps (MPSC) with representatives from the other services.

Numbers of detainees held during the past three years is given below:

MCTC Detainees 2011–2013

Sentence length	FY 2011–12	FY 2012–13
Under 60 days	490	320
61 to 112 days	130	80
113 days to 6 months	110	60
6 months to 1 year	50	40
1 year to 18 months	10	10
18 months to 24 months	10	10

CHAPTER 6 – MISCELLANEOUS

THE SERVICES HIERARCHY

Officer Ranks

Army	*Navy*	*Air Force*	*NATO Code*
Field Marshal	Admiral of the Fleet	Marshal of the RAF	OF-10
General	Admiral	Air Chief Marshal	OF-9
Lieutenant-General	Vice-Admiral	Air Marshal	OF-8
Major-General	Rear-Admiral	Air Vice Marshal	OF-7
Brigadier	Commodore	Air Commodore	OF-6
Colonel	Captain	Group Captain	OF-5
Lieutenant-Colonel	Commander	Wing Commander	OF-4
Major	Lieutenant-Commander	Squadron Leader	OF-3
Captain	Lieutenant	Flight-Lieutenant	OF-2
Lieutenant/2Lt	Sub-Lieutenant	Flying/Pilot Officer	OF-1
Officer Cadet	Midshipman		OF(D)

Non Commissioned Ranks

Army	*Navy*	*Air Force*	*NATO Code*
Warrant Officer 1	Warrant Officer 1	Warrant Officer	OR-9
Warrant Officer 2	Warrant Officer 2		OR-8
Staff/Colour Sergeant	Chief Petty Officer	Flight Sergeant/Ch Tech (1)	OR-7
Sergeant	Petty Officer	Sergeant	OR-5
Corporal	Leading Rate	Corporal	OR-4
Lance Corporal			OR-3
Private Cl 1 -3	Able Rating	Leading Aircraftsman (2)	OR-2
Private Cl 4/Junior		Aircraftsman	OR-1

Note: (1) Chief Technician; (2) May include Junior Technician and Senior Aircraftsman.

UK ARMED FORCES PAY 2013–2014

The following table shows the average pay based on the rates for 2013–2014.

Other ranks are allocated to either higher or lower pay spines in accordance with their trade. These are rates for the other ranks lower pay spine – officer pay is not affected by pay spines. Service ranks equate to the NATO rank designations above.

Rank	*Pay from 1 April 2013*
OR-1/OR-2	£17,689–£21,991
OR-3	£21,292–£24,472
OR-4	£26,668–£30,138
OR-5	£30,312–£34,452
OR-7	£33,555–£38,055
OR-8	£38,638–£40,023
OR-9	£40,544–£44,561

OF-1	£24,861–£33,029
OF-2	£38,295–£45,541
OF-3	£48,238–£57,771
OF-4	£67,701–£78,393
OF-5	£82,123–£90,302
OF-6	£98,000–£100,97

The table does not include the specialist pay rates for medical officers, chaplins, pilots etc. Pay for Admirals, Generals and Air Marshals is determined by the Civil Service Top Salaries Review Board.

THE MOD'S CIVILIAN STAFF

The three uniformed services are supported by the civilian staff of the MoD. On 1 April 2013 there were approximately 65,400 civilian personnel employed by the MoD. This figure has fallen from 316,700 civilian personnel in 1980. The current total civilian staff figure is a reduction of 20,450 since 1 April 2010.

During early 2013 MoD civilian staff were employed in the following budgetary areas:

Navy Command	2,030
Land Command	11,410
Air Command	5,550
Joint Forces Command	3,920
Head Office & Corporate Services	7,300
Defence Equipment and Support	12,550
Defence Infrastructure Organisation	5,290
Royal Fleet Auxiliary	1,900
MoD Trading Funds (1)	7,170
Locally Engaged Civilians (2)	8,250
Unallocated	30
Total	65,400

Note: MoD Trading Funds include the Defence Science and Technology Laboratory, The Meteorological Office, Hydrographic Office and Defence Support Group. (2) The majority of locally engaged civilians are employed in Germany. This number will fall quickly as the withdrawal gathers pace.

Earlier in the decade the UK MoD stated that "The Department remains committed to a process of civilianisation. Increasingly, it makes no sense to employ expensively trained and highly professional military personnel in jobs which civilians could do equally well. Civilians are generally cheaper than their military counterparts and as they often remain longer in post, can provide greater continuity. For these reasons, it is our long-standing policy to civilianise posts where possible and so release valuable military resources to the front line whenever it makes operational and economic sense to do so".

In general, MoD Civil Servants work in a parallel stream with their respective uniformed counterparts. There are some 'stand alone' civilian agencies of which the QinetiQ is probably the largest.

THE UNITED KINGDOM DEFENCE INDUSTRY

Despite uncertainties over future defence commitments and pressure on defence spending, the United Kingdom's Defence Industry has proved to be a remarkably resilient and successful element of the UK's national manufacturing base.

Historically, the UK defence industry has possessed the capability and competence to provide a wide range of advanced systems and equipment to support our own Armed Forces. This capability, matched with their competitiveness, has enabled UK companies to command a sizeable share of those overseas markets for which export licence approvals are available. At home, UK industry has consistently provided some 75 per cent by value of the equipment requirements of The Ministry of Defence. In simple terms, in recent years UK industry has supplied £8 – £9 billion worth of goods and services for our Armed Forces annually.

The United Kingdom's defence companies are justifiably proud of their record in recent years in the face of fierce overseas competition. Reductions in the UK's Armed Forces and the heavy demands on our remaining Service personnel, who face an unpredictable international security environment, make it inevitable that considerable reliance will be placed upon the support and surge capacity offered by our comprehensive indigenous defence industrial base. Without this effective industrial base, the ability of UK to exert independence of action or influence over collective security arrangements would be constrained. It is essential that government policies ensure that industry retains the necessary capabilities to support our forces in a changing world.

During 2012 UK defence exports totalled approximately £8.8 billion, a figure that was an increase of over 60 per cent on the previous year, and the largest increase for five years. These figures confirm the UK as the second most successful defence exporter after the United States, with a 20 per cent share of the global defence export market. Defence export results were reinforced by sales of Typhoon and Hawk aircraft – the Typhoon programme alone supporting an estimated 8,600 jobs in the UK.

As importantly, the defence industry is not only a major employer but it is also the generator of high technology that is readily adaptable to civilian use in fields such as avionics and engine technology. The future of the UK's defence industry will almost certainly have to be properly planned if it is to remain an efficient and essential national support organisation in times of crisis. A look at MoD payments to contractors during FY 2011–2012 identifies some of the larger manufacturers.

Major Contractors Listing by Holding Company

Over £500 million
Agustawestland Ltd
AWE Management Ltd
BAE Systems (Operations) Ltd
BAE Systems Marine Ltd
HP Enterprise Services Defence & Security UK Ltd
BAE Systems Surface Ships Ltd
NETMA
Defence Science & Technology Laboratory

£250–£500 million
Aspire Defence Ltd
BAE Systems Global Combat Systems Munitions Ltd
BAE Systems PLC
British Telecommunications PLC
Debut Services Ltd
Paradigm Secure Communications Ltd
Devonport Royal Dockyard Ltd
QinetiQ Ltd
General Dynamics United Kingdom Ltd
Rolls-Royce PLC
MBDA UK Ltd
Rolls-Royce Power Engineering PLC

100–£250 million

Airbus Operations Ltd
Annington Receivables Ltd
Babcock Dyncorp Ltd
Babcock Land (Whitefleet Management) Ltd
Babcock Marine (Clyde) Ltd
BAE Systems Global Combat Systems Ltd
BAE Systems Integrated System Technologies Ltd
Boeing Company (The)
BP Oil International Ltd
Carillion Enterprise Ltd
Defence Support Group (DSG)
Pride (Serp) Ltd
Holdfast Training Services Ltd
Purple Foodservice Solutions Ltd
Kellogg Brown & Root Ltd
Reserve Forces and Cadets Associations2
Lockheed Martin Aerospace Systems Integration Corporation
Serco Ltd
MAN Truck & Bus UK Ltd
Sodexo Ltd
Marshall of Cambridge Aerospace Ltd
SSE Energy Supply Ltd
Meteorological Office
Thales Optronics Ltd
Modern Housing Solutions (Prime) Ltd
Thales UK Ltd
Office of Communications (OFCOM)
United States Government
Organisation For Joint Armaments Co-Operation Executive Admin

Note: Payments to the companies listed may include payments made to subsidiaries or contractors.

QINETIQ

(Formerly known as the Defence Evaluation & Research Agency)

From 1 April 1995, the Defence Evaluation & Research Agency (DERA) assumed the responsibilities of its predecessor the Defence Research Agency (DRA). DERA changed its title to QinetiQ on 2 July 2001.

The name QinetiQ has been derived from the scientific term, kinetic (phonetic: ki'ne tik), which means 'relating to or caused by motion'. This in turn comes from the Greek, kinetikos based on 'kineo' which means 'to move'.

Following the 2001 restructuring, certain functions of DERA, encompassing the majority of the organisation's capabilities for defence and security and amounting to approximately three quarters of DERA, were formed into QinetiQ Limited, an entity which is a wholly-owned subsidiary of QinetiQ Group plc. In February 2006 QinetiQ was listed on the London Stock Exchange.

A quarter of QinetiQ has been retained within the MOD as the Defence Science and Technology Laboratory (DSTL) to manage the research programme and the International Research Collaboration, along with other sensitive areas such as CBD (Chemical & Biological Defence), Porton Down.

The main business areas of QinetiQ are in the UK, US and Australia providing procurement and technical support to nations seeking to procure new capabilities. In addition, through their technical support services QinetiQ can provide technology transfer and local training for sovereign states wishing to create national facilities and capability.

The Group employs about 14,000 people of which some 6,400 are in North America, and operates around 20 UK sites with major technology facilities at Farnborough, Boscombe Down and Malvern. QinetiQ 's global revenue was £1,366 million in the year to 31 March 2013 (UK – £480.3; US £620.8; Other 226.7).

About 60 per cent of the group's UK employees are graduates and more than 700 hold PhDs. More than half of the employees in the UK are focussed on research, invention, development and application of new technology. There are strategic partnerships with 13 UK universities, and 30 QinetiQ staff have visiting professorships.

THE MOD'S LAND HOLDINGS

The Ministry of Defence (MoD) is one of the largest landowners in the UK with a diverse estate of some 240,000 hectares (1 per cent of the UK land mass) and is valued at over £15 billion. Typically,approximately £1.5bn per year is spent on maintenance and new construction. Some of these costs are offset against income from tenants and other land users.

The Defence Infrastructure Organisation (DIO) is the MoD Agency responsible for the management of the defence estate and provides services to support all aspects of a large and very diverse estate.

The estate is made up of:

◆ Built Estate which occupies around 80,000 hectares and is made up of naval bases, barracks/camps, airfields, research and development installations, storage and supply depots, communications facilities, around 49,000 Service Families Accommodation and town centre careers offices.

◆ The Rural Estate occupies around 160,000 hectares which includes 21 major armed forces training areas 39 minor training areas, small arms ranges, test and evaluation ranges and aerial bombing ranges.

◆ Significant overseas estate in Germany, Cyprus, the Falkland Islands and Gibraltar with major overseas training facilities in Canada, Norway, Poland and Kenya.

◆ There are 179 Sites of Special Scientific Interest (SSSIs) across the rural estate that is managed by the MoD, the largest number in Government ownership.

◆ There are currently around 650 listed buildings and 1057 scheduled monuments across both the built and rural estate. The defence estate includes the largest proportion of statutorily protected buildings held by the government, 43% of all government heritage properties.

CODEWORDS AND NICKNAMES

A Codeword is a single word used to provide security cover for reference to a particular classified matter, eg 'CORPORATE' was the Codeword for the recovery of the Falklands in 1982. In 1990 'GRANBY' was used to refer to operations in the Gulf and 'Op HERRICK' is used for current UK operations in support of NATO forces in Afghanistan. 'Op ELLAMY' is the Codeword for UK participation in the military intervention in Libya during 2011. A Nickname consists of two words and may be used for reference to an unclassified matter, eg 'Lean Look' referred to an investigation into various military organisations in order to identify savings in manpower.

DATES AND TIMINGS

When referring to timings the British Army uses the 24 hour clock. This means that 2015 hours (pronounced twenty fifteen hours) is in fact 8.15pm. Soldiers usually avoid midnight and refer to 2359 or 0001 hours. Time zones present plenty of scope for confusion! Exercise and Operational times are expressed in Greenwich Mean Time (GMT) which may differ from the local time. The suffix Z (Zulu) denotes GMT and A (Alpha) GMT + 1 hour. B (Bravo) means GMT + 2 hours and so on.

The Date Time Group or DTG can be seen on military documents and is a point of further confusion for many. Using the military DTG 1030 GMT on 20 April 2007 is written as 201030Z APR 07. When the Armed Forces relate a days and hours to operations a simple system is used:

a. D Day is the day an operation begins.
b. H Hour is the hour a specific operation begins.
c. Days and hours can be represented by numbers plus or minus of D Day for planning purposes. Therefore if D Day is 20 April 2012, D-2 is 18 April and D + 2 is 22 April. If H Hour is 0600 hours then H+2 is 0800 hours.

PHONETIC ALPHABET

To ensure minimum confusion during radio or telephone conversations difficult words or names are spelt out letter by letter using the following NATO standard phonetic alphabet:

ALPHA – BRAVO – CHARLIE – DELTA – ECHO – FOXTROT – GOLF – HOTEL - INDIA – JULIET – KILO – LIMA – MIKE – NOVEMBER – OSCAR – PAPA - QUEBEC – ROMEO – SIERRA – TANGO – UNIFORM – VICTOR – WHISKEY – X RAY – YANKEE – ZULU.

OPERATION BANNER – NORTHERN IRELAND

The 1st Bn The Prince of Wales' Own Regiment was the first unit to be deployed in Northern Ireland in August 1969 closely followed by The 1st Royal Green Jackets.

During the worst period of The Troubles between 1972 and 1973, 27,000 military personnel were stationed in Northern Ireland, the majority of them Army. These military personnel were supported by over 13,000 personnel from the Royal Ulster Constabulary.

Over the course of Operation Banner, 763 servicemen and women were killed as a direct result of terrorism. This includes 651 Army and Royal Marine personnel; one Royal Naval Serviceman; 50 members of the former Ulster Defence Regiment and later Royal Irish Regiment; 10 members of the Territorial Army with 51 military personnel murdered outside Northern Ireland. Some 6,116 members of the Army and Royal Marines were wounded over the period.

At one stage there were 106 military bases or locations in Northern Ireland, however, following the first Provisional IRA cease-fire in September 1994, 80 per cent of these were closed. The closure of the bases was accelerated after the Good Friday Agreement of April 1998.

The process of steadily reducing military presence began on 1 August 2005 and Operation Banner officially ended on 31 July 2007. It was superseded on 1 August 2007 by Operation Helvetic, a garrison of no more than 5,000 military personnel in 10 locations, trained and ready for deployment worldwide.

The names of the UK service personnel who lost their lives during Operation Banner are listed on the Armed Forces Memorial, Staffordshire. The Memorial, which opened to the public in October 2007, remembers all those killed on duty in conflicts or on training exercises, by terrorist action or on peacekeeping missions – www.forcesmemorial.org

Korea: 765
Northern Ireland: 763 (1)
Malaya: 340
The Falklands: 255
Palestine: 784 (2)
Iraq 2003–2009: 179
Cyprus: 105
Aden: 68
Egypt: 54
Balkans: 48
The Gulf 1990: 47
Yangtse River: 46
Oman & Dhofar: 24
Suez: 22
Borneo: 126
Kenya: 12
Sierra Leone: 1

Notes:

(1) Figure for Northern Ireland includes military deaths on the UK mainland and Germany attributed to Irish terrorism. In 1972 171 service personnel were killed.
(2) Source – Commonwealth War Graves Commission. This figure includes service personnel deaths by accident in theatre – about 80% were killed in action and does not include deaths of members of the Palestinian Police.
(3) As of mid 2013 a total of 401 UK Service personnel had been killed in Afghanistan since October 2001 as a result of enemy action (444 from all causes).

QUOTATIONS

Young officers and NCOs may find some of these quotations useful on briefings etc: There are two groups – Military and General.

Military

"It's not the bullet that's got my name on it that concerns me; it's all them other ones flyin' around marked 'To Whom It May Concern.'"

Rifleman – Afghanistan 2011

Young officers are always taught that the first battle they will fight is that for the respect of their men.

Anon

"Never be sad about becoming an old soldier – there are thousands who wished they had the chance. "

Anon

"You may not be interested in war, but war is interested in you."

Leon Trotsky – 1879 – 1940

"Before all else, be armed."

Machiavelli 1469–1527

"All warfare Is based on deception."

Sun Tzu – about 600 BC

"Tactics without Strategy is just noise before defeat"

"War is delightful to those who have no experience of it. "

Ersamus 1456–1536

"Any government has as much of a duty to avoid war as a ship's captain has to avoid a shipwreck. "

Guy de Maupassant 1850–1893

"The human factor will decide the fate of war, of all wars. Not the Mirage, nor any other plane, and not the screwdriver, or the wrench or radar or missiles or all the newest technology and electronic innovations. Men – and not just men of action, but men of thought. Men for whom the expression 'By ruses shall ye make war' is a philosophy of life, not just the object of lip service."

Israeli Air Force Commander Ezer Weizman 1924 – 2005

"In 1944 Major Digby Tatham-Warter won the DSO commanding a company of 2 Para at Arnhem when he led a bayonet charge wearing a bowler hat and carrying an umbrella. When he was told that it would be useless against German fire he replied "But what if it rains"."

"Anyone wanting to commit American ground forces to the mainland of Asia should have his head examined."

General Douglas MacArthur 1880–1964

"They used to say professionals talk logistics and then tactics. Today, real professionals talk command, control and communications, then logistics and after that tactics."

General Sir David Richards to the House of Commons Defence Committee (February 2009)

"In 1920 King Amunullah of Afghanistan made a state visit to London. As his coach rolled down The Mall towards Buckingham Palace two Cockney bystanders watched proceedings:

First Cockney: 'ose that in the coach then?
Second Cockney: Its the King of Arfghanistan!
First Cockney: 'ose the King of the other Arf then?"

"Having lost sight of our objectives we need to redouble our efforts."

Anon

"During the Second World War Air Marshal Sir Arthur (Bomber) Harris was well known for his glorious capacity for rudeness, particularly to bureaucrats. "What are you doing to retard the war effort today" was his standard greeting to senior civil servants."

"The military value of a partisan's work is not measured by the amount of property destroyed, or the number of men killed or captured, but the number he keeps watching."

Confederate Cavalry Leader – John Singleton Mosby 1833-1916

"Keep shouting Sir, we'll find you. Keep going down hill – Don't cross the river!"

LCpl Thomas Atkins

"It is foolish to hunt the tiger when there are plenty of sheep around."

Al Qaeda Training Manual 2002

"Information is something that you do something with. Data is something that just makes officers feel good! I keep telling them but nobody listens to me."

US Army Intelligence specialist – CENTCOM Qatar 2003

"If you torture data sufficiently it will confess to almost anything."

Fred Menger – Chemistry Professor (1937–)

"If you tell someone what needs doing, as opposed to how to do it, they will surprise you with their ingenuity."

General Patton 1885–1945

"An appeaser is one who feeds a crocodile in the hope it will eat him last."

Winston Churchill 1874–1965

"More delusion as a solution."

US State Department Official – Baghdad March 2005

"If you claim to understand what is happening in Iraq you haven't been properly briefed."

British Staff Officer at Coalition HQ 2004

"If you can keep your head when all about you are losing theirs and blaming it on you – you'll be a man my son."

Rudyard Kipling 1865–1936

"If you can keep your head when all about you are losing theirs – you may have missed something very important."

Royal Marine – Bagram Airfield 2002

"Admiral King commanded the US Navy during the Second World War. His daughter wrote – "He was the most even tempered man I ever met – he was always in a rage. In addition, he believed that civilians should be told nothing about a war until it was over and then only who won. Nothing more!"

"We trained very hard, but it seemed that every time we were beginning to form up in teams, we would be reorganised. I was to learn in later life that we tend to meet any new situation by reorganising, and a wonderful method it can be for creating an illusion of progress, while producing confusion, inefficiency and demoralisation."

Caius Petronius 66 AD

"A few honest men are better than numbers."

Oliver Cromwell 1599–1658

"The beatings will continue until morale improves."

Attributed to the Commander of the Japanese Submarine Force in 1944

"When other Generals make mistakes their armies are beaten; when I get into a hole, my men pull me out of it."

The Duke of Wellington 1759–1852

"Take short views, hope for the best and trust in God."

Sir Sydney Smith 1764–1840

"There is no beating these troops in spite of their generals. I always thought them bad soldiers, now I am sure of it. I turned their right, pierced their centre, broke them everywhere; the day was mine, and yet they did not know it and would not run."

Marshal Soult 1769–1851 (French Army) – Commenting on the British Infantry at Albuhera in 1811

"There can be no government without an army,
No army without money,
No money without prosperity,
And no prosperity without justice and good administration."

Muslim scholar Ibn Qutayba – 9th Century

"More powerful than the march of mighty armies is an idea whose time has come."

Victor Hugo 1802 – 1885

"Its always best to leave a party before the fight starts."

John Sergeant – 19 November 2008

"No one is foolish enough to choose war instead of peace. In peace sons bury fathers – in war fathers bury sons."

Herodotus – about 440 BC

"What experience and history teach us is this – that people and governments have never learned anything from history, or acted upon any lessons they might have drawn from it."

Georg Hegel 1770–1831

"Better ten years of repression than one night of mob mayhem."

Old Muslim proverb

"Why plan when panicking is so much more fun."

UN administrator in the Congo during 2006 when pressed for his lack of planning for an imminent operation

"You can get a lot more done with a kind word and a gun than you can with a kind word alone."

Attributed to Al Capone

"This is the right way to waste money!"

PJ O'Rourke – Rolling Stone Magazine (Watching missiles firing during an exercise)

"Pale Ebenezer thought it wrong to fight,
But roaring Bill, who killed him, thought it right."

Hiliare Belloc 1873–1952

"Everyone wants peace – and they will fight the most terrible war to get it."

Miles Kington – BBC Radio 4th February 1995

"War is a competition of incompetence – the least incompetent usually win."

General AAK Niazi (Pakistan) – after losing Bangladesh in 1971.

"In war the outcome corresponds to expectations less than in any other activity."

Titus Livy 59 BC – 17AD

"Nothing is so good for the morale of the troops as occasionally to see a dead general."

Field Marshal Slim 1891–1970

"It makes no difference which side the general is on."

Unknown British Soldier

"At the end of the day it is the individual fighting soldier who carries the battle to the enemy; Sir Andrew Agnew commanding Campbell's Regiment (Royal Scots Fusiliers), giving orders to his infantrymen before the Battle of Dettingen in 1743 shouted; "Do you see yon loons on yon grey hill? Well, if ye dinna kill them, they'll kill you! "

"The only time in his life that he ever put up a fight was when we asked for his resignation."

A comment from one of his staff officers following French General Joffre's resignation in 1916.

"How can the enemy anticipate us when we haven't got a clue what we are doing?"

Pte Thomas Atkins (Basrah 2006)

"Never disturb your enemy while he is making a mistake."

Mrs Saatchi explained her 12 month silence after her husband started living with Nigela Lawson by quoting Napoleon's dictum

"This is just something to be got round – like a bit of flak on the way to the target."

Group Captain Leonard Cheshire VC 1917–1992 – Speaking of his incurable illness in the week before he died.

"Awards are like haemorrhoids: in the end every asshole gets one".

Frederick Raphal (author born 1931)

GENERAL QUOTES

"All rumours are true, especially when your boss denies them."

Dogbert – Build a better life by stealing office supplies

"If a miracle occurs and your boss finally completes your performance appraisal, it will be hastily prepared, annoyingly vague and an insult to whatever dignity you still possess."

Dogbert – Clues for the clueless

"Put all your friends in private offices and all of your wretched slaves in cubicles".

Roman General Dogbertius Dilbert – Thriving on vague objectives

"You got to look on the bright side, even if there ain't one."

Dashiell Hammett – Author 1894–61

"Don't worry about people stealing an idea. If it's original you will have to ram it down their throats."

Howard Aiken 1900–1973 (Howard Aiken completed the Harvard Mark II, a completely electronic computer, in 1947).

Homer Simpson's advice to his son Bart:
Homer to Bart: "These three little sentences will get you through life":

Number 1: "Oh, good idea boss".
Number 2: (whispers) "Cover for me".
Number 3: "It was like that when I got here".

"Democracy means government by the uneducated, while aristocracy means government by the badly educated".

GK Chesterton 1874–1936

"From the naturalistic point of view, all men are equal. There are only two exceptions to this rule of naturalistic equality: geniuses and idiots".

Mikhail Bakunin 1814–1876

"The greatest evil is not done in those sordid dens of evil that Dickens loved to paint ... but is conceived and ordered (moved, seconded, carried, and minuted) in clear, carpeted, warmed, well-lighted offices, by quiet men with white collars and cut fingernails and smooth-shaven cheeks who do not need to raise their voices. We should remember that...Evil flourishes where good men do nothing".

CS Lewis 1898–1963

'We're menaced by what I might call 'Fabio-Fascism', by the dictator-spirit working away quietly behind the facade of constitutional forms, passing a little law here, endorsing a departmental tyranny there, emphasizing the national need for secrecy elsewhere, and whispering and cooing the so-called 'news' every evening over the (BBC) radio, until opposition is tamed and gulled."

EM Forster 1979–1970

"The incompetent always present themselves as experts, the cruel as pious, sinners as excessively devout, usurious as benefactors, the small minded as patriots, the arrogant as humble, the vulgar as elegant and the feebleminded as intellectual.

Carlos Ruiz Zafon – (from The Angels Game 2006)

"Tell the truth and run".

Old Yugoslav Proverb

"The credit belongs to one who strives valiantly and errs often, because there is no effort without error or shortcoming. Even if such a person fails, he fails while daring greatly, so his place shall never be with those cold and timid souls who know neither victory nor defeat".

US President Theodore Roosevelt (1858–1919)

"All you need in this life is ignorance and confidence. Success is then assured."

Marl Twain 1835–1910

"In this country nobody really seems to know anything about anything anymore".

From the New York Times during the financial crisis of September 2008

"Avoid 'toxic colleagues' who stop you doing your job by whinging and complaining and diverting you from getting things done. Keep away from people who try to belittle your ambition. Small people always do that, but the really great make you feel that you too, can achieve something great".

Mark Twain 1835–1910

"The more corrupt a state; the more numerous its laws".

Tacitus AD 89

"Clear language, reflects clear thought."

George Orwell (1903–1950)

"It's like the old hooker said. I really enjoy the work – it's the stairs that are getting me down"

Elaine Stritch – Actress 2003

"The primary function of management is to create the chaos that only management can sort out. A secondary function is the expensive redecoration and refurnishing of offices, especially in times of the utmost financial stringency".

Theodore Dalrymple 'The Spectator' 6 November 1993.

"Success is generally 90% persistence".

Anon

"It is only worthless men who seek to excuse the deterioration of their character by pleading neglect in their early years".

Plutarch – Life of Coriolanus – Approx AD 80

"They say hard work never hurt anybody, but I figured why take the chance".

US President Ronald Regan 1911–2004

"To applaud as loudly as that for so stupid a proposal means that you are just trying to fill that gap between your ears".

David Starkey – BBCRadio 4 (Feb 1995)

"Ah, these diplomats! What chatterboxes! There's only one way to shut them up – cut them down with machine guns. Bulganin, go and get me one!"

Joseph Stalin 1878–1953 – As reported by De Gaulle during a long meeting.

"Whenever I hear about a wave of public indignation I am filled with a massive calm".

Matthew Parris – The Times 24th October 1994

"It is a general popular error to imagine that the loudest complainers for the public to be the most anxious for its welfare."

Edmund Burke 1729–1797

"The men who really believe in themselves are all in lunatic asylums."

GK Chesterton 1874–1936

"What all the wise men promised has not happened and what all the dammed fools said would happen has come to pass".

Lord Melbourne 1779–1848

"When we have finally stirred ourselves to hang them all, I hope that our next step will be to outlaw political parties outside Parliament on the grounds that, like amusement arcades, they attract the least desirable members of our society."

Auberon Waugh 1939–2001 (in The Spectator 1984)

Extracts from Officer's Annual Confidential Reports

"Works well when under constant supervision and cornered like a rat in a trap."

"He has the wisdom of youth, and the energy of old age."

"This Officer should go far – and the sooner he starts, the better."

"This officer is depriving a village somewhere of its idiot."

"Only occasionally wets himself under pressure."

"When she opens her mouth, it seems that this is only to change which ever foot was previously in there."

"He has carried out each and every one of his duties to his entire satisfaction."

"He would be out of his depth in a car park puddle."

"This young man has delusions of adequacy."

"When he joined my ship, this Officer was something of a granny; since then he has aged considerably."

"This Medical Officer has used my ship to carry his genitals from port to port, and my officers to carry him from bar to bar."

"Since my last report he has reached rock bottom, and has started to dig."

"She sets low personal standards and then consistently fails to achieve them."

"His men would follow him anywhere, but only out of curiosity."

"This officer has the astonishing ability to provoke something close to a mutiny every time he opens his mouth".

"His mother should have thrown him away and kept the stork".

"I cannot believe that out of 10,000 sperm his was the fastest".

"The most complementary thing that I can say about this officer is that he is unbearable".

FINALLY

Drill instructor to an embarrassed officer cadet who appears to be completely incapable of identifying left from right – "Tell me Sir, as an outsider, what is your opinion of the human race?

Overheard at the RMA Sandhurst

Extracts from the Devils Dictionary 1911

Accuracy: A certain uninteresting quality generally excluded from human statements.

Armour: The kind of clothing worn by a man whose tailor is a blacksmith.

Colonel: The most gorgeously apparelled man in a regiment.

Education: That which discloses to the wise and disguised from the foolish their lack of understanding.

Enemy: A designing scoundrel who has done you some service which it is inconvenient to repay.

Foe: A person instigated by his wicked nature to deny one's merits or exhibit superior merits of his own.

Foreigner: A villain regarded with various degrees of toleration, according to his conformity to the eternal standard of our conceit and the shifting ones of our interest.

Freedom: A political condition that every nation supposes itself to enjoy in virtual monopoly.

Friendless: Having no favour to bestow. Destitute of fortune. Addicted to utterance of truth and common sense.

Man: An animal so lost in rapturous contemplation of what he thinks he is as to overlook what he ought to be. His chief occupation is the extermination of other animals and his own species.

Overwork: A dangerous disorder affecting high public functionaries who want to go fishing.

Peace: In international affairs a period of cheating between two periods of fighting.

Plunder: To wrest the wealth of A from B and leave C lamenting a vanished opportunity.

Republic: A form of government in which equal justice is available to all who can afford to pay for it.

Resign: A good thing to do when you are going to be kicked out.

Revelation: Discovering late in life that you are a fool.

Robber: Vulgar name for one who is successful in obtaining the property of others.

Zeal: A certain nervous disorder affecting the young and inexperienced.

ABBREVIATIONS

The following is a selection from the list of standard military abbreviations and should assist users of this handbook.

AWOL	Absent without leave
ACE	Allied Command Europe
Adjt	Adjutant
admin	Administration
AD	Air Defence / Air Dispatch / Army Department
ADA	Air Defended Area
ADP	Automatic Data Processing
AFCENT	Allied Forces Central European Theatre
AIFV	Armoured Infantry Fighting Vehicle
Airmob	Airmobile
ATAF	Allied Tactical Air Force
armd	Armoured
ACV	Armoured Command Vehicle
AFV	Armoured Fighting Vehicle
AMF(L)	Allied Mobile Force (Land Element)
APC	Armoured Personnel Carrier
APDS	Armour Piercing Discarding Sabot
ARV	Armoured Recovery Vehicle
AVLB	Armoured Vehicle Launched Bridge
AP	Armour Piercing / Ammunition Point / Air Publication

APO	Army Post Office
ARRC	Allied Rapid Reaction Corps
ATGW	Anti Tank Guided Weapon
ATWM	Army Transition to War Measure
arty	Artillery
BE	Belgium (Belgian)
BEF	British Expeditionary Force (France – 1914)
BGHQ	Battlegroup Headquarters
BiH	Bosnia and Herzogovina
Bn	Battalion
Bty	Battery
BC	Battery Commander
BG	Battle Group
Bde	Brigade
BAOR	British Army of the Rhine
BFG	British Forces Germany
BFPO	British Forces Post Office
BMH	British Military Hospital
BRSC	British Rear Support Command
C3I	Command, Control, Communications & Intelligence.
CCP	Casualty Collecting Post
CCS	Casualty Clearing Station
CASEVAC	Casualty Evacuation
CAD	Central Ammunition Depot
CEP	Circular Error Probable/Central Engineer Park
CEPS	Central European Pipeline System
CET	Combat Engineer Tractor
CGS	Chief of the General Staff
CinC	Commander in Chief
CIMIC	Civil Military Co-operation
COMMS Z	Communications Zone
CVD	Central Vehicle Depot
CW	Chemical Warfare
COS	Chief of Staff
CP	Close Protection/Command Post
CAP	Combat Air Patrol
c sups	Combat Supplies
CV	Combat Vehicles
CVR(T) or (W)	Combat Vehicle Reconnaissance Tracked or Wheeled
comd	Command/Commander
CinC	Commander in Chief
CPO	Command Pay Office/Chief Petty Officer
CO	Commanding Officer
Coy	Company
CQMS	Company Quartermaster Sergeant
COMSEN	Communications Centre
CCM	Counter Counter Measure
DAA	Divisional Administrative Area
DF	Defensive Fire
DPA	Defence Planning Assumptions
DK	Denmark

DISTAFF	Directing Staff (DS)
Div	Division
DAA	Divisional Administrative Area
DMA	Divisional Maintenance Area
DS	Direct Support/Dressing Station
DTG	Date Time Group
ech	Echelon
EME	Electrical and Mechanical Engineers
ECCM	Electronic Counter Measure
EDP	Emergency Defence Plan
EMP	Electro Magnetic Pulse
engr	Engineer
EOD	Explosive Ordnance Disposal
ETA	Estimated Time of Arrival
EW	Early Warning/Electronic Warfare
Ex	Exercise
FRG	Federal Republic of Germany
FGA	Fighter Ground Attack
FUP	Forming Up Point
FAC	Forward Air Controller
FEBA	Forward Edge of the Battle Area
FLET	Forward Location Enemy Troops
FLOT	Forward Location Own Troops
FOO	Forward Observation Officer
FR	France (French)
FRT	Forward Repair Team
FUP	Forming Up Place
GDP	General Defence Plan
GE	German (Germany)
GR	Greece (Greek)
GOC	General Officer Commanding
GPMG	General Purpose Machine Gun
HAC	Honourable Artillery Company
HE	High Explosive
HEAT	High Explosive Anti Tank
HESH	High Explosive Squash Head
HVM	Hyper Velocity Missile
Hy	Heavy
IFF	Identification Friend or Foe
II	Image Intensifier
IGB	Inner German Border
IO	Intelligence Officer
INTSUM	Intelligence Summary
ISTAR	Intelligence, surveillance, target acquisition and reconnaissance
IRG	Immediate Replenishment Group
IR	Individual Reservist
IS	Internal Security
ISAF	International Security Assistance Force (Kabul)
ISD	In Service Date
IT	Italy (Italian)
IW	Individual Weapon

JFHQ	Joint Force Headquarters
JHQ	Joint Headquarters
JSSU	Joint Services Signals Unit
KFOR	Kosovo Force (NATO in Kosovo)
LAD	Light Aid Detachment (REME)
L of C	Lines of Communication
LLAD	Low Level Air Defence
LO	Liaison Officer
Loc	Locating
log	Logistic
LRATGW	Long Range Anti Tank Guided Weapon
LSW	Light Support Weapon
MAOT	Mobile Air Operations Team
MBT	Main Battle Tank
maint	Maintain
mat	Material
med	Medical
mech	Mechanised
MFC	Mortar Fire Controller
MNAD	Multi National Airmobile Division
NE	Netherlands
MO	Medical Officer
MP	Military Police
MPSC	Military Provost Staff Corps
MoD	Ministry of Defence
MovO	Movement Order
MT	Military Tasks
MV	Military Vigilance
NAAFI	Navy, Army and Air Force Institutes
NADGE	NATO Air Defence Ground Environment
NATO	North Atlantic Treaty Organisation
NCO	Non Commissioned Officer
NL	Netherlands
NO	Norway (Norwegian)
NOK	Next of Kin
NORTHAG	Northern Army Group
NTR	Nothing to Report
NBC	Nuclear and Chemical Warfare
NYK	Not Yet Known
OP	Observation Post
OC	Officer Commanding
OCU	Operational Conversion Unit (RAF)
OIC	Officer in Charge
OOTW	Operations Other Than War
ORBAT	Order of Battle
POL	Petrol, Oil and Lubricants
P info	Public Information
PJHQ	Permanent Joint Head Quarters
Pl	Platoon
PO	Portugal (Portuguese)

PUS	Permanent Under Secretary
QGE	Queens Gurkha Engineers
QM	Quartermaster
RAP	Rocket Assisted Projectile/Regimental Aid Post
RJDF	Rapid Joint Deployment Force
RTM	Ready to Move
RCZ	Rear Combat Zone
R & D	Research and Development
Recce	Reconnaissance
Regt	Regiment
RHQ	Regimental Headquarters
RMA	Rear Maintenance Area/Royal Military Academy
RSA	Royal School of Artillery
RSME	Royal School of Mechanical Engineering
RTU	Return to Unit
SACUER	Supreme Allied Commander Europe
SATCOM	Satellite Communications
SDR	Strategic Defence Review
SFOR	Stabilisation Force (NATO in Bosnia)
2IC	Second in Command
SH	Support Helicopters
SHAPE	Supreme Headquarters Allied Powers Europe
SITREP	Situation Report
SIB	Special Investigation Branch
SMG	Sub Machine Gun
SLR	Self Loading Rifle
SMG	Sub Machine Gun
SNCO	Senior Non Commissioned Officer
SP	Spain (Spanish)
Sqn	Squadron
SP	Self Propelled/Start Point
SSM	Surface to Surface Missile
SSVC	Services Sound and Vision Corporation
STA	Surveillance and Target Acquisition
STOL	Short Take Off and Landing
TOT	Time on Target
TCP	Traffic Control Post
tpt	Transport
tp	Troop
TCV	Troop Carrying Vehicle
TLB	Top Level Budget
TU	Turkish (Turkey)
TUL	Truck Utility Light
TUM	Truck Utility Medium
UAV	Unmanned Air Vehicle
UCAV	Unmanned Combat Air Vehicle
UK	United Kingdom
UKMF	United Kingdom Mobile Force
UNCLASS	Unclassified
UNPROFOR	United Nations Protection Force

UXB	Unexploded Bomb
US	United States
U/S	Unserviceable
VCDS	Vice Chief of the Defence Staff
veh	Vehicle
VOR	Vehicle off the Road
WE	War Establishment
wh	Wheeled
WIMP	Whinging Incompetent Malingering Person
WMR	War Maintenance Reserve
WO	Warrant Officer
wksp	Workshop
X	Crossing (as in roads or rivers)

CHARLES HEYMAN (EDITOR)

A former infantry officer, Charles Heyman served in the British Army between 1962 and 1986, with tours of active service in Borneo, Cyprus, Malaysia and Northern Ireland. Between active service tours he served as a Regimental Officer (commanding a Combat Team in Germany) and as a General Staff Officer in the Headquarters of the 1st British Corps. Before leaving the British Army in 1986 he spent two years as a lecturer in Defence Studies at the Royal Air Force College (Cranwell).

Since leaving the British Army Charles Heyman has been specialising in threat and general military and security analysis. Initially working as a consultant for various NATO Defence Ministries, by the early 1990s he was leading research teams for Jane's Information Group. From 1995 until 2003 he was the editor of Jane's World Armies and from 1994 to 2000 the editor of Jane's Police and Security Handbook. In addition, from 1995 until 2004 he was the Senior Defence Analyst for Jane's Consultancy Group and took part in over 200 defence related consultancy projects.

Charles Heyman has extensive experience in the Balkans, and during the recent campaigns in Iraq and Afghanistan he was a regular contributor to the BBC World Service, Sky News, National Public Radio in the USA and the Australian and Canadian Broadcasting Corporations. During the past five years he has written articles for a variety of newspapers that include The Times, The Scotsman, Sunday Express and the Sydney Morning Herald. He remains the author of the Armed Forces of the United Kingdom and The British Army Guide published by Pen & Sword. During recent NATO operations in Libya he was a regular contributor for both the BBC and Sky News.

He is a member of the International Institute for Strategic Studies (IISS) and currently the Managing Director of R&F International Defence & Security Consultancy.

E Mail – Charles.Heyman@Yahoo.co.uk

This publication was produced by R&F (Defence) Publications

Editorial Office Tel 07889 886170
E Mail: charles.heyman@yahoo.co.uk
Website: www.armedforces.co.uk
Editor: Charles Heyman

Other publications in this series are:
The Royal Air Force Pocket Guide 1994-95
The British Army Guide 2012–2013 (12th Edition)
The Territorial Army – Volume 1 1999

Further copies can be obtained from:
Pen & Sword Books Ltd
47 Church Street
Barnsley S70 2AS
Telephone: 01226 734222   Fax: 01226-734438

7th Edition October 2013

HMSO Core Licence Number CO2W0004896
Parliamentary License Number P2006000197
PSI Licence Number C2006009533